Silver Burdett Ginn Science
DiscoveryWorks

Silver Burdett Ginn

Parsippany, NJ   Needham, MA

Atlanta, GA   Deerfield, IL   Irving, TX   Upland, CA

Authors

William Badders
Science Resource Teacher
Cleveland Public Schools
Cleveland, OH

Lowell J. Bethel
Professor of Science Education
The University of Texas at Austin
Austin, TX

Victoria Fu
Professor of Child Development
Virginia Polytechnic Institute and
State University
Blacksburg, VA

Donald Peck
Director, Center for Elementary Science
Fairleigh Dickinson University
Madison, NJ

Carolyn Sumners
Director of Astronomy and Physics
Houston Museum of Natural Science
Houston, TX

Catherine Valentino
Senior Vice President for
Curriculum Development
Voyager Expanded Learning
West Kingston, RI

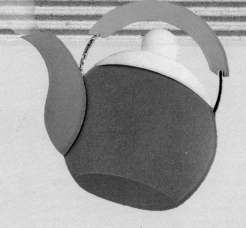

Consulting Author

R. Mike Mullane
Astronaut, retired
Albuquerque, NM

Acknowledgements appear on page H43, which constitutes an extension of this copyright page.

Silver Burdett Ginn
A Division of Simon & Schuster
299 Jefferson Road, P.O. Box 480
Parsippany, NJ 07054-0480

ISBN 0-382-41637-6   ISBN 0-382-33384-5

7 8 9 10 11 12 13 14 RRD 05 04 03 02 01 00 99 98

CONTENTS

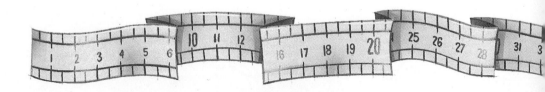

UNIT B

Properties of Matter

THEME: SCALE

UNIT D

Magnetism and Electricity

THEME: MODELS

GET READY TO INVESTIGATE!   D2

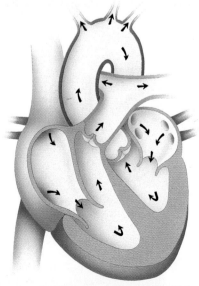

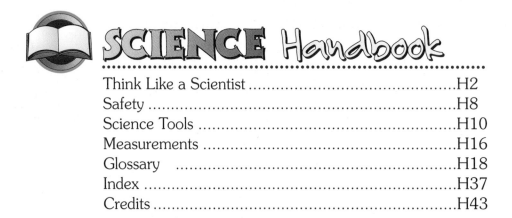

SCIENCE Handbook

UNIT A

EARTH'S LAND RESOURCES

Theme: Constancy and Change

GET READY TO

OBSERVE & QUESTION

How do wind and ice shape the land?

Look around you. Careful observation may reveal odd and unusual landforms. How do forces such as wind and ice produce such unusual shapes?

EXPERIMENT & HYPOTHESIZE

What do people throw away and where does it go?

Building a model landfill and doing other hands-on activities will help you investigate how well this method of trash disposal works.

INVESTIGATE!

RESEARCH & ANALYZE

As you investigate, find out more from these books.

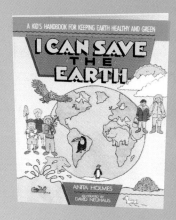

A KID'S HANDBOOK FOR KEEPING EARTH HEALTHY AND GREEN

I CAN SAVE THE EARTH

ANITA HOLMES

ILLUSTRATED BY DAVID NEUHAUS

- **I Can Save the Earth** by Anita Holmes (Julian Messner, 1993). This book will show you what part you can play in saving Earth.

- **One Day in the Desert** by Jean Craighead George (HarperCollins, 1983). This book will tell you about what a wall of water did in a place where you thought that there was almost no water.

WORK TOGETHER & SHARE IDEAS

What's your plan for the wise use of resources?

As you investigate, you'll work together to identify and find out about natural resources. Your goal is to make exhibits that tell the location of natural resources in your state, how easy they are to obtain, and the best plan for developing and conserving them. Look for the Unit Project Links for ideas to help you with this project.

CHAPTER 1

THE SHAPE OF THE LAND

Have you seen pictures or movies that show whitewater rafting? Were the riders paddling wildly through a canyon in a crashing, speeding river? You know that rivers can be very powerful forces. But did you know that such forces help to shape the land?

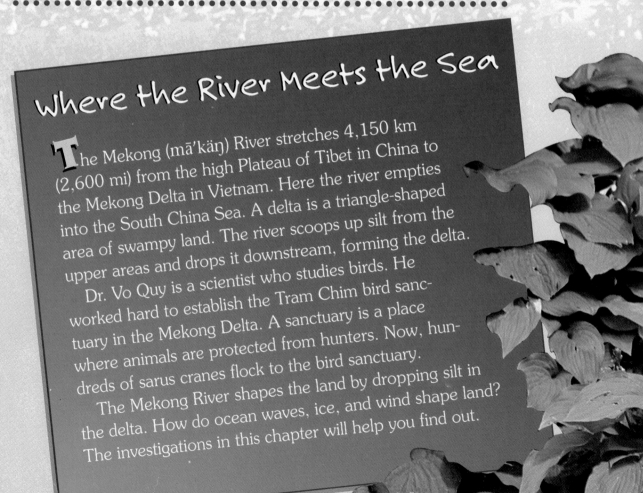

Where the River Meets the Sea

The Mekong (mā'käŋ) River stretches 4,150 km (2,600 mi) from the high Plateau of Tibet in China to the Mekong Delta in Vietnam. Here the river empties into the South China Sea. A delta is a triangle-shaped area of swampy land. The river scoops up silt from the upper areas and drops it downstream, forming the delta.

Dr. Vo Quy is a scientist who studies birds. He worked hard to establish the Tram Chim bird sanctuary in the Mekong Delta. A sanctuary is a place where animals are protected from hunters. Now, hundreds of sarus cranes flock to the bird sanctuary.

The Mekong River shapes the land by dropping silt in the delta. How do ocean waves, ice, and wind shape land? The investigations in this chapter will help you find out.

Dr. Vo Quy (*top*) works to protect birds such as the sarus crane (*bottom*).

HOW DOES MOVING WATER SHAPE THE LAND?

A gentle rain falls. You watch puddles form and water trickle along the ground. How can these small streams of water affect the land? In this investigation you'll find out how Earth's land is shaped by water.

Activity

Hills and Valleys

Hills and valleys don't look as if they'd ever change. But they do. Find out how moving water can change them.

MATERIALS

- goggles
- large baking pan
- sand
- coffee cans with holes in the bottom
- metric ruler
- pitcher
- water
- *Science Notebook*

SAFETY

Wear goggles during this activity. Clean up any spills immediately.

Procedure

1. Pile damp sand in one end of a baking pan. Shape the sand so that it forms first a hill, next a steep slope, and then gradually an area that is nearly flat. Shape the sand down to a thin edge a short distance from the other end of the pan.

2. Use a coffee can with holes in the bottom as your rain-maker. Have a group member hold the rainmaker a few centimeters above the top of the hill. Fill a pitcher with water. **Predict** what will happen to the sand if you make the "rain" fall on the top of the hill. **Record** your prediction in your *Science Notebook*.

Step 3

3. Then **test** your prediction. Pour the water into the rainmaker. **Observe** the water as it flows down the hill. **Describe** where the water makes a "stream," a "river," and an "ocean."

4. **Make a drawing** of what you observe. Draw arrows to point out the stream, river, and ocean areas. Then add the labels *stream, river,* and *ocean* to your drawing.

5. With your group, **experiment** with different-shaped hills. Try using more than one rainmaker. **Make drawings** of what you observe.

Analyze and Conclude

1. How do your observations compare with your prediction?

2. **Compare** the shape of the valley that the stream made near the top of the hill with the shape of the valley that the river made near the bottom of the hill.

3. Study the drawing you made. What can you **infer** about how moving water changes the shape of the land over which it moves?

UNIT PROJECT LINK

In shaping land, moving water can create places of scenic beauty—natural resources that people can enjoy. Local, state, and national parks are often in such places. With your group, make a list of scenic places in your state. Collect pictures of them if you can. Display the pictures to show others some of the beautiful places that can be visited in your state.

Activity

At the Beach

Where does sand on a beach come from? Where does it go? Find out how moving water affects sand on a beach.

MATERIALS

- goggles
- large baking pan
- sand
- pitcher
- water
- metric ruler
- 12 to 15 pebbles (about 1 cm in diameter)
- *Science Notebook*

SAFETY //////

Wear goggles during this activity. Clean up any spills immediately.

Procedure

1. Pile damp sand in one side of a baking pan. Shape the sand into a beach.

2. Fill a pitcher with water. Slowly pour the water into the other side of the pan until the water is about 3 cm deep.

3. Place a ruler in the water, at the side of the pan opposite the sand. Make waves by moving the ruler slightly back and forth.

4. **Observe** what happens to the beach. **Record** your observations in your *Science Notebook*.

5. Make a jetty by piling up pebbles in a line that extends from the middle of the shoreline into the water about 5 cm, as shown.

Step 3

Step 5

A8

6. With your group, **predict** what will happen to the waves and the beach if you make waves that hit the jetty. Explain your prediction.

7. Use the ruler again to make waves. **Observe** what happens when waves strike the jetty. **Record** your observations.

Analyze and Conclude

1. From your observations in step 4, **infer** how waves can change a shoreline.

2. **Compare** the changes you observed in step 4 with those you observed in step 7. How did your prediction compare with your observations?

3. **Hypothesize** how a jetty changes the movement of sand. **Give evidence** to support your hypothesis.

INVESTIGATE FURTHER!
EXPERIMENT
Hypothesize whether the direction from which the waves come makes a difference in what happens to a beach. Make a plan to find out, and then carry it out. Share your findings with your class.

SCIENCE IN LITERATURE

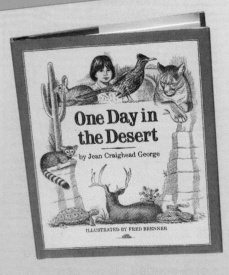

ONE DAY IN THE DESERT
by Jean Craighead George
Illustrated by Fred Brenner
HarperCollins, 1983

Water can change the shape of a beach. But how can water affect a desert? With these words, Jean Craighead George tells what it's like to experience a flash flood in a desert: "Water came bubbling and singing down the arroyo. It filled the riverbed from bank to bank, then rose like a great cement wall. . . ." An arroyo (ə roi'ō) is a dry channel that moving water has carved. On this day a sudden rainstorm fills the arroyo.

In *One Day in the Desert*, you'll read how Bird Wing, a young Papago Indian, and the plants and animals of the desert face the power of a wall of water.

Carving the Land

You may have watched water flow along the ground after a rainstorm. Gravity, the force that pulls you toward Earth, causes the water to flow downhill until it finds a low spot. There the water forms a puddle. Often a puddle is muddy from soil that the rainwater picked up and carried with it. The process just described takes place on a much larger scale all over the world. It is called erosion (ē rō′zhən).

Partners That Shape the Land

Erosion is the process by which broken-down rock material is carried from one place to another by moving water, wind, or moving ice. Water causes more erosion on Earth than wind and moving ice combined.

Have you ever scraped your knee in a fall? Land can also be scraped— by materials that are carried by water. Over time, erosion and an- other process, called weathering, work together to wear away the land. **Weathering** is the process by which rock is broken into smaller pieces. The small pieces of rock in soil are formed by weathering.

OVER STEEP LAND Fast-moving rivers can carve deep valleys. Rivers often join before reaching the ocean.

ACROSS A VALLEY FLOOR As a river approaches the ocean, it winds in a string of S-shaped curves across a valley floor. On the inside of each curve, the river deposits some of the material it is carrying.

Breaking Up, Wearing Down

Have you ever watched sugar dissolve in a glass of water? Some rocks contain materials that dissolve in water. When some materials in a rock dissolve, the whole rock is made weaker. Then it's easier to break the rock into pieces.

Sometimes, gases from the air help to weaken rocks. Certain gases mix with water to make a weak acid. The acid dissolves certain materials in rocks, making the rocks weaker. Then the rocks are more easily broken down by moving water.

From Trickle to River

When rain falls on a hill or mountainside, some soaks into the ground. The rest of the rainwater trickles down the slope. Several trickles may join to form a brook. Several brooks may join to form a stream. Streams join to form a river. Small rivers join larger ones.

A river and the waterways that drain into it are called a **river system.** The map below shows some rivers of the Mississippi River system. It's the largest river system in the United States.

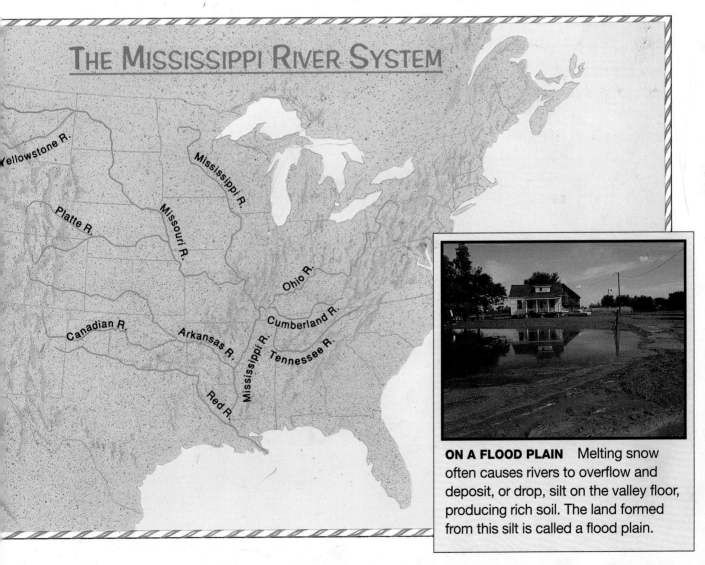

THE MISSISSIPPI RIVER SYSTEM

Yellowstone R.

Mississippi R.

Platte R.

Missouri R.

Ohio R.

Canadian R.

Cumberland R.

Arkansas R.

Mississippi R.

Tennessee R.

Red R.

ON A FLOOD PLAIN Melting snow often causes rivers to overflow and deposit, or drop, silt on the valley floor, producing rich soil. The land formed from this silt is called a flood plain.

Rushing down a slope, a stream or river can move soil, sand, gravel, and rocks. The materials that are carried by moving water are called **sediments**. You saw sandy sediment carried by "rainwater" in the activity on pages A6 and A7.

Fast-flowing rivers can move even small boulders. As boulders and rocks are carried along, they crash into each other and into rocks along riverbanks. Chips of rock break off. Over time, moving water grinds rocks into grains of sand or tiny particles, called clay and silt.

How River Valleys Form

Just as a metal file wears away hard material, a fast-moving river can carve a deep, steep-sided valley.

Over time the river valley deepens and widens.

As water batters the sides of the valley, the water breaks up rock and soil and carries them away. At some point the soil above the eroded sides of the valley caves in. This widens the river valley even more.

When Water Slows Down

When a river reaches the ocean, the water slows down. Then the water loses energy and can no longer carry all its sediments. The river deposits, or drops, the sediments. They build up along the banks and bottom of the river. As you can see below, when a river empties into the ocean, sediments form a flat plain called a **delta** (del′tə). ■

The Mississippi Delta ▼

A SATELLITE VIEW OF THE DELTA
Look for a clue to why deltas are named after the triangle-shaped Greek letter *delta*.

The Changing Shoreline

When you look at a map of the world, you can see the thousands of kilometers of shoreline, the area where the ocean meets the land. Coastal areas are among the most beautiful places in the world. But these areas are under constant attack by water and wind.

Wearing Away the Shoreline

Moving water and wind are the major causes of weathering and erosion. And nowhere on Earth is the land more exposed to moving water and wind than along shorelines.

Waves are driven onto the shore by the wind and by tides, the regular rise and fall of Earth's ocean water. Along rocky shorelines, sand and small rocks carried by the waves grind against large rocks. This grinding breaks down the rocks and wears them away. It also helps to form interesting rock shapes along rocky shorelines.

The water brought in by a wave rushes back toward the ocean. Along sandy shorelines, waves remove sand from some places and deposit it in other places, often very far away.

Shorelines around the world are constantly being changed by wind and water. ▼

A13

In fact, sand can be deposited hundreds of kilometers from where it was removed. Some sandy beaches change with the seasons. During the winter, strong winds produce waves that are steep and close together. These waves remove more sand from the shore than they wash in. In summer, gentler waves deposit more sand on beaches than they remove.

Building Up the Shoreline

Sometimes, sand carried by a current along the shoreline moves past a headland. A **headland** is a natural piece of land that extends out into the water. The headland may be at the mouth, or opening, of a bay. A **bay** is a body of water that is partly enclosed by land but has an opening, called a mouth, connecting the water to the ocean.

Sand is washed along an ocean shore by waves. When the sand reaches a headland, the headland directs the sand across the mouth of the bay. Over time the sand may build up and form features such as the barrier island shown. Such narrow islands stretch for hundreds of kilometers along the Atlantic and Gulf coasts of the United States.

A Tug of War at the Shore

As the ocean and land interact, movement and change are normal. This is especially true for beach areas. Beach areas can change a lot almost overnight. If no people lived in these areas, the natural changes would go almost unnoticed. However, people do live in these areas. Some of the world's largest cities are found near the shore.

Headland and bay ▼

Barrier island ▼

▲ **Sea wall and jetty**

In the United States, many people live and work on many of the barrier islands along the Atlantic and Gulf coasts. In addition, millions of tourists visit these beaches each year. These areas can be greatly damaged or even destroyed by the strong winds and huge waves that occur during severe storms.

People have thought of different ways to protect shore areas, such as building jetties and sea walls. When you did the activity on pages A8 and A9, you built a jetty out of pebbles.

A jetty, shown above, is a structure built to stop the movement of sand. Water that strikes a jetty slows and drops the sand it is carrying.

The ways for saving or restoring beaches are costly. Most of them will not work over a long period. And none can completely protect people or property from fierce storms, such as hurricanes. What is your answer, then, to this question: Who's winning the tug of war at the shore—people or nature? ■

INVESTIGATION 1

1. Suppose you wanted to build a house at the shore. Would you choose to build it on a rocky shore or a sandy beach? Give reasons for your answer.

2. Describe at least two land shapes that are formed by moving water.

A15

HOW DO WIND AND ICE SHAPE THE LAND?

When you're hot and sweaty, wind and ice can cool you off. In winter they may keep you from playing outdoors. But wind and ice can do something more. They can shape the land. In this investigation you'll find out how.

Activity

Blowin' in the Wind

The word desert can make you think of huge dry areas and hills of sand called sand dunes. What part does wind play in shaping a desert landscape? Find out in this activity.

MATERIALS

- goggles
- tray or pan
- dry sand
- metric ruler
- cardboard box
- hair dryer
- timer
- craft sticks
- *Science Notebook*

SAFETY

Wear goggles during this activity. Be careful not to burn yourself when using the hair dryer. Use the coolest setting.

Procedure

1. **Make a model** of a desert. With your group, spread a layer of dry sand in a tray. The layer should be about 2 cm deep. The sand is your "desert."

2. Set one end of the tray in a cardboard box. The box is to keep the sand from blowing around the room.

3. Use a hair dryer as a source of wind. Set the dryer for the coolest temperature. Hold the dryer so that the wind *gently* blows along the surface of the sand, as shown on the next page. Continue directing wind onto the sand for 15 to 20 seconds.

4. **Observe** the surface of the sand. **Record** your observations in your *Science Notebook*.

Step 3

5. Spread the sand out evenly again. Lay several sticks on top of the sand, as shown. **Talk with your group** and together **predict** what the surface of the sand will look like if you repeat step 3.

Step 5

6. Record your prediction and **give reasons** for predicting as you did. Then **test** your prediction and **record** what you observe.

Analyze and Conclude

1. Compare the surface of the desert produced in step 3 with the surface produced in step 6.

2. How did your prediction compare with what you observed in step 6?

3. What role do the sticks play in helping to shape a desert surface? **Infer** what must happen in order for a sand dune to form.

INVESTIGATE FURTHER!

EXPERIMENT

Smooth out your desert sand. Put plants in the desert. Then use the hair dryer to blow wind along the surface of the sand for 15 to 20 seconds. Record your observations. Infer the effect plants have on the erosion of sand in desert areas.

Activity

Gigantic Frozen Sandpaper

Have you ever seen what sandpaper can do to a piece of wood? In nature a huge mass of ice called a glacier can do the same thing to rock. Find out how ice shapes the land.

MATERIALS

- goggles
- small baking pan
- sand
- pebbles
- pitcher
- water
- freezer
- flat rock
- towel
- *Science Notebook*

SAFETY

Wear goggles during this activity. Clean up any spills immediately.

Procedure

1. **Make a model** of a glacier. Scatter a handful of sand and pebbles in a small pan. Add water to the pan until it is two-thirds full. Then carefully place the pan in a freezer.

2. After the water has frozen solid, remove the block of ice from the pan. The ice is your "glacier" (glā'shər).

Step 1

Step 3

3. Using a towel to protect your hands, place the glacier, sandy side down, on a flat rock. With your group, **predict** what will happen if you press down hard on the glacier and move it back and forth over the rock. **Record** your prediction in your *Science Notebook*.

4. Using the towel again to protect your hands, **test** your prediction. **Observe** what happens to the rock. **Record** your observations.

Analyze and Conclude

1. **Compare** your observations with your prediction.

2. **Hypothesize** what a real glacier would do to Earth's surface as the glacier moves over it. **Give reasons** to support your hypothesis.

INVESTIGATE FURTHER!

RESEARCH

The movement of glaciers forms grooves in Earth's surface. Use an encyclopedia or other reference book to find out the effect a glacier had on Kelley's Island in Lake Erie. Report your findings to your class.

Sand Blasted

Wind is not as powerful as moving water. But, like water, wind can change the shape of land. Have you ever had wind blow sand into your eyes? Then you know that wind can carry sediment.

Wind Blows Away the Land

The stronger the wind, the more sediments it can carry. Wind must blow at least 18 km/h (11 mph) just to move sand along the ground. Stronger winds are needed to lift sand and carry it less than a meter above the ground.

In areas with loose sand and fine soils, wind can blow these materials away. The wind is even more likely to erode materials during dry periods, when most of the plants in an area may die off. In some areas, wind erosion can be prevented or reduced by windbreaks. Windbreaks may be fences, shrubs, grass, or trees—anything that can slow down the wind.

Wind Carves the Land

Wind erodes Earth's surface by removing sand and silt from one place and depositing them in another. The sediments that wind carries also erode Earth's surface. As wind-blown grains of sand move along the ground, they act as sandblasters—chipping, cutting, and polishing.

DUNES THAT MOVE Where winds blow steadily in the same direction, dunes migrate, or move, as much as 30 m (100 ft) a year. Dunes can even bury towns and forests. ▼

Wind Builds Up the Land

The sediments that wind picks up from one surface are deposited on another. That surface is then built up.

Wind will carry its load of sediments until something like a boulder, a bush, or a fence slows it down. Think back to the activity on pages A16 and A17, in which you used a hair dryer to model wind blowing across sticks on a desert. When an object on a desert slows down the wind, the wind deposits some of the sediments it carries. Often piles of sand are deposited in one place, forming hills called **sand dunes**.

◀ **Desert sand dunes**

Sand dunes are formed on desert floors, on dry sandy flood plains, and along shorelines. Dunes vary in size. In the Sahara, in North Africa, sand dunes cover an area larger than the state of Texas. Small beach dunes may be 1–2 m (3–7 ft) high. Dunes in the Sangre de Cristo Mountains, in Colorado, are nearly 300 m (1,000 ft) high.

To carve buttes, polish rock, and make sand dunes move, wind has to attack, wear down, and carry away pieces of Earth's surface. Then the pieces have to be deposited somewhere else. All of these activities take a lot of sandblasting!

BUTTE Erosion by windblown sand can help shape the surfaces of rock formations such as this butte (byo͞ot). A butte is a narrow-topped hill with very steep, clifflike sides. ▼

Glaciers– Nature's Bulldozers

A bulldozer pushes soil, trees, stumps, and rocks ahead of it as it moves. Nature has its own "bulldozers." They are called glaciers. A **glacier** is a huge mass of moving ice that forms over land. Glaciers form in cold regions, where more snow falls in winter than melts in summer. In such places the snow piles up, becomes heavy, and turns to ice. As shown in the pictures below, there are two kinds of glaciers—continental and valley.

How Glaciers Move

As unlikely as it may seem, glaciers do move. The great weight of the ice causes a continental glacier to flow outward in all directions from its center. Gravity is the main force that makes glaciers move.

Some glaciers move only a few centimeters a day. Others move a few meters a day. No matter how slowly a glacier moves, the surface beneath the glacier is changed by the huge amount of ice moving across it.

CONTINENTAL GLACIERS Also called ice sheets, these gigantic masses of ice are found only in Greenland and Antarctica. ▼

VALLEY GLACIER Also called alpine (al'pīn) glaciers, these thick "rivers" of ice form in high mountain ranges. ▼

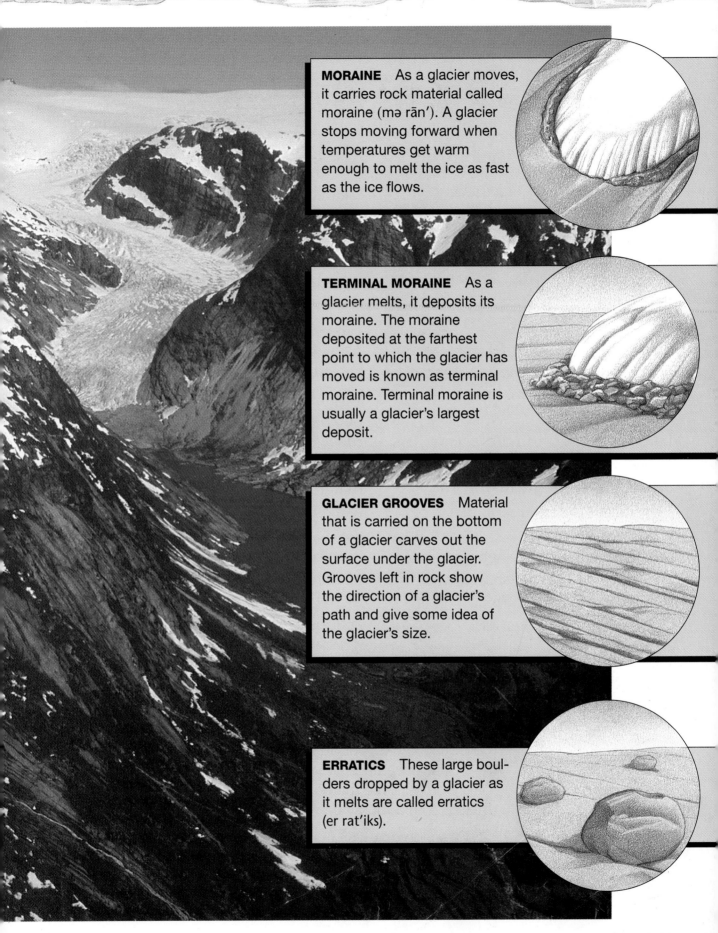

MORAINE As a glacier moves, it carries rock material called moraine (mə rān'). A glacier stops moving forward when temperatures get warm enough to melt the ice as fast as the ice flows.

TERMINAL MORAINE As a glacier melts, it deposits its moraine. The moraine deposited at the farthest point to which the glacier has moved is known as terminal moraine. Terminal moraine is usually a glacier's largest deposit.

GLACIER GROOVES Material that is carried on the bottom of a glacier carves out the surface under the glacier. Grooves left in rock show the direction of a glacier's path and give some idea of the glacier's size.

ERRATICS These large boulders dropped by a glacier as it melts are called erratics (er rat'iks).

▲ This peak, known as the Matterhorn, was carved by glaciers.

What Ice Leaves Behind

In places where a huge mass of ice once moved, signs of its presence and its power are left behind. These signs include deep U-shaped valleys, pointed peaks, sharp ridges, steep cliffs, lakes, and waterfalls.

Often two or more valley glaciers move down a mountain at the same time. The glaciers grind away at the rocky structure between them, producing narrow ridges with ragged edges. Around the mountain near its top, the glaciers carve out bowl-shaped holes. This action produces a pyramid-shaped peak, called a horn. Perhaps the most famous horn is the Matterhorn, located in the Alps between Switzerland and Italy.

Like wind and moving water, glaciers shape the land in two ways. As a glacier moves across the land, it carries away tons of material. Later, when the glacier stops moving and begins to melt, it deposits its load of sediments.

A glacier does more than just push materials from one place to another. Its action shapes mountains, carves valleys, and leaves huge boulders and piles of rocks along its path. Some of the most beautiful landscapes in the world have been produced by the actions of nature's bulldozers. ■

INVESTIGATION 2

1. Suppose a giant snowball rolled down a hill, collecting sticks, pebbles, and soil on its way. Then warm weather arrived and melted the snowball. Compare the material left when the snowball melted with a moraine.

2. Describe one way that wind shapes land and one way that glaciers shape land.

REFLECT & EVALUATE

WORD POWER

bay   river system
delta   sand dune
erosion   sediment
glacier   weathering
headland

On Your Own
Review the terms in the list. Then use as many terms as you can in a labeled diagram that shows one way that land can be shaped by moving water, wind, or moving ice.

With a Partner
Write a clue for each term in the list. Then challenge your partner to write the correct term for each clue.

BUILD YOUR PORTFOLIO

Imagine that you are a boulder on the side of a mountain. You roll into a rushing mountain stream and . . . .Tell the story of your journey from this point to the sea.

Analyze Information

Use this photograph of the Grand Canyon to explain how the canyon was formed.

Assess Performance

Plan an experiment to find out what will happen if a stream forms on each side of a mountain. After your teacher has reviewed your plan, carry out the experiment. Compare your results with those of others.

Problem Solving

1. Suppose you are drawing different landscape scenes for a calendar. Describe some land shapes formed by moving water, wind, or moving ice that you might draw in a desert or mountain scene.

2. Think about what happens to sediments when water in which they are carried is slowed down. How does this explain why a barrier island might form near a headland?

3. Describe one way that a delta and a terminal moraine are alike.

CHAPTER 2

THE IMPORTANCE OF NATURAL RESOURCES

One of the resources we get from the land is coal. Why is coal important? Because it's a fuel that, when burned, can be used to produce electrical energy. What other natural resources come from the land? Why are they important?

To Save the Streams

When the stream near Joan Sims's West Virginia home suddenly turned orange, she was shocked! Then she found out that the color was caused by a harmful material called acid. The acid was draining from a nearby coal mine. The acid was so harmful that it killed all stream life.

To find ways to keep streams free of acids, Joan Sims formed a group called Living Streams. With help from the public, the coal industry, and the Division of Energy, the group worked to stop coal mining in areas from which acid was draining. Happily, acids have been removed from several streams.

Do other fuels cause environmental problems? Are there other sources of energy that can be used? These important questions are discussed in the investigations in this chapter.

Coming Up

◄ Joan Sims works to keep streams clean.

WHY IS SOIL AN IMPORTANT RESOURCE?

Soil is a valuable natural resource. A natural resource is any material from Earth that can be used by people. Where does soil come from? How do we use it? How can we make sure we'll always have enough? Find out!

Activity

Little Ones From Big

You can make soil the way a mountain stream does. Find out how.

- -

MATERIALS
- goggles
- rock chips
- water
- 2 plastic jars, 1 with screw lid
- timer
- filter paper
- funnel
- hand lens
- *Science Notebook*

SAFETY
Wear goggles during this activity. Clean up any spills immediately.

Procedure

Wash some rock chips with water. Fill a plastic jar one-third full of chips. Cover them with water. Screw the lid on tightly. With a partner, take three 1-minute turns each, shaking the jar hard to model a mountain stream.

Place filter paper in a funnel. Stand the funnel in a plastic jar. **Predict** what you would see if you poured the water through the filter. Then **test** your prediction. Use a hand lens to **observe** the material on the paper. **Record** your observations in your *Science Notebook*.

Analyze and Conclude

Compare your prediction with what you observed. **Infer** how mountain streams help to make soil.

Activity
Saving Soil

Do plants help to keep soil from being washed away? Find out in this activity.

MATERIALS

- goggles
- 2 baking pans
- topsoil
- piece of sod
- 2 wooden blocks
- 2 coffee cans, each with holes in their bottoms
- 2 pitchers
- water
- *Science Notebook*

SAFETY

Wear goggles during this activity. Clean up any spills immediately.

Procedure

1. Place soil in one baking pan and sod in another. Sod is soil with grass growing in it. Set one end of each pan on a wooden block so that the pans are sloped.

2. **Predict** how rain might affect the soil in each pan. **Record** your prediction in your *Science Notebook*.

3. Use coffee cans with holes in their bottoms as rain-makers. Hold the rainmakers over the pans.

4. Have two other members empty equal amounts of water into the rainmakers as shown. **Observe** each pan. **Record** your observations.

Analyze and Conclude

1. **Compare** your observations with your predictions.

2. **Infer** how soil might be kept from washing away during a rainstorm.

Step 4

Gully!
It's Soil Erosion

The word *soil* means different things to different people. A construction worker sees soil as material that can be moved by digging. To a farmer, soil is the loose surface material in which plants with roots can grow. To a person who is doing laundry, soil is dirt to be washed from clothing.

Soil—A Limited Resource

Geologists (jē äl'ə jists) are scientists who study the materials that make up Earth. To a geologist, **soil** is the loose material that covers much of Earth's land surface. If

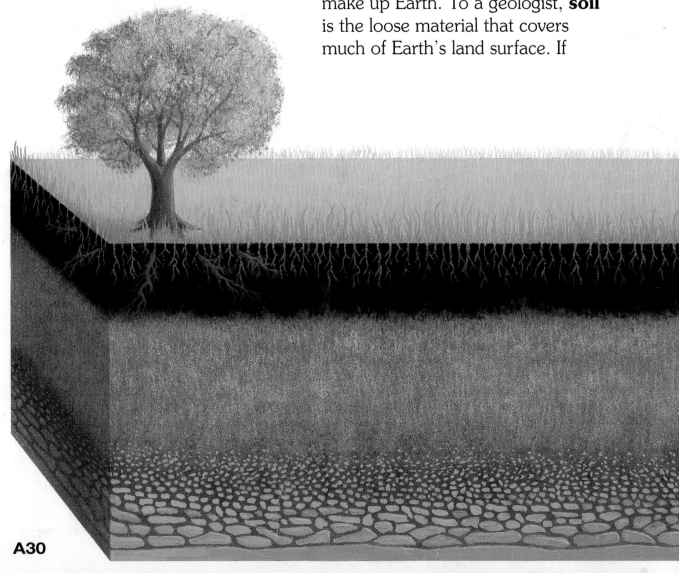

you've ever watched a building crew dig a big hole, it may seem that the soil goes on forever. Actually, the layer of soil that covers the land is very thin compared with the thick layer of rock that's under the soil.

Soil is a natural resource. A **natural resource** is any useful material from Earth. Some other natural resources are trees, petroleum (pə-trō'lē əm), air, and water.

The most important thing about soil is that plants can grow in it. Without plants, life as we know it couldn't exist. That's because plants are the source of food for living things on Earth.

Soil doesn't just happen. A well-developed soil is made up of layers that take many years to form. A side view of the different layers, called a soil profile, is shown below.

Using Soil Wisely

The greatest cause of soil loss is erosion by running water. When rain falls on bare soil, it runs across the surface carrying soil with it. Gullies, or miniature river valleys, are formed in the soil. With each new rainfall, the gullies get bigger and deeper, and more soil is carried away.

Conservation (kän sər vā'shən) is the wise use of natural resources. There are many things people can do to conserve soil. The most important is to leave plants growing where they are whenever possible.

A SOIL PROFILE

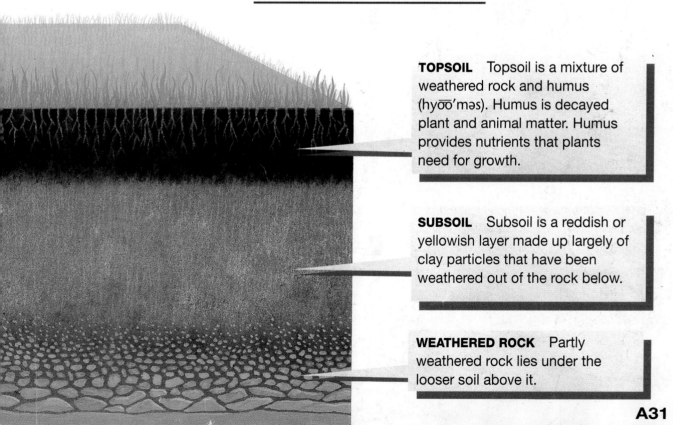

TOPSOIL Topsoil is a mixture of weathered rock and humus (hyoo'məs). Humus is decayed plant and animal matter. Humus provides nutrients that plants need for growth.

SUBSOIL Subsoil is a reddish or yellowish layer made up largely of clay particles that have been weathered out of the rock below.

WEATHERED ROCK Partly weathered rock lies under the looser soil above it.

CONTOUR PLOWING Contour plowing is plowing hilly land in a way that follows the shape of the land. This practice slows rainwater as it runs downhill, giving it time to sink into the soil. ▶

◀**STRIP CROPPING** Strip cropping is planting a cover crop in strips between rows of crops. A cover crop is a crop, such as clover, that grows quickly. The closely planted cover crop absorbs rainfall. Then the rainfall will not run off the land and erode the soil.

Plants, such as trees and grass, provide protection against soil erosion. Remember what you observed in the activity on page A29 about the way "rain" affected sod and soil. The sod, with grass growing in it, lost less soil when it was "rained" on. Plant roots hold soil in place. Some of the ways to protect soil from erosion are described on these two pages.

Conserving soil is hard work. But soil is important. The word *soil* has different meanings. But probably the one most important to you is that soil is a natural resource that helps to produce food.

DAM BUILDING Dam building helps slow or stop the formation of gullies. Dams may be built with boulders, small trees, tree branches, bushes, or boards. Water that would have run into a gully, thus carrying soil away, is stopped by a dam. ▶

▲ **TERRACING** Terracing is the building of terraces, or steplike ridges, in hilly areas to prevent or slow down water runoff.

UNIT PROJECT LINK

As you study this chapter, write and design a class newsletter that informs others about the need to conserve natural resources, such as soil. Choose natural resources that are important in your own community. Distribute the newsletter locally.

INVESTIGATION 1

1. Suppose your town wants a park, but the only land available is bare and full of gullies. Make a plan to convince the town leaders that the available land can be used to make the park.

2. Explain how the processes of weathering and erosion relate to soil.

WHY ARE ROCKS AND MINERALS IMPORTANT?

Below the layers of soil exists a wealth of materials that we use to build everything from computers to roads. What are these materials? Rocks and minerals! In this investigation you'll learn how we get and use these materials.

Activity

Exploring Minerals

You can explore the different properties of minerals. Then decide how these properties make the minerals useful.

MATERIALS
- assorted labeled mineral samples
- hard tile
- magnet
- *Science Notebook*

- - - - - - - - - - - - - - - - - - - -

Procedure

1. **Observe** the labeled minerals your teacher has displayed—magnetite (mag′-nə tīt), hematite (hem′ə tīt), chalcopyrite (kal kō pī′rīt), sphalerite (sfal′ər īt), gypsum (jip′səm), and quartz (kwôrts). In your *Science Notebook*, **make a chart** like the one shown. In the first column write the names of the minerals.

MINERAL	PROPERTIES			
	Hardness	Shiny	Makes a Streak	Attracted to a Magnet

2. A softer mineral can be scratched by a harder one. With your group, handle the minerals and **predict** their hardness, from softest to hardest. Then rub the minerals together to test them. Under *Hardness* in your chart, write a letter from *A* to *F* to tell each mineral's hardness, with *A* representing the softest and *F* the hardest.

Step 2

3. Minerals that are shiny, like a coin, are said to have metallic luster. **Observe** each of the minerals. Under *Shiny*, write *yes* if the mineral has a metallic luster. Write *no* if it doesn't.

4. Some minerals leave a colored streak when they are rubbed on a hard tile. Rub each mineral on a hard tile. Under *Makes a Streak*, write *yes* if the mineral makes a streak. Write *no* if it doesn't.

5. **Test** each mineral with a magnet. Under *Attracted to a Magnet*, write *yes* if the mineral is attracted to the magnet. Write *no* if it isn't.

6. Go on a scavenger hunt. Use reference books to find out what materials come from the minerals. **Record** your findings.

Analyze and Conclude

1. Which of the minerals is the hardest? Which is the softest? **Compare** your results with your predictions.

2. **Infer** which property might be common to all minerals.

3. Use what you learned in this activity to explain how the different properties of mineral resources make them useful for different things.

Activity

Being Polite About Resources

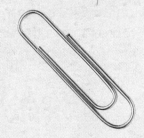

MATERIALS

- small plastic bowl
- paper clips to repre-sent the total supply of a natural resource
- 3 role cards
- *Science Notebook*

Suppose at dinner your favorite food is passed. To be polite, you must take only your fair share. In this activity you'll find out why being polite about mineral resources is important, too.

Procedure

1. You will play a game in which a bowl of paper clips at your work station represents the total supply of a metal resource that is present in Earth's crust today. Place the role cards face down on the table. Each group member selects one card. Hold up your card so that the other group members can read it. The card tells you the name of your generation group—parent, children, or grandchildren—and how many people are in that group.

Step 1

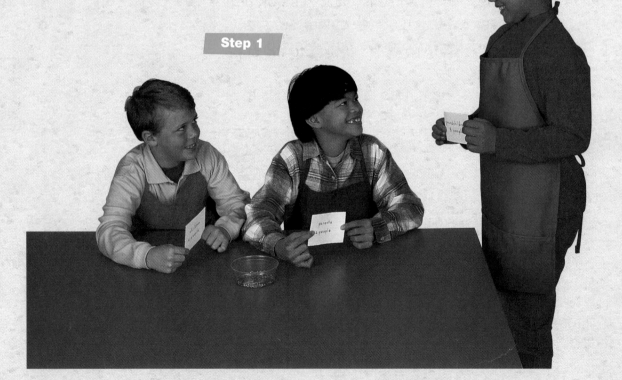

2. When your turn comes, take five paper clips for each person in your generation group. The student with the "Parent" card goes first.

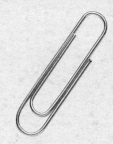

Step 2

3. The student with the "Children" card goes next, followed by the student with the "Grandchildren" card.

Analyze and Conclude

1. Describe the results of this activity.

2. Based on the results, what can you **infer** about the number of paper clips that represent a fair share of the world's present supply of this metal?

3. **Hypothesize** about what would happen to the supply of the metal in several more generations.

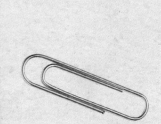

INVESTIGATE FURTHER!

TAKE ACTION

Make a list of items that you use that are made of metals—for example, paper clips. Brainstorm with members of your group to think of some ways that you can help to make sure that people in future generations will have their fair share of metal resources. Record your ideas in your *Science Notebook* and share them with your classmates.

Minerals Through the Ages

People have always found ways to use materials that are taken from the ground. Some of these materials are called minerals. Metals come from a group of minerals that contain metal ore, or rock that can be mined to obtain metals.

Suppose no one had ever found out how to use metals. You wouldn't be sitting at a desk, because there would be no desks. There would be no desks because there would be no metal tools for making desks. Look at the time line to discover some things people have learned about minerals over time.

THE STONE AGE
2 million years ago to 4000 B.C.

58,000 B.C.
People in what are now Europe, the Middle East, and North Africa shape flint, a mineral, into spear points for hunting. They shape other rocks into tools for scraping hides.

7000 B.C.
People in what is now China make stone spades for digging up plants and roots. In what is now North America, people use stone tools for woodworking.

THE BRONZE AGE
4000 B.C. to 1000 B.C.

4000 B.C.
The Egyptians and Sumerians find that gold and silver are easy to hammer and shape. They also use copper alloys (al'ɔɪz). An alloy is a mixture of metals. Bronze, for example, is an alloy of copper and tin.

500 B.C.
The use of bronze for weapons, armor, and tools is widespread. Better ways to make bronze are developed.

THE INDUSTRIAL AGE
1700 to the 1900s

1770s

The Industrial Revolution begins in the textile, or cloth, industry in Great Britain and later spreads to the rest of Europe and to America. Machines replace hand methods. Factories are built. In 1789, Samuel Slater, a British textile worker, opens the first factory in the United States.

1800

The first copper-and-zinc battery is invented.

1874

A steel bridge that spans the Mississippi River is built at St. Louis, Missouri. This bridge is the first major steel structure in the United States.

1912

Stainless steel is invented. Its ability to resist rusting makes it an ideal material for surgical instruments and kitchen utensils.

THE IRON AGE
1000 B.C. to A.D. 1700

350 B.C.

In China, ironworks produce better tools for farming and stronger weapons. At ironworks, iron is separated from the rock it's in.

1452

Metal plates are used for printing. These plates are usually made of copper.

1668

The first cast-iron pipeline is used in Versailles, France, to supply water to the city.

THE INFORMATION AGE
1960 to the 1990s

1960s

Computers help guide spacecraft to the Moon and back.

1981

The silicon chip is invented and used in computers.

1990s

Scientists are finding newer and better ways to use metals and other minerals. For example, gold is used in making very small computers called microcomputers.

2000

A39

From Rocks to Riches

The next time you look at jewelry, spend a coin, or pedal away on your bicycle, think a minute. Where did the materials that were used to make those objects come from? The materials came from rocks. The next time you pick up a rock, look at it carefully. It may contain a little iron, copper, lead, or even gold!

Where Rocks Are Found

Earth is made up of layers. The thinnest, outermost layer is called Earth's crust. It is made mostly of rock. The thickest parts of the crust are the continents (kän'tə nənts). The thinnest parts are the ocean floors.

The surface of Earth's crust may be covered with rocks or soil or water or plants. But if you were to dig down far enough at any place on the surface, you'd find solid rock.

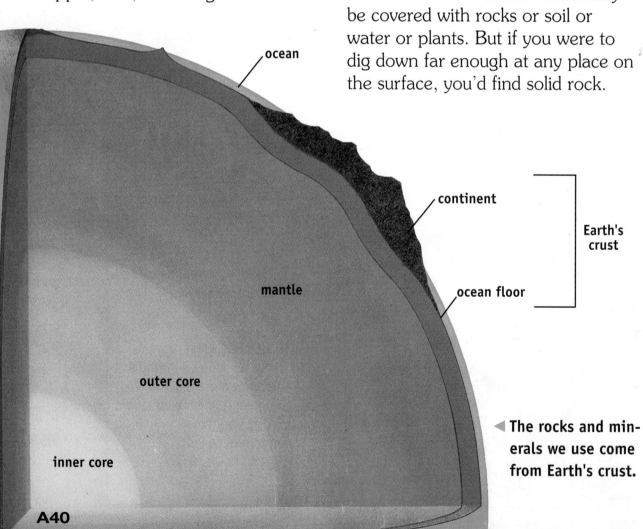

ocean

continent

Earth's crust

mantle

ocean floor

outer core

inner core

◀ The rocks and minerals we use come from Earth's crust.

◀ **Many items you use came from or are minerals.**

An Inside Look at Rocks

Rock is a solid material made up of one or more minerals. Recall that a **mineral** is a natural solid found in Earth's crust. Just as different foods can make up a cookie, different minerals can make up a rock. Most rocks are made up of at least two kinds of minerals.

Uses of Rocks

The way rocks are used depends on their properties. For example, granite (gran'it) is a very hard rock. Because it doesn't weather easily, it's commonly used as a building material. Marble is a rock used for its beauty. Many of the most famous statues are carved from marble.

Uses of Minerals

Rocks may be valuable because of the minerals they contain. If you tried to list all the uses of minerals, your list couldn't fit on all the pages in this book. In fact, you might need a whole sheet of paper just to list the things in your classroom that are made from minerals.

Lead in your pencil is made from the mineral graphite (graf'īt). Chalk is a mineral called calcite (kal'sīt). The salt you sprinkle on food is a mineral called halite (hal'īt).

If you look closely at a rock, you may see specks of different minerals. ▶

Minerals in Ore

All the metals in your classroom come from minerals found in ores. An **ore** is a rock that can be mined for the minerals it contains.

Most minerals come from ores. Some rocks are made up of a single mineral. Rock salt, for example, is rock made up of the mineral halite. Rock salt is an ore that is mined for its one mineral—salt.

Metals are perhaps the most valuable substances that come from ores. Iron, copper, aluminum, gold, and tin are some metals found in ores. Obtaining pure metals from ores is a long and costly process. The first step in this process is to find an ore deposit, or place where there is a large amount of ore. The pictures on page A43 show what is done after a metallic ore deposit is found.

Resources Worth Saving

Some natural resources can be replaced fairly easily. For example, an area that once had trees can be replanted with trees that can grow in a fairly short time. A resource that can be replaced is called a **renewable resource.**

Unfortunately, many of our natural resources, such as metallic ores, can't be replaced. A natural resource

SCIENCE IN LITERATURE

A KID'S HANDBOOK FOR KEEPING EARTH HEALTHY AND GREEN

I CAN SAVE THE EARTH

ANITA HOLMES
ILLUSTRATED BY
DAVID NEUHAUS

I CAN SAVE THE EARTH
by Anita Holmes
Illustrated by David Neuhaus
Julian Messner, 1993

Think of all the kids who might read *I Can Save the Earth*. Think about the many family members and friends they have. Now you get an idea about how *I Can Save the Earth* can really work. This book is filled with ideas about small things you, your family, and your neighbors can do to save Earth's natural resources.

Read pages 76–84 to find out how one day in 1970 changed the way people in our country take care of Earth. You'll find out how you can convince even more people to "save the Earth."

1 First a metallic ore is mined, or dug out of the ground.

2 The ore is taken from the mine to a crusher.

3 The ore is crushed and the valuable metal is collected.

4 The pure metal is taken away to be used.

that can't be replaced is called a **nonrenewable resource.** Nonrenewable resources should be conserved. Otherwise, people some-day will have to do without them.

That's what happened to the paper clip "resource" in the activity on pages A36 and A37. This same thing could happen to actual mineral resources. ■

INVESTIGATION 2

1. Pretend you have discovered a new mineral. Name the mineral and describe its properties. Then explain how the mineral can be used.

2. Write a short paragraph that explains why rocks are important resources.

WHY ARE ENERGY RESOURCES SO IMPORTANT?

People need energy for many things—to move things, to make things, and to keep themselves warm or cool. In this investigation you'll explore how people get energy to meet their current needs, and you'll think about what fuels might be used in the future.

Activity

Sun-Toasted Marshmallows

You can feel the energy from the Sun on a hot, sunny day. Can you make this energy work for you? Find out as you try to make a Sun-powered marshmallow toaster.

Procedure

1. Glue a sheet of aluminum foil to a square of cardboard to make a sun reflector. Repeat this procedure to make two more reflectors.

2. Carefully bend one reflector into a V shape. Bend another reflector into a U shape. Keep the third reflector flat. Tape a thermometer to each of three wood dowels.

3. Talk with your group members and **predict** which thermometer will show the highest temperature if you place the reflectors in sunlight and hold a thermometer in the center of each. Be sure you can explain why you made the prediction you did. **Record** your prediction in your *Science Notebook*.

4. **Test** your prediction and **record** your observations.

5. **Predict** whether the time of day will make a difference in the temperature readings. **Record** your predictions and then test them. **Record** your observations.

6. Use your results from step 4 and step 5 to **design** a solar cooker that will toast a marshmallow.

7. After getting your teacher's approval, **test** your design. Carefully put a marshmallow on a wood dowel. Hold the dowel so that the marshmallow is in the center of your solar cooker. Wait for your marshmallow to cook. **Record** your results.

Analyze and Conclude

1. Which produced the highest temperature, the flat, the V-shaped, or the U-shaped reflector? **Compare** your results with your prediction.

2. At what time of day was the temperature the highest? **Compare** your results with your predictions.

3. What kind of energy heated your marshmallow?

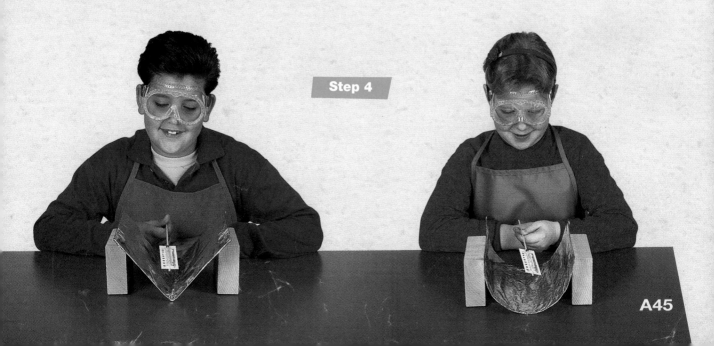

Step 4

Fuels Around the World

What is happening when a car engine starts up and hamburgers sizzle on a grill? Fuel is being burned to produce energy, usually heat energy. People around the world burn different kinds of fuels to produce energy.

Fuel From Living Things

Wood has been used as a fuel for thousands of years. It's still an important fuel in some parts of the world. Wood, of course, comes from trees. A tree stores energy that is released when wood is burned.

In some areas, solid animal waste, called dung, is burned as fuel. The energy in dung comes from energy stored in plants that are eaten by animals. Dung is used in the United States, too. An electric power plant in California uses cow manure as fuel!

WORLD SOURCES OF FOSSIL FUELS

Oil
Natural Gas
Coal

Fossil Fuels

Much of the energy that people use comes from burning fossil fuels. **Fossil fuels**—natural gas, coal, and petroleum, also called crude oil—are fuels made from the remains of once-living things. Peat, another fuel, comes from the remains of ancient swamp plants. In time and with enough pressure, peat can change into coal.

Supply and Demand

As you can see from the map and graphs, the world's fossil fuels are not shared equally. What country today uses the most petroleum? the most natural gas? the most coal?

Fossil fuel use per person is even less equal. The average person in the United States uses about 47 times as much petroleum as the average person in India. And per person the United States uses more than three times as much coal as does China.

Fossil fuels are nonrenewable resources, so people must conserve them. Suppose all people used as much fossil fuel as do people in the United States. Imagine how quickly fossil fuels would disappear. In the future more people might use solar energy, the kind you used in the activity on pages A44 and A45. This kind of fuel will never run out. ■

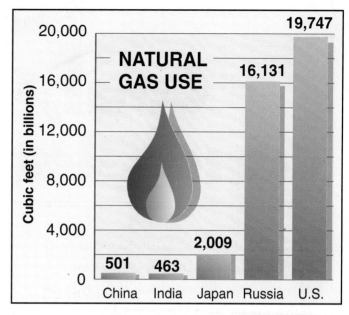

NATURAL GAS USE

Cubic feet (in billions)

China	501
India	463
Japan	2,009
Russia	16,131
U.S.	19,747

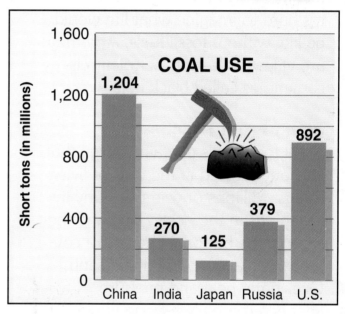

COAL USE

Short tons (in millions)

China	1,204
India	270
Japan	125
Russia	379
U.S.	892

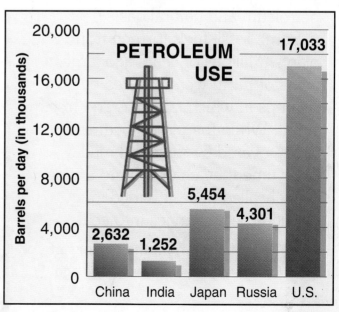

PETROLEUM USE

Barrels per day (in thousands)

China	2,632
India	1,252
Japan	5,454
Russia	4,301
U.S.	17,033

Coal, Gas, and Black Gold

Did you eat food cooked on a stove or ride in a bus or car today? Then you used fossil fuel, which is fuel made from once-living things. It's hard to imagine what life would be like without fossil fuels. And they are valuable. In fact, petroleum is sometimes called black gold.

Fuels From Fossils

All fossil fuels contain energy that was once stored in the cells of living things. Millions of years ago tiny living things in the ocean died and then sank to the bottom. They were covered with layers of mud and sand. Over time, heat and pressure changed these once-living things into petroleum and natural gas.

Some fossil fuels formed from plants. Millions of years ago large areas of Earth were covered by swamps in which tall ferns and trees stood. When the plants died, they were covered by sand and mud. Over time they changed into a type of fuel called peat. If buried long enough, peat changes into coal.

Coal is made from the remains of plants that lived long ago. ▶

Bad News About Fossil Fuels

The fuels that people use can't be replaced in those people's lifetimes. For example, a quantity of natural gas takes millions of years to form. But that same quantity can be burned in a very short time.

Petroleum is also being used up rapidly. And it's difficult to find and costly to remove from the ground.

Coal, mainly found in North America, Asia, and Australia, is more

Land that is strip-mined (*left*) is ripped up by power shovels. The same land can be restored (*right*).

plentiful than oil or natural gas. But even coal won't last forever.

If people had all the fossil fuels they needed, there would still be problems. For example, coal mining destroys huge stretches of land. Mine operators try to repair the damage. But repairing the land may take a long time.

Burning fossil fuels puts extra carbon dioxide and other gases into the air. Carbon dioxide acts like the glass in a greenhouse. Carbon dioxide traps and holds heat close to Earth. Some scientists fear that too much carbon dioxide in the air will change climates on Earth.

Good News About Fossil Fuels

The supply of fossil fuels decreases steadily. So it's possible to determine about when we might run out of them before that ever happens.

▲ To find coal buried deep underground, miners dig hundreds of meters into Earth's surface.

And that's part of the good news—fossil fuel supplies are dependable.

Because fossil fuels are formed and stored in the ground, they can be removed as they are needed. They can also be transported.

A small amount of a fossil fuel has a great deal of energy. This energy can be used to warm rooms or heat water or power machines.

New Energy Sources

Do you remember how long it took to cook the marshmallow in your solar cooker? Possibly the marshmallow didn't cook at all. Your cooker used **solar energy**, or energy from the Sun.

Sunlight is a cheap, clean energy. Solar energy is being used more today than ever before. The Sun heats water for over half the homes in Israel. In Cyprus almost all the homes use solar energy to heat water.

As Earth's supply of fossil fuels runs low, people will continue to search for cleaner and better sources of energy. New energy sources include the wind, energy from inside Earth, and sea water. Chances are that sea water might become the most important fuel source in the future. ■

A windmill farm uses the wind as a source of energy. ▼

INVESTIGATION 3

1. Choose one of these kinds of energy—solar energy, wind energy, or energy from inside Earth. Explain why using that kind of energy might be better than using energy from fossil fuels.

2. Name the three main fossil fuels and tell why they should be conserved.

REFLECT & EVALUATE

WORD POWER

conservation
fossil fuel
mineral
natural resource
nonrenewable resource
ore
renewable resource
rock
soil
solar energy

On Your Own
Review the terms in the list. Then write one new thing you learned about each term.

With a Partner
Write each term in the list on one side of an index card and the definition on the other side. Use the cards to quiz your partner.

PORTFOLIO

Make a booklet about nonrenewable resources. Look for pictures of products made from these resources. Include the pictures in your booklet.

Analyze Information

Study the picture. Describe how natural resources are being conserved.

Assess Performance

Fill a plastic jar halfway with soil that contains no stones. Fill the jar with water. Predict how the sediments will settle if you shake the jar and then let it sit until the water is clear. Test your prediction. Measure the layers. Make a bar graph to show the depth of each layer.

Problem Solving

1. Why should you recycle aluminum cans?

2. Why is it important for farmers to prevent soil erosion?

3. Cars are being designed to use less fuel and burn fuel more cleanly. Why is this important?

CHAPTER 3

THE PROBLEM WITH TRASH

Trash—it's what becomes of many of our land resources. In fact, Americans throw out enough trash every day to fill 63,000 garbage trucks. Where does all the trash go? And how does trash affect our natural resources?

A Trash Detective

William Rathje is an unusual kind of archaeologist (är kē äl'ə jist). An archaeologist is a scientist who digs up buried objects and studies them to learn about the people who left them. Rathje is sometimes called a garbologist. He is part of a team who digs up, sorts, and catalogs garbage from old landfills and dumps. When the team dug up garbage that had been buried for 40 years, they made these discoveries about two of the items found.

- Newspapers were still readable.
- Hot dogs were still recognizable.

These and other discoveries have led people to think about new ways to dispose of, or get rid of, wastes. As you explore the investigations in this chapter, think about how you dispose of wastes. Can you make some changes?

Coming Up

◀ Dr. Rathje is a scientist who studies garbage.

A53

WHAT DO PEOPLE THROW AWAY AND WHERE DOES IT GO?

Think of a 13-story building the size of a football field. Americans produce enough trash to fill 10,000 of these buildings every year. Where do we put it all? In Investigation 1 you'll find out!

Activity

Looking at Trash

Think about the trash your family throws away. What materials make up the trash most people throw away? Find out!

MATERIALS

- goggles
- plastic gloves
- bag of trash
- newspaper
- *Science Notebook*

SAFETY

Wear goggles during this activity. Wear plastic gloves when handling trash.

Procedure

1. Your teacher will give your group a bag of trash that a family might dispose of. Before the bag is opened, **talk with your group** and **predict** what material most items will be made of. **Record** your prediction in your *Science Notebook*.

2. Carefully empty the bag onto newspaper and **examine** the trash. **Classify** the trash into groups based on the material each item is made of.

Step 2

3. Make a chart like the one shown. Count and record the number of trash items in each group.

Group (Material Item Is Made Of)	Item of Trash

4. Analyze the data in your chart. Then make a bar graph to show your data.

Analyze and Conclude

1. Which material was most of the trash made of?

2. How did your prediction compare with what you found out?

3. Resources were used to make the materials in the trash. What resources were being thrown away?

INVESTIGATE FURTHER!

EXPERIMENT

Make a list of all the trash that is produced by your class during the school day. Classify the trash and then make a large bar graph of the results. What material would you infer is thrown away in schools in the greatest amount?

Activity
Making a Landfill

Many towns dispose of trash in a landfill. What happens to trash buried in a land-fill? Build a model and find out!

Procedure

1. Look at different items of trash. **Predict** what will happen to each kind of waste after it has been buried for two weeks.

2. Spread newspaper on your work surface. Work with your group to **build a model** landfill as shown in the cutaway drawing. Press down the layers. End with a layer of soil on top.

Step 2

3. Set the landfill on a tray where it won't be disturbed.

4. Each day sprinkle the landfill with 60 mL of "rain" as shown on the next page.

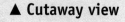

plastic wrap

soil

trash

shoebox

▲ Cutaway view

5. At the end of two weeks, dump the wastes onto newspaper. **Record** in your *Science Notebook* any changes you **observe**.

Analyze and Conclude

1. **Compare** your results with your predictions.

2. **Infer** what happens to the different items of trash buried in a landfill.

3. What material served as a liner in your model land-fill? **Hypothesize** what would happen if wastes were buried in the ground without a liner.

INVESTIGATE FURTHER!

EXPERIMENT

Bury trash in a model landfill for three months. Predict what will happen. Check your predictions. Infer what happens to trash in a landfill over long periods of time.

Trashing Trash

"It's time to take out the trash!" Do you ever hear that reminder? People produce a lot of trash. The average American produces 1.8 kg (4 lb) of trash each day.

Look at the graph. It shows the kinds of trash a town produces and how much space each kind takes up. Which kind of trash is missing?

A TOWN'S TRASH

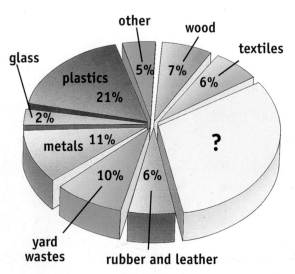

glass
other 5%
wood 7%
textiles 6%
plastics 21%
2%
metals 11%
?
10%
6%
yard wastes
rubber and leather

Trash can be a problem. It's ugly, smelly, and can be harmful to living things. Let's take a look at where trash goes, what problems it can cause, and how people try to prevent those problems.

Trashing Trash in the Past

Until recently, most trash was put in dumps far away from people. These dumps were usually holes in the ground that were covered over when they were filled. But dumps have many drawbacks. The wastes in

TRASH Trash is brought to the landfill by trucks. The trash is spread in a layer and squeezed together to take up less room.

uncovered dumps attract birds, rats, mice, flies, and other disease-carrying animals. Dumps also smell bad, and rainwater moving through a dump picks up harmful chemicals. If this water reaches underground drinking water supplies, the water becomes unsafe to drink.

Today most places have laws against simply dumping trash. Instead the Environmental Protection Agency (EPA) suggests four ways of dealing with trash—bury it, burn it, make new things out of it, or make less of it.

In the activity on pages A56 and A57, you saw how landfills are made. A **landfill**, like a dump, is a large hole that is filled with trash over time. But landfills are built to keep trash from harming the environment. Examine the layers in the landfill picture below. How is the trash kept from getting outside the landfill? How is this landfill like your model?

When a landfill is full, it can be covered over, planted with grass, and made into a park or used for other purposes. Some cities build recreational areas on old landfills.

BURYING TRASH IN A LANDFILL

SOIL Each layer of trash in the landfill is covered with soil. The soil helps reduce odors and keep animals away.

CLAY OR PLASTIC LINER In a sealed landfill, a waterproof liner of plastic or clay keeps liquids in the trash from leaking out of the landfill and into the surrounding soil.

The Problem With Landfills

Building landfills isn't the perfect solution to the trash problem. There are strict laws about how landfills should be built and run. These laws make it costly to run a landfill. And because people don't like to live near landfills, it's hard to find places to put new landfills.

There's another problem with landfills. For many years, people thought that trash in a landfill decayed, or rotted, very fast. But think back to Dr. Rathje and his team of garbologists. They found out that trash in a landfill doesn't decay quickly at all.

In a landfill the trash is squeezed together so tightly that there is very little air or water around it. Without air and water, very little decay occurs. In fact, Dr. Rathje has found that the products everyone thought were the first to rot—paper products—are very slow to rot. He also found that paper products take up the most space in landfills.

Look back at the circle graph on page A58. Did you think that paper makes up the largest amount of trash? How does that compare with your results from the activity on pages A54 and A55 in which you classified trash?

SCIENCE IN LITERATURE

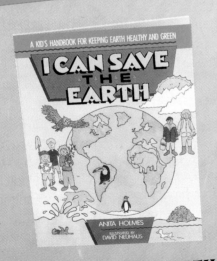

I CAN SAVE THE EARTH
by Anita Holmes
Illustrated by David Neuhaus
Julian Messner, 1993

- A thrown-away aluminum can will barely change at all—even after 500 years!
- The highest point of land on the east coast of the United States is a pile of garbage!

These are just two of the "trashy" facts you'll find in *I Can Save the Earth* by Anita Holmes. Investigate ways to reduce the amount of garbage you send to landfills by reading pages 33–45. Then use what you learned to make your own list of startling facts about what people throw away.

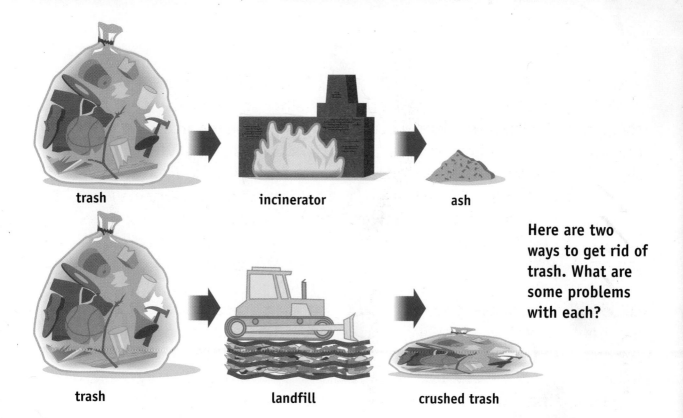

trash   incinerator   ash

trash   landfill   crushed trash

Here are two ways to get rid of trash. What are some problems with each?

What About Burning Trash?

Getting rid of trash by burning it is called **incineration** (in sin ər-ā'shən). Burning trash reduces the amount of material that needs to be disposed of. And the heat produced by burning the trash can be used to make electricity. But today less than one tenth of all the trash in the United States is burned. This is because burning causes smoke. The smoke can contain harmful materials that make the air dirty. The ash itself may also contain harmful materials and must be disposed of carefully.

What Else Can We Do?

As you can see, burning and burying trash offer some solutions, but they aren't perfect. Remember the EPA's other ideas? In Investigation 3 you'll explore how you can make new things out of trash and how you can make less trash. ■

INVESTIGATION 1

1. Imagine that you are in charge of getting rid of your town's trash. If you had to choose between burning it and burying it, which method would you use? Give reasons for your choice.

2. If you were to examine the contents of a town's garbage bags, what type of trash would you expect to find most of? Explain your answer.

INVESTIGATION 2

HOW CAN TRASH AFFECT RESOURCES?

Some trash isn't "lucky" enough to end up in a landfill or incinerator. It's thrown out of car windows, dropped on city streets, or piled up in illegal dumps. Find out in Investigation 2 what effects this trash has on our environment.

Activity

A Litter Walk

MATERIALS
• *Science Notebook*

SAFETY
Do not pick up trash.

Trash thrown on the ground is litter. How does litter affect your school's environment?

Procedure

Take a walk outdoors to look for litter. In your *Science Notebook*, **make a list** of the kinds of litter you see. When you return to the classroom, work with your group to decide how you would like to classify the litter. Using the categories your group decides on, **classify** the litter on your list. **Make a chart or bar graph** to help you **analyze your data**. Share your results with the class.

Analyze and Conclude

1. What material was most litter made of? What else did you learn about litter?

2. How was the litter affecting the environment? **Infer** how litter can waste resources.

Activity

Clean It Up!

Oil is a natural resource. Find out two ways spilled oil affects Earth.

Procedure

1. Half-fill a plastic cup with sand. Pour 20 mL of vegetable oil on the sand. The vegetable oil represents motor oil.

2. After an hour, **observe** the oily sand. **Discuss with your group** ways to remove the oil from the sand. **Predict** which method will best clean up the oil.

3. **Make a plan** to test one of your ideas. Show the plan to your teacher and then carry it out. Note how long you work to remove the oil. **Record** all your results in your *Science Notebook*.

Step 1

Analyze and Conclude

1. How well did your plan work? **Hypothesize** whether your plan would work on a real oil spill on land. Explain.

2. Motor oil is made from crude oil, a natural resource. How does throwing away used motor oil affect the amount of crude oil available as a resource?

INVESTIGATE FURTHER!

RESEARCH

Find out about the methods used to clean up oil spills. Research one of the following: the 1989 Exxon *Valdez* spill into Prince William Sound, Alaska; the 1993 Braer tanker spill off the Shetland Islands into the North Sea; or another spill.

Don't Teach Your Trash to Swim!

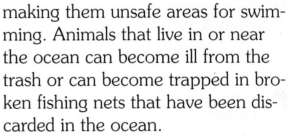

STS
SCIENCE
TECHNOLOGY
& SOCIETY

You might think that litter is only a problem on land. But littering is a big problem in the ocean, too. For centuries, sailors have thrown their garbage over the sides of their boats. And for a long time, trash produced in coastal cities was taken out to sea and dumped.

Ocean dumping does more than make the water dirty. Trash that's dumped at sea washes up on beaches, making them unsafe areas for swimming. Animals that live in or near the ocean can become ill from the trash or can become trapped in broken fishing nets that have been discarded in the ocean.

But some fishers are trying very hard to change their habits. In Newport, Oregon, fishers bring their garbage back to land. There it is sorted and disposed of properly. Some fishers are even picking up the trash they see floating in the ocean. They are hoping that their motto— Don't teach your trash to swim!— catches on. ■

◀ **These plastic objects were found in the nest of this albatross. Birds are attracted to colorful plastics, which are harmful if eaten.**

Trashing Resources

The Earth is full of treasures. Soil, rocks and minerals, water, and petroleum are all natural resources we get from the land. Sometimes people add unwanted materials to the environment, causing **pollution** (pə-lōo′shən). The unwanted materials are called **pollutants**.

People cause pollution when they improperly dispose of trash. Look at the picture below. It shows how pollutants can seep into the ground from oil cans that have been disposed of improperly. Trace the oil as it moves through the ground and into the water. What will happen to the soil in this area? How will the environment of the stream change?

Think back to the activity you did on page A63. How easy will it be to clean up the oil from the soil?

Hazardous Wastes

There are many materials that can harm soil or water supplies. They include motor oil, paint, pesticides, many cleaning supplies, and chemicals from the inside of batteries. These pollutants are called hazardous wastes. **Hazardous wastes** are wastes that can pollute the environment even in small amounts.

Improper disposal of trash can pollute the environment. ▼

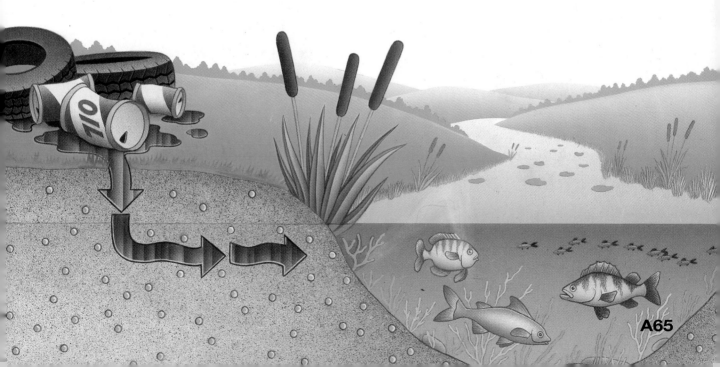

▲ **Littering reduces natural resources and harms the environment.**

PETROLEUM Plastics are made from petroleum, or crude oil. Since this is a non-renewable resource, every time you throw away a plastic bottle the amount of available petroleum is reduced. How does throwing away plastic harm the environment? ▶

Hazardous wastes in soil or drinking water can cause diseases.

Litter—An Ugly Trash Problem

Litter is solid waste, or trash, that is discarded on the ground or in water.

Littering can hide the beauty of the land and be harmful to living things. Some animals are attracted to and collect litter to feed to their young. This can cause serious health problems in the young animals.

◀ **PAPER** Paper is made from trees. Even though we can plant more trees, it takes time for them to grow. And processing trees into paper produces many pollutants.

◀ **METALS** Aluminum cans are made from metal. This picture shows what aluminum ore looks like when it is mined. Mining aluminum is expensive and uses energy. How would reusing the aluminum in cans reduce pollution?

Littering also reduces the amount of available resources. Think back to the litter you saw on your litter walk in the activity on page A62. What resources were being thrown away? Look at the pictures on these pages to see some other ways that littering wastes resources. ■

INVESTIGATION 2

1. Pretend that you are a detective. Look for evidence of land pollution in your community. Record your observations. Then suggest the cause and how this pollution might be prevented.

2. Name two ways that trash can affect available natural resources.

INVESTIGATION 3

HOW CAN YOU HELP SOLVE THE TRASH PROBLEM?

"Please take out the trash!" How many times a week do you hear that? How can your family reduce the amount of trash it produces? Find out in Investigation 3.

Activity

Recycling Old News

Have you ever noticed the words **Made From Recycled Paper** *on a product? In this activity you'll recycle paper.*

Procedure

1. Tear a sheet of newspaper into small pieces. Place the pieces in a plastic container and cover them with water. Let the mixture stand overnight.

2. Place the soaked paper into an electric blender. Add water to cover the paper. With the help of your teacher, blend the water and paper until a smooth mixture is formed. This is called paper pulp.

Step 2

3. Place window screening in the bottom of a flat tray. Then quickly pour the pulp onto the screen.

4. Lift the screen straight up out of the tray. There should be an even layer of pulp on the screen.

Step 4

5. Set the screen on several layers of newspaper to absorb water from the pulp.

6. Place a sheet of wax paper over the pulp. Use a heavy book to press the water out of the pulp.

7. Remove the book. Holding the wax paper and the screen, turn them upside down. Remove the screen. Let the pulp sit overnight. **Talk with your group** and together **predict** what the new paper will be like.

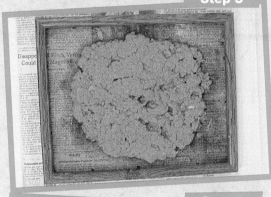

Step 5

8. The next day carefully remove your new paper. Allow it to dry thoroughly. Try writing, drawing, or painting on your paper.

Analyze and Conclude

1. Describe the paper you made. How does it compare with your prediction? Next time, what would you do differently?

2. Infer how using old newspapers to make new paper helps conserve resources.

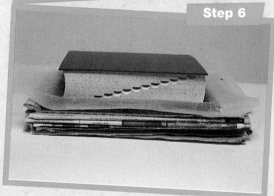

Step 6

INVESTIGATE FURTHER!

EXPERIMENT

Make more recycled paper. Add things such as food dye or pieces of colored thread to the pulp. When the paper is dry, you might wish to cut it into an attractive shape, write a poem on it, decorate it, and give it as a gift.

Activity

The Rethink Link

MATERIALS
• Science Notebook

You've heard of the three R's—reading, 'riting, and 'rithmetic. Now you'll learn about the four R's—reduce, reuse, recycle, and rethink. They can help you find ways to save resources.

- -

Procedure

1. The pictures on this page show some ways to save resources. Think of a way to save resources that you would like to try. **Make a plan** for what you'll do and show it to your teacher.

2. **Predict** how your plan will work. **Record** your prediction in your *Science Notebook.* Carry out the plan. Then share your results.

Analyze and Conclude

1. **Compare** your results with your prediction.

2. How will your plan help save resources?

▲ Collect leaves and grass clippings for compost.

▲ Have a yard sale to sell items that you no longer use.

▲ Use a sponge or cloth instead of paper towels.

▲ Start a recycling center in your home.

Activity

A Second Life for Trash

MATERIALS
- street map of your community
- telephone directory
- colored markers
- *Science Notebook*

How can you reduce your household trash? In this activity you'll identify places to take items for recycling and reuse.

Procedure

1. Study a street map of your community. With your group, **predict** how many places there are to take items for recycling or reuse.

2. Use a local telephone directory to **identify** recycling centers and stores that sell used items.

3. Use colored markers to mark on your map the location of each place you identify.

4. **Make a chart** like the one below in your *Science Notebook*. **Record** in your chart information about each place you marked on your map.

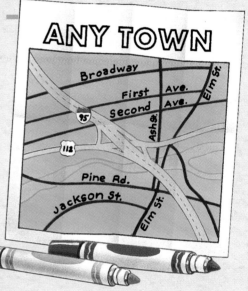

WHERE TO RECYCLE AND REUSE			
Name and Address	**Telephone Number**	**Kinds of Items Accepted**	**Payment Given for Items**

Analyze and Conclude

1. What kinds of items can be accepted for recycling or reuse in your community?

2. **Compare** your prediction with the number of places you found.

3. How does recycling or reusing help conserve resources?

Conserving Resources

Have you ever given away clothing that you've outgrown or toys that you no longer play with? If you have, you were conserving resources. Using materials that otherwise would be thrown away is what conserving resources is all about.

Today many communities recycle paper, aluminum cans, glass, and plastic items. They try to save resources and reduce the amount of trash going into landfills.

Study the time line. As you can see, conserving resources by recycling and reusing materials is not a new idea at all.

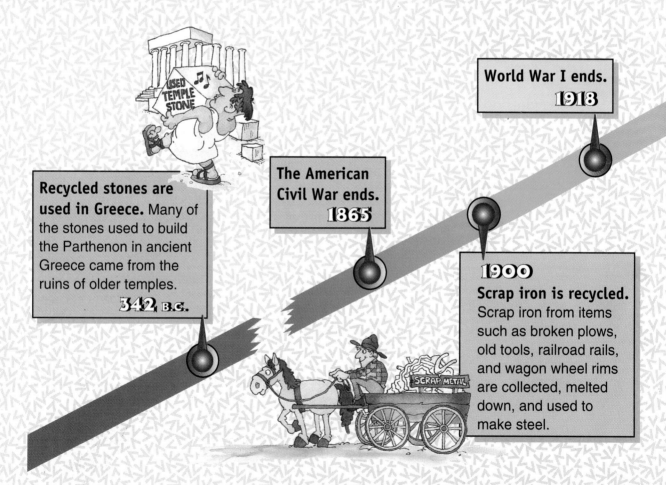

Recycled stones are used in Greece. Many of the stones used to build the Parthenon in ancient Greece came from the ruins of older temples.
342 B.C.

The American Civil War ends.
1865

World War I ends.
1918

1900
Scrap iron is recycled. Scrap iron from items such as broken plows, old tools, railroad rails, and wagon wheel rims are collected, melted down, and used to make steel.

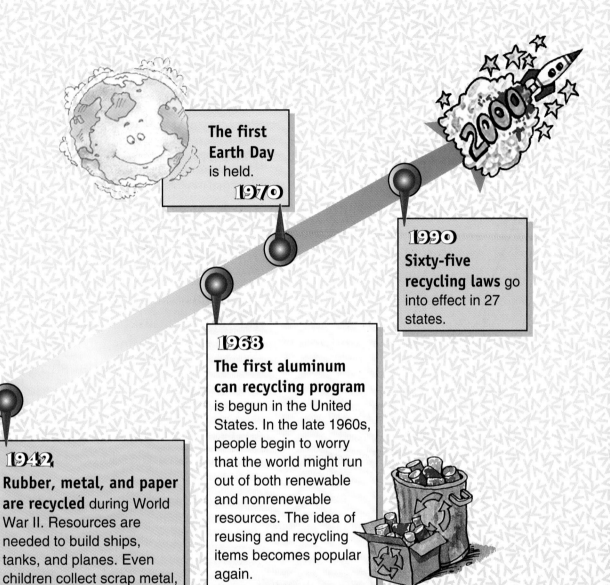

The first Earth Day is held.
1970

1990
Sixty-five recycling laws go into effect in 27 states.

1968
The first aluminum can recycling program is begun in the United States. In the late 1960s, people begin to worry that the world might run out of both renewable and nonrenewable resources. The idea of reusing and recycling items becomes popular again.

1942
Rubber, metal, and paper are recycled during World War II. Resources are needed to build ships, tanks, and planes. Even children collect scrap metal, old rubber tires, tin foil, and tin cans for recycling.

UNIT PROJECT LINK

Choose one resource in your state. Use the information in Investigation 1 to figure out how much of this resource is thrown away. Make a plan for reducing this amount. Then carry out your plan.

Recycling How It's Done

Each day, Americans make enough trash to fill two football stadiums. This trash could be reduced by half if people would **recycle**, or process items and use them again.

Recycling begins at home when recyclables are separated from the rest of the trash and collected. But what happens next? That depends on the kind of material being recycled. When you made recycled paper, you saw some of the steps in that process. Let's see how plastic, aluminum, and glass are recycled.

Recycling Plastic

The diagram below shows the stages in recycling plastics. Although many plastic bottles look alike, they may contain different materials. That's why the plastics industry created a number code that shows what kind of plastic an item is made of. As you can see in the picture on the next page, the code is stamped on the bottom of plastic containers.

1 Recyclable plastic items are carried along a belt.

2 Items are chopped into small pieces and dropped into a flotation tank.

3 The pieces of plastic are washed in the tank. Dirt and nonplastic items, which sink, are separated from the floating plastic pieces.

4 The plastic pieces are dried in a dryer.

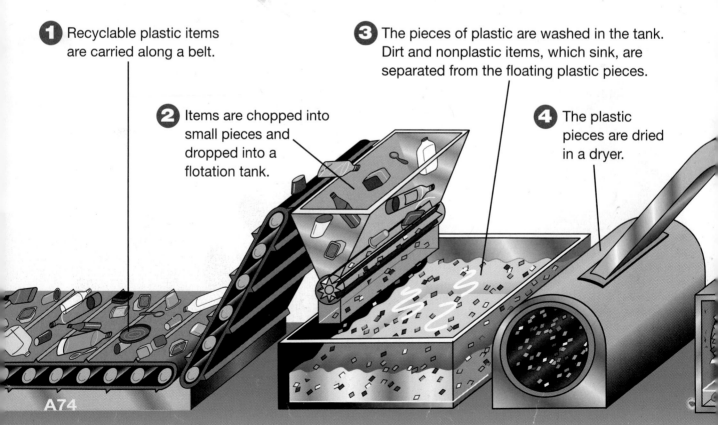

Recycling Plastics

Code	Original Plastics	New Products
1	soft-drink bottles, peanut-butter jars, frozen-food trays	surfboards, film, skis, carpets, soft-drink bottles
2	detergent bottles, milk and water jugs, toys	flowerpots, trash cans, stadium seats, toys
3	shampoo bottles, clear food wrap	floor mats, pipes, hoses, mud flaps on trucks
4	bread bags, frozen-food bags, grocery bags	grocery and other types of bags
5	ketchup bottles, yogurt cups, other food containers	food trays, car battery parts
6	videocassette cases, plastic spoons, food trays, foam cups	trash cans, egg cartons, hangers
7	packages with many layers of materials	plastic lumber

The plastic coded 1 is called PET or PETE. PET is used to make plastic soda bottles. It is the easiest plastic to recycle. The plastic coded 2, called HDPE, is also easy to recycle. Look at the table above to find out what products are made from the plastics you recycle.

▲ **Number code on plastic container**

5 The plastic pieces are melted, filtered, and shaped into strands.

6 The plastic strands are chopped into small bead-shaped pieces that are bought by manufacturers, who make new plastic products from them.

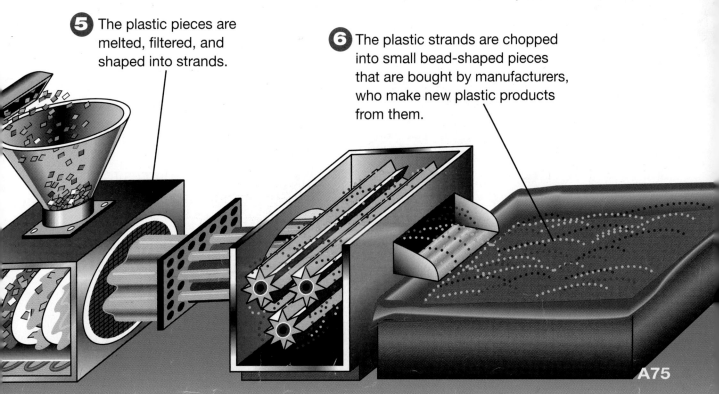

A75

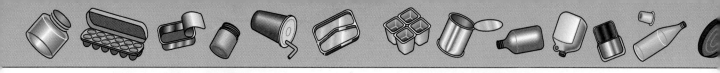

Recycling Glass

1. Used glass bottles are sorted by color and checked for metal caps.

2. The bottles are crushed into small pieces.

3. The glass pieces are cleaned and mixed with sand, soda ash, and limestone.

4. The mixture is melted, and the melted glass is shaped and cooled.

Recycling Aluminum

1. Aluminum cans are crushed.

2. The crushed cans are melted.

3. The liquid aluminum is poured into molds and cooled.

Recycling Glass

Some types of glass—such as that used in light bulbs, windows, and auto headlights—can't be recycled. These types of glass can cause damage to a glass furnace when they're mixed with glass bottles. Study the process used to recycle glass bottles.

Recycling Aluminum

Aluminum cans may be melted down to make new cans. The steps above show the process of recycling aluminum cans. How does it compare with recycling glass and plastics?

Recycling materials helps save resources. However, recycling is not free. It takes energy resources to collect the materials and run the machines used in recycling. But the energy used to recycle materials is usually less than what is needed to make the same materials from scratch. ∎

The Wrap Trap

When you did the activity on page A70, you made a plan to reduce, reuse, or recycle. All the methods shown in the activity help solve the problem of too much trash. And they help conserve natural resources. But one of the most important things you can do to help reduce the amount of trash is to rethink. Rethinking is making choices *before* you buy or use a product.

Wrap Rap

Packaging is the wrappings and containers of items for sale.

▲ Layers of packaging keep products fresh, safe, and unbroken. They also add to the trash problem.

Think back to the trash and litter you analyzed in Investigations 1 and 2. How many of those items were wrappings or containers? In the United States about one third of the trash in landfills comes from packaging. Think about the many products for sale and their wrappings. Could less wrapping have been used? Why not just stop making packaging? The answer is that packaging serves many purposes.

Look at the diagram. It shows some of the purposes for packaging and some examples. What other examples can you think of?

You Decide

Many of the items people buy are wrapped several times. Some bags of snack food come packed within larger bags. Fruit is often put on paper or plastic-foam trays and then covered with plastic wrap.

How can you help with the "wrap trap" of overpackaging? You have a choice of products when you go shopping. If you choose products wisely, you can help reduce the amount of trash in landfills.

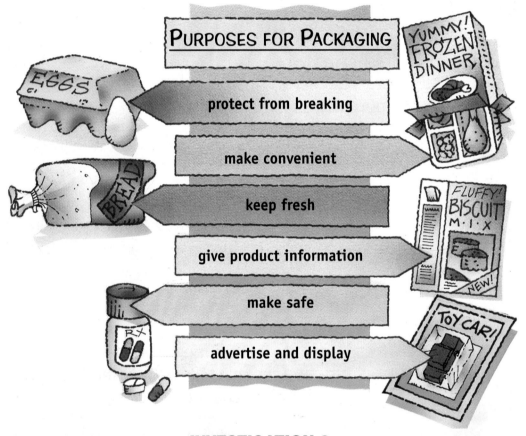

PURPOSES FOR PACKAGING

- protect from breaking
- make convenient
- keep fresh
- give product information
- make safe
- advertise and display

INVESTIGATION 3

1. Most people agree that reducing the amount of packaging would help conserve natural resources and save space in landfills. Why is it difficult to reduce packaging?

2. What are four ways that you can help reduce trash? Describe them.

REFLECT & EVALUATE

WORD POWER

hazardous waste
incineration
landfill
litter
packaging
pollutant
pollution
recycle

 On Your Own
Write a definition for each term in the list.

 With a Partner
Mix up the letters of each term in the list. Provide a clue for each term and challenge your partner to unscramble the terms.

PORTFOLIO

Make a poster that will encourage people to conserve natural resources. Use the words *reduce*, *reuse*, *recycle*, and *rethink*.

Analyze Information

Study the drawing. Then use the drawing to describe how newspapers are recycled.

scraps of used paper
paper pulp
recycling bin
ink being removed
bleach being added
newspaper

pulp being rolled into sheets of paper

Assess Performance

Design the least amount of packaging that will keep four cookies from breaking. Plan a way to test your packaging.

Problem Solving

1. How is reusing materials simpler than recycling them? List five items and describe how you can reuse them.

2. A town is having trouble with unsafe drinking water. How might a garbage dump be related to this problem?

3. The word *recycle*, like the word *bicycle*, contains the word *cycle*. *Cycle* comes from a Greek word that means "circle." Knowing this, explain why recycling won't work if people don't buy things that are made from recycled materials.

A79

Throughout this unit you've investigated questions related to Earth's land resources. How will you use what you've learned and share that information with others? Here are some ideas.

Hold a Big Event
to Share Your Unit Project

Help plan a natural resources exhibit about your state's natural resources. Invite other classes to the exhibit. Distribute suggestions at the exhibit about how your state's resources might be used wisely.

Experiment

Plan a long-term project based on an activity in this unit. You might want to keep your model landfill for several months and see what does (or doesn't) decay. You may want to start a collection made up of local rocks. Set up a plan for your experiment and show it to your teacher before you begin.

Research

Choose a topic from this unit to learn more about. You might investigate a stream or pond in your area to find out how much sediment it contains. You might collect more samples of things made from minerals. Whichever topic you choose, share your information by writing a report or setting up a display.

Take Action

Make a plan to reduce, reuse, or recycle trash. Then put your plan into action. You might set up a home recycling center. If your community has curbside recycling, you might help carry the bags outside each week. Or you might encourage your neighbors to recycle.

UNIT B

PROPERTIES OF MATTER

Theme: Scale

GET READY TO

OBSERVE & QUESTION

What are chemical changes?

Look around you—things are always changing. How are some chemical changes helpful, while others can cause problems?

EXPERIMENT & HYPOTHESIZE

How can matter be described?

Studying different kinds of matter will help you recognize properties. Through hands-on activities you'll learn how these properties are used to describe objects and materials.

INVESTIGATE!

RESEARCH & ANALYZE

As you investigate, find out more from these books.

- **Marie Curie** by Leonard Everett Fisher (Macmillan, 1994). Find out how this famous scientist spent years investigating a certain kind of matter. Her efforts led to the discovery of radioactivity.

- **From Glasses to Gases: The Science of Matter** by Dr. David Darling (Dillon Press, 1992). Read this book to learn that some kinds of matter may not be what they seem.

WORK TOGETHER & SHARE IDEAS

How can you use what you know about matter to set up a science museum?

Working together you'll have a chance to creatively apply what you've learned to set up a science museum. Look for the Unit Project Links for suggested matter mysteries that can be used as displays in your museum.

CHAPTER 1

DESCRIBING MATTER

What do a snowflake, a flower, a dinosaur skeleton, and the Moon have in common? They are all made up of the same stuff—matter. It's the stuff the universe is made of. It's the stuff that we see. Sometimes it's the stuff we *don't* see.

What's the Matter?

Here is a famous poem by Christina Rossetti. Find five things made of matter named in the poem.

The Wind
Who has seen the wind?
Neither I nor you;
But when the leaves hang trembling
The wind is passing through.
Who has seen the wind?
Neither you nor I;
But when the trees bow down their heads
The wind is passing by.

Did you name I, you, leaves, trees, and wind? Yes, wind—an invisible kind of matter! Read on. You'll discover more amazing things about matter in this chapter.

Coming Up

◀ Although you can't see wind, you can't fly a kite without it.

INVESTIGATION 1

HOW CAN MATTER BE DESCRIBED?

Did you know that you and this page are made of the same stuff? That stuff is called matter. Everything around you, even air, is made of matter. In this investigation you'll find out what matter is and how it can be described.

Activity

Describing Things

What features of a baseball bat would you use to describe it? Anything that can be used to describe an object is called a property of that object. In this activity you'll use properties to describe and classify objects.

MATERIALS

• bag of assorted objects
• *Science Notebook*

Procedure

1. Your teacher will give your group a bag with several objects in it. Empty the bag onto your desk.

2. **Observe** the objects and decide what you can tell about them just by looking at them. In your *Science Notebook*, **make a chart** like the one shown. **Record** the name of each object and what you can tell about it.

Object	Description

3. Now pick up each object and study it. Think of new information that you can **infer** about the object by handling it. Add the new information to the description of that object in your chart.

B6

4. Find out if some of the objects share certain properties. To do this, you can **classify** the objects—divide the large group of objects into smaller groups based on shared properties. **Record** the properties you chose to classify the objects.

Analyze and Conclude

1. What properties could you describe by just looking at the objects?

2. What other properties were you able to describe after handling the objects?

3. **List** some other properties that you might use to describe objects. **Hypothesize** what objects or materials might have these properties.

INVESTIGATE FURTHER!

EXPERIMENT

The ability to float in water is a property of many objects. Examine the objects used in the activity. Predict which of the objects will float and which will sink. Test your predictions by placing each object in a bucket of water.

Activity
Similar but Different

MATERIALS
- assortment of num-
  bered balls
- *Science Notebook*

A baseball bat and a toothpick are both made of the same matter—wood. But the bat contains more wood than the toothpick. How do you know? Can you always tell how much matter is in an object from its size?

Step 3

Procedure

1. Look at the numbered balls. Using the numbers, **rank** the balls in order of size, from largest to smallest, in your *Science Notebook*.

2. Now **make inferences** about the amounts of matter in the balls. **Predict** the order of the balls, from the one having the most matter to the one having the least. **Record** your prediction, using the numbers.

3. Check your prediction by picking up the balls and **comparing** how heavy they are. Using the numbers, **rank** the balls in order, from heaviest to lightest.

Analyze and Conclude

1. What properties do all the balls have in common? What can you tell about the different balls just by looking at them? What did you learn by lifting them?

2. What property did you use in making your prediction about which ball contains the most matter and which contains the least matter?

3. **Compare** your prediction about the amount of matter in the balls with your observations. What can you **infer** about the relationship between the size of an object and the amount of matter it contains?

B8

Activity

Move Over

Does all matter take up space? Can two things be in the same place at the same time? Find out.

Procedure

1. Half-fill a narrow plastic jar with water. Use a grease pencil to mark the level of the water on the side of the jar. Pour the water into a dry cup.

2. Place a marble in the jar. Pour the water from the cup back into the jar and mark the level of the water. Pour the water, but not the marble, back into the cup.

3. Place a second marble in the jar. **Talk with your group** and together **predict** where the level of the water will be if you pour it back into the jar now. **Record** your prediction in your *Science Notebook*.

4. Mark the predicted level on the side of the jar. Then check your prediction by pouring the water from the cup back into the jar. **Record** your results.

Step 2

Analyze and Conclude

1. What information did you use to make your prediction in step 3? How did your prediction compare with your result in step 4?

2. Did you use the same amount of water in each step of the activity? If so, why did the level of the water in the jar change?

3. From your results, **infer** whether two things can be in the same place at the same time. Give reasons why you think as you do.

B9

Matter, Matter Everywhere

Imagine you're home alone at night and all the lights go out. As you sit in the dark, you hear a strange creaking sound in another part of the house. You grab a flashlight and go to investigate.

As you shine the light around, different things come into view. You even see dust in the air. Finally, you notice a cabinet door swinging slowly back and forth on rusty hinges. You can relax. You've found the source of the squeak.

What Is Matter?

Everything you saw as you shined the light around the house, even the

dust in the air, was matter. **Matter** is anything that has mass and takes up space.

Just about everything you can think of is matter. Think about the different kinds of matter that you described in the activity on pages B6 and B7. If you can see it, smell it, or taste it, it's matter. Matter can also be invisible, as air is.

A Matter of Mass

Look at the many different things around you. These things are all matter, but they don't all contain the same *amount* of matter. Recall the balls you investigated in the activity on page B8. Some balls felt heavier than others because they contained different amounts of matter. They had different masses.

Mass is a measure of the amount of matter something contains. The more matter an object or material contains, the greater its mass will be.

◀ **Air in the glass keeps the paper towel from getting wet. What does this tell you about air?**

▲ **How many objects in this picture are made of wood? Do they all have the same mass? How do you know?**

A Matter of Volume

In addition to having mass, matter also takes up space. The amount of space that matter takes up is called **volume**. Even the smallest bit of matter you can think of has volume.

Look at a piece of chalk. You can see that it takes up space. You could measure its volume quite easily. Now think about the chalk dust in the tray that is under the chalkboard. Does a single speck of this dust take up space? Does it have mass? The answer is yes, even though these properties are hard to measure because of the tiny size of the specks.

As you go about your daily routine, keep those specks of chalk dust in mind. Everywhere you look, there is matter, some as big as a mountain, some so small you can't even see it. Matter is, indeed, everywhere.

UNIT PROJECT LINK

Make your first Matter Mysteries display. Collect several objects that can be measured in different ways. Make up a challenging question about these objects for visitors to your museum to answer. The question should challenge the visitor to order the objects by mass or volume (size). Describe the materials used in each object. Name the property or properties that make each material useful for the purposes shown.

Making Materials Useful

You are probably familiar with the story of Cinderella. One of the most important parts of the story deals with a glass slipper.

Useful Properties

How would you describe glass? You might use such words as *hard, solid, clear,* and *breakable*. All of these things are properties of glass. A **property** is something that describes matter.

The idea of making a slipper out of glass is silly. The kind of matter used to make an object is chosen for its useful properties. Slippers and other kinds of footwear are made from materials that are flexible, or easy to bend.

Kinds of Properties

There are two kinds of properties that describe matter—physical (fiz′i-kəl) and chemical (kem′i kəl). The **physical properties** of a material are those characteristics that can be seen or measured without changing the material.

You can identify the physical properties of a material by using your five senses. Odor, color, shape, and texture are physical properties.

What's wrong with this picture? ▼

B12

▲ Name the materials used in each object. Describe properties that make each material useful for the purposes shown.

The **chemical properties** of a material are characteristics that can only be seen when the material changes and new materials are formed. A chemical property of wood is its ability to burn. This property makes wood a useful fuel. As wood burns, it changes. It is no longer wood. The wood is "gone," and other materials are left.

So the next time you put on your sneakers or look through a window, think about the materials those objects are made of. Ask yourself what properties made those materials right for the job. ■

INVESTIGATION 1

1. Look at this list: hammer, ice cube, mirror, rubber balloon. For each object, identify the property or properties that make the material that the object is made of useful.

2. Imagine that you are going on a trip to the South Pole. Name two nonfood items you would bring with you and tell why each would be useful.

INVESTIGATION 2

HOW CAN MATTER BE MEASURED?

Do you know how tall you are? You probably do, because you've been measured. Measuring is one way to describe matter. In Investigation 2 you'll learn how to make measurements of matter using different measuring tools.

Activity

A Balancing Act

A rock contains matter—but how much matter? How can you measure the amount of matter in an object?

Procedure

Step 1

1. Place a small rock in the pan on the left side of a balance. **Observe** what happens. Add objects from bag *A* to the other pan until both pans contain the same amount of matter. **Infer** how you will know when this happens. **Record** your inference and your results in your *Science Notebook*.

2. Leave the rock in its balance pan. Remove the objects from the other pan. Replace them in bag *A*.

3. Look at the objects in bag *B*. **Talk with your group.** Then together **predict** how many objects from bag *B* it will take to balance the rock. Be sure that you can explain why you made the prediction you did. **Record** your prediction.

4. Use objects from bag *B* to **measure** the amount of matter in the rock. **Record** your results.

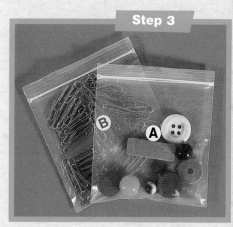

Step 3

Analyze and Conclude

1. Name the objects used in step 1 to find the amount of matter in the rock.

2. How many objects from bag *B* were used to equal the amount of matter in the rock? **Compare** your results with your prediction.

3. Which measurement is easier for telling about the amount of matter in the rock, the one made in step 1 or the one made in step 4? Explain your answer.

SCIENCE IN LITERATURE

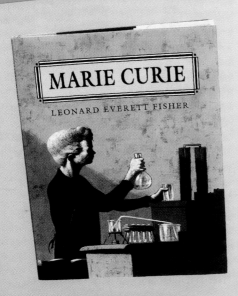

MARIE CURIE
by Leonard Everett Fisher
Macmillan, 1994

Marie Curie had a mysterious lump of rock that glowed in the dark. She was determined to find out all she could about its properties. Curie tested the rock in her lab. After a year she decided that the rock was a kind of matter never before identified. She described how the strange matter gave off energy—a property she called radioactivity.

Marie Curie lived about 100 years ago at a time when most girls never thought of becoming scientists. Find out what she named the two kinds of matter she discovered. Read the story of her life in *Marie Curie* by Leonard Everett Fisher.

B15

Activity

Wider or Taller?

When people stand with their arms out-stretched, are they wider than they are tall, or taller than they are wide? Use a measuring tool to find out.

- -

Procedure

1. Work with a partner. One partner will be the model. The other will be the marker. The model will stand, arms outstretched, with his or her back against the chalk-board. The marker will use a piece of chalk to mark the model's height and arm span, as shown. Arm span is the width from the tip of one hand to the tip of the other.

Step 1

2. **Select** an object to use as a measur-ing tool. Don't select the same tool that your partner does. Using the floor and the marks on the chalkboard, use your mea-suring tool to **measure** the model's height and arm span. **Record** your results in your *Science Notebook*. **Compare** your results with those of your partner.

3. Repeat step 2, this time using the *same* measuring tool that your partner does to measure the height and arm span. **Predict** how your measurements will compare with those of your partner. **Record** your prediction and then check it.

Analyze and Conclude

1. Which was greater, the model's height or the model's arm span?

2. Which measurements were easier to compare, those made in step 2 or those in step 3? Explain your answer.

Activity
How Much?

Suppose that you could have as much gold dust as you could carry in a single container. If you had three containers, how could you find out which would hold the most? Could you tell by just looking?

MATERIALS
- goggles
- newspaper
- 3 plastic containers of different sizes and shapes
- grease pencil
- small plastic cup
- sand
- *Science Notebook*

SAFETY //////
Wear goggles during this activity. Clean up spills immediately.

Procedure

1. Spread newspaper on your work area. Place three containers on the newspaper. Use a grease pencil to label the containers *A, B, C,* with a different letter for each container.

2. Study the containers. **Infer** which can hold the most matter. **Record** your inference in your *Science Notebook.*

3. The amount of sand or other matter that a container can hold is the **volume** of the container. **Write a plan** to find out how much matter each container can hold. Show the plan to your teacher. Carry out your plan and **record** your results.

Step 2

Analyze and Conclude

1. Which container can hold the most matter? How did your results compare with your inference?

2. Which container has the greatest volume? How do you know?

B17

Measuring Systems

You may not realize it, but you measure things every day. How do you know when it's time to go to school or go home? You look at a clock. You usually know what day it is because you see it on a calendar, another way to measure time. Whenever you weigh yourself or check your height, you're measuring.

You measure ingredients when you make lemonade or cocoa. How did people of long ago measure things? You'll have to go back in time to see for yourself.

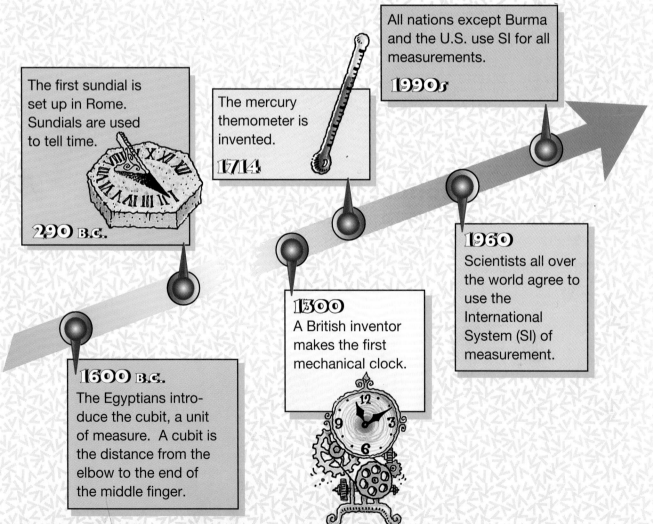

All nations except Burma and the U.S. use SI for all measurements.

1990s

The first sundial is set up in Rome. Sundials are used to tell time.

290 B.C.

The mercury themometer is invented.

1714

1960
Scientists all over the world agree to use the International System (SI) of measurement.

1300
A British inventor makes the first mechanical clock.

1600 B.C.
The Egyptians introduce the cubit, a unit of measure. A cubit is the distance from the elbow to the end of the middle finger.

The Metric System

Imagine that you and a group of friends are planning to build a clubhouse. You receive permission from your parents, draw up your plans, and collect your materials.

On the first day of work, each member of your group shows up with a homemade ruler. Nobody's units match anybody else's units! What do you think your clubhouse will look like if measurements are made with these rulers?

In the activity on pages B14 and B15 and the one on page B16, you discovered the importance of using standard units to make measurements. A **standard unit** is one that is agreed on and used by everyone. When all members of your group used the *same* objects to make measurements, you were using standard units—standard, at least, for those activities.

Measuring Systems

To accurately describe matter, it is necessary to use a set of standard units to measure such properties as size, mass, volume, and temperature. Such a set of standards is known as a system of measurement.

At the present time, there are two widely used systems of measurement—the metric system and the English system. The metric system is used in just about *every* country—except the United States and Burma. Almost everyone in this country uses the English system.

Why is the clubhouse so crooked? ▼

English System Units

Length	Weight (mass)	Volume
mile (1,760 yards)	ton (2,000 pounds)	gallon (4 quarts)
yard (3 feet)	pound (16 ounces)	quart (2 pints)
foot (12 inches)	ounce	pint (16 ounces)

How Many Inches in a Mile?

The English system of measurement includes such units as feet and inches, pounds and ounces, quarts and pints, and degrees Fahrenheit.

The problem with the English system is the way its units vary. The table above lists some units used to measure length (or distance), weight, and volume in the English system.

As the table shows, there is no logical relationship between units, even for measurements of the same property. For example, suppose you want to find out how many inches are in one mile. You must know how many feet are in one mile and how many inches are in one foot. Then you need to do a lot of multiplying.

The Metric System

The **metric system** is a system of measurement that is based on the

number 10 and multiples of 10. In other words, it is a decimal system.

The metric system of measurement was introduced in France during the 1790s and is used by most people in the world today. In 1960, scientists worldwide agreed to use a modern version of the metric system. This system is known as the International System of Units, abbreviated SI.

BALANCE Balances are used to measure mass. An object of unknown mass placed in one pan is balanced by objects of known mass placed in the other pan. ▼

METERSTICK AND METRIC RULER
Metersticks and metric rulers are used to measure length, or distance. The scale of this meterstick is divided into centimeters and millimeters. ▼

90 91 92 93 94 95 96 97 98   8 99 1

Because the metric system is a decimal system, it's easy to learn. And it's easier to use than the English system. The table below shows some basic units of measurement in the metric system and their symbols. The pictures show some measuring tools. You can learn more about how these tools are used by reading pages H12–H15 in the Science Handbook.

Metric System Units

Measurement	Unit	Symbol
length	meter	m
mass	gram	g
volume	liter	L
temperature	degree Celsius	°C

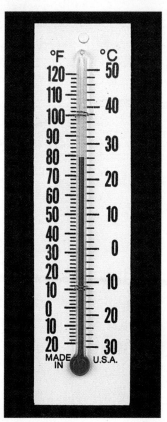

▲ **THERMOMETER** Thermometers are used to measure temperature. The thermometer shown here has two temperature scales.

GRADUATED CYLINDER Graduated cylinders, or graduates, are used to measure volumes of liquids. The scale of a graduate is divided into milliliters. ▶

Metric Prefixes

Prefix	Meaning	Symbol	Example
kilo-	one thousand	k	1 kilometer (km) = 1,000 m
deci-	one tenth	d	1 decimeter (dm) = 0.1 m
centi-	one hundredth	c	1 centimeter (cm) = 0.01 m
milli-	one thousandth	m	1 millimeter (mm) = 0.001 m

One thing that makes the metric system easy to use is a set of prefixes. A *prefix* is a syllable added to the beginning of a word to give the word a new meaning. Think of the word *triangle*. The prefix *tri-* means "three." So *triangle* means "three angles."

The table above lists the prefixes used in the metric system. It gives their meanings, their symbols, and examples of how they are used.

How do the prefixes help to make using the metric system easy? The same prefixes are used with all the basic units. So you know that a kilogram is equal to 1,000 grams and a kiloliter is equal to 1,000 liters. You also know that 5 kilograms is equal to 5,000 grams. Similarly, a centimeter is equal to $\frac{1}{100}$ of a meter, or 0.01 meter. How many centimeters are in 5 meters?

Scientists have chosen the metric system because it's simple, it's accurate, and it's known worldwide. Much of a scientist's time is spent making observations and measurements. By using the same system of measurement—SI—scientists can easily compare their work with that of other scientists, no matter what nation they're from. ■

INVESTIGATION 2

1. Suppose you want to move a desk into your bedroom. What properties of the desk will you have to measure?

2. You want to make enough fruit punch to fill a large punch bowl. What property of the bowl do you need to measure? How would you make the measurement?

REFLECT & EVALUATE

WORD POWER

chemical properties
mass
matter
metric system
physical properties
property
standard unit
volume

On Your Own
Review the terms in the list. Then use as many terms as you can in a paragraph about ways to describe matter.

With a Partner
Write a definition for each term in the list. Have your partner match each definition to the correct term.

PORTFOLIO

Find examples of everyday items that make use of metric measurements in the U.S. Cut out pictures or make drawings of five things you find and use the pictures to make a poster.

Analyze Information

Study the materials in the photograph. List as many properties of each material as you can. Then describe the properties that make each material useful for the purpose shown in the photograph.

Assess Performance

Design and carry out an activity to help you determine which is easier to use, the metric system or the English system. Report your results and conclusions.

Problem Solving

1. Suppose you wanted to find the length and mass of your science textbook. What tools would you use to make these measurements? In what units would you record your measurements?

2. How could you use a balloon and a balance to show that air is matter?

3. Suppose you need to find the mass of a jar of paste. You have a balance and a box of washers to use as masses. Each washer has a mass of 2 g. It takes 41 washers to balance the jar of paste. What is the mass of the jar?

B23

CHAPTER 2

OBSERVING STATES OF MATTER

Have you ever wanted to catch a cloud? Did you ever wonder how water turns to ice? Are you curious about what a rainbow is made of? In this chapter you'll investigate the forms of things around you and how those forms can change.

Solving Earth's Mysteries

In the 1930s a boy named Fred roamed the land of his ancestors. He and his family lived the way Navajos had for hundreds of years. They hunted, fished, and picked wild herbs. Practicing Navajo medicine was their work.

As he traveled, young Fred wondered about the world around him. He wondered how mountains form and what lightning is. He questioned how things work. Though he didn't know it, Fred was already a scientist.

Today, Dr. Fred Begay still asks questions about how the world works. That is his job as a physicist (fiz′ə sist). A physicist is a scientist who studies matter and energy.

As you move through the investigations in this chapter, be a scientist like young Fred Begay. Think about the way things are made. Question how things work. Explore the mysteries of matter and energy.

Coming Up

◀ Dr. Fred Begay, physicist

WHAT IS MATTER LIKE?

Your friend is having a birthday party. There are cookies, juice, and balloons. These things are all made of matter, but each is different. In this investigation you'll find out about the states of matter and what kinds of matter exist.

Activity

States of Matter

Does juice change shape when poured from a carton into a glass? Do all kinds of matter change in the same way? Compare the property of shape in three states of matter.

MATERIALS

- 5 objects of different shapes and sizes, labeled *A–E*
- 3 plastic containers of different shapes, labeled 1–3
- plastic soda bottle filled with water
- small inflated balloon
- *Science Notebook*

SAFETY

Clean up spills immediately.

Procedure

1. **Observe** objects *A* through *E*. Press down on each object with your thumb and **observe** what happens to the object. Pick up each object, handle it, and describe its properties. **Record** your descriptions in your *Science Notebook*.

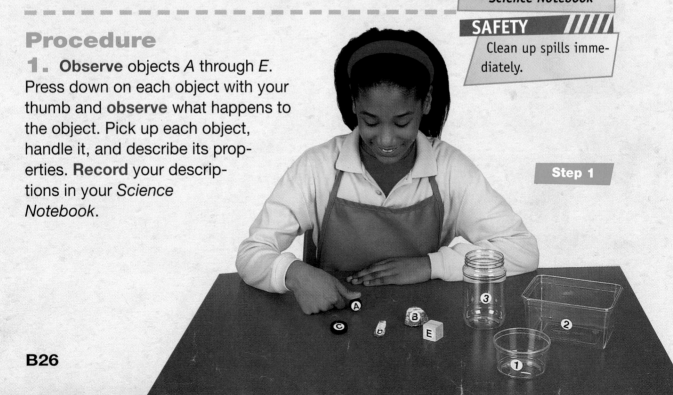

Step 1

2. Place each object, one at a time, into each of the containers. Each time, gently shake the container and its contents. **Observe** and **record** any changes in the objects. Remove the objects from the containers.

3. Pour water from the bottle into the containers to fill them, one at a time. **Observe** what happens to the shape of the water in each container. **Record** your findings.

Step 3

4. **Observe** and **record** what happens to the matter inside an inflated balloon when you press on it with your hand and when you stop pressing on it. **Predict** what will happen to the air inside the balloon when you untie the balloon. **Record** your prediction.

5. Hold the balloon and carefully undo the twist tie on the neck of the balloon. **Observe** and **record** what happens to the air inside the balloon.

Analyze and Conclude

1. The objects used in steps 1 and 2 are all solids. Based on your observations, what can you **infer** about the shape and volume of a solid?

2. From your observations of liquid water, what can you **infer** about the shape and volume of a liquid?

3. Air is a mixture of gases. From your observations in steps 4 and 5, what can you **infer** about the shape and volume of a gas?

UNIT PROJECT LINK

With your group, brainstorm a list of materials that can be presented in a form or state different from that in which they are normally found. Choose three materials from your list and prepare a display of these materials (either pictures or actual materials) in their unusual form or state. Create signs inviting visitors to your science museum to learn the identities of the materials.

Activity

Invisible Matter

Did you ever enter a front doorway and know what was cooking in the kitchen? How did the smell get from the kitchen to your nose? Find out how one state of matter behaves.

MATERIALS
- goggles
- small plastic bottle (stoppered) containing vanilla extract
- large wide-mouthed plastic jar
- timer
- *Science Notebook*

SAFETY /////
Wear goggles during this activity. Clean up any spills immediately.

Procedure

1. Put your nose over the opening of a large plastic jar to find out if you smell any odor. **Record** your observations in your *Science Notebook*.

2. Remove the stopper from a bottle of vanilla extract. Put your nose over the bottle to see if you smell any odor. **Record** your observations.

3. Place the opened bottle of vanilla extract at arm's length on your desktop. Have a group member quickly place a large jar upside down over the bottle of vanilla.

4. Leave the jar undisturbed over the bottle for about one minute.

5. Pick up the jar and put your nose to the opening to see if you smell any odor. **Record** your observations.

Step 2

Step 3

Analyze and Conclude

1. How did the jar smell before it was placed over the bottle of vanilla extract?

2. How did the jar smell after it was placed over the bottle? **Compare** your observations from steps 2 and 5. **Talk with your group** and **hypothesize** about what happened. Give reasons for your hypothesis. What do your observations tell you about matter?

More About Matter

Can you identify the kind of matter being described in this riddle?

You can see it and skate on it, but you can't pour it.

You can see it and pour it, but you can't skate on it.

You can't see it or pour it or skate on it, but it can fog up a mirror.

Did you answer "water"? If you did, you're correct.

States of Matter

The riddle describes some properties of water in three different forms. These forms—liquid, solid, and gas—are called **states of matter**. The state of a sample of matter is a physical property of that sample.

Look at the pictures below of the three different states of matter. As you read about each state, think back to what you observed in the activities on pages B26–B28.

SOLIDS A **solid** is matter that has a definite volume and a definite shape.

LIQUIDS A **liquid** is matter that has a definite volume but no definite shape. Liquids take the shape of their containers.

GASES A **gas** is matter that has no definite volume or shape. A gas spreads out to fill its container.

A Closer Look at Matter

It might surprise you to learn that scientists discovered much of what is known about matter by studying gases. Remember how the odor of vanilla spread out from its container in the activity on page B28? Such observations led scientists to conclude that all matter is made up of tiny bits, or particles.

The particles that make up matter are much too small to be seen, even with a powerful microscope. But even though scientists can't see them, they know that the particles are always moving. This explains how the vanilla particles moved out of the bottle and spread through the large jar to your nose. The drawings show the arrangement of particles in the three states of matter.

Back to Basics

Think of all the different kinds of matter there are in the world. It might surprise you to learn that there are only 109 basic kinds of matter, called elements (el'ə mənts). An **element** is any material made up of only one kind of matter.

Elements are made up of very tiny particles called atoms. An **atom** is the smallest part of an element that has the properties of that element. All of the atoms in a given element are the same. For example, all the atoms in a piece of iron are iron atoms. Iron atoms are different from

▲ Particles in a solid are packed closely together. The particles can only vibrate, or move back and forth, in a very small space. This explains why a solid holds its shape.

the atoms that make up any other element.

Symbols for Elements

When scientists study matter and its changes, they record their observations. To save time and space, scientists use chemical symbols. A **chemical symbol** is one or two letters that stand for the name of an element. The table shows the names and symbols of some elements.

Element & Symbol		Element & Symbol	
oxygen	O	iron	Fe
hydrogen	H	gold	Au
iodine	I	helium	He

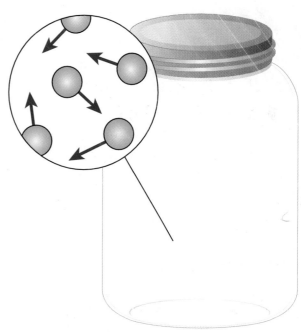

▲ Particles in a liquid are farther apart and move faster than those in a solid. They can move past each other, allowing the liquid to take the shape of its container.

▲ Particles in a gas are farther apart and move faster than particles in solids or liquids. As the particles move, they spread out in all directions, filling their container.

SCIENCE IN LITERATURE

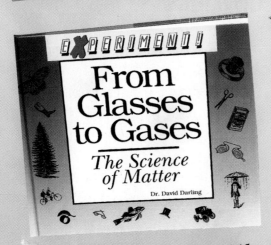

FROM GLASSES TO GASES
THE SCIENCE OF MATTER
by Dr. David Darling
Dillon Press, 1992

What's the slowest flowing liquid on Earth? You might pick it up at dinnertime tonight! Can't guess? It's ordinary glass! Find out what makes glass a liquid and not a solid on page 22 of the book *From Glasses to Gases* by David Darling.

From Glasses to Gases is loaded with facts and experiments about solids, liquids, and gases. Read on pages 23–29 about how water has a "skin" that insects can run across. Then pick one of the experiments to try. (Make sure you have the permission of an adult before you begin!)

A Precious Metal

Babies and children are often described as *precious*, meaning "dear" or "beloved." Some elements—particularly metals such as gold—are also said to be precious. The term is used to describe certain elements because they are valuable, not because they're beloved.

The main reason that gold is valuable is because it's rare. Only a few places in the world have large deposits of gold. In the past, people have gone to great lengths to obtain some of that gold. The map below shows the location of some of the best-known gold discoveries in history.

The discovery of gold has changed many places. Tiny towns and remote villages have been turned into bustling communities just because gold was found nearby. In 1886 the discovery of gold in South Africa led to war between the British and a group of Dutch settlers called Boers. ■

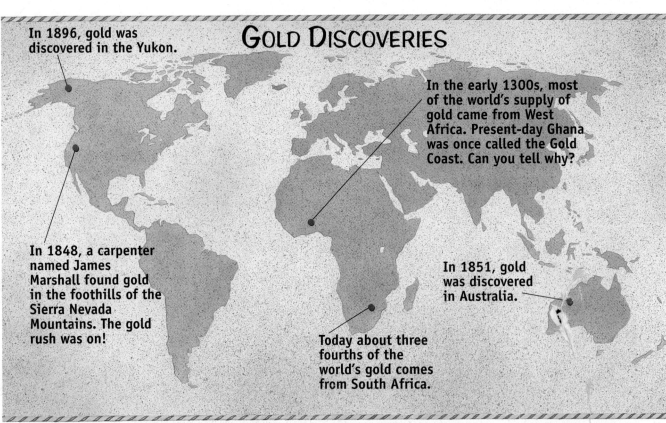

GOLD DISCOVERIES

In 1896, gold was discovered in the Yukon.

In the early 1300s, most of the world's supply of gold came from West Africa. Present-day Ghana was once called the Gold Coast. Can you tell why?

In 1848, a carpenter named James Marshall found gold in the foothills of the Sierra Nevada Mountains. The gold rush was on!

In 1851, gold was discovered in Australia.

Today about three fourths of the world's gold comes from South Africa.

Compounds
They're Elementary

Picture yourself on a spaceship headed for a planet in a distant solar system. When you arrive, you discover that all matter is in the form of elements—the same elements found on Earth. Would you want to live there, even if you could?

You possibly could breathe the air, because there would be oxygen present. You might find a lot of gold or silver lying around, but you wouldn't find soil or rubber or cloth.

Most importantly, you wouldn't find many of the things you need to live. No water and no living things! So, even though all the natural elements were there, you wouldn't want to stay around very long.

Building Blocks

As you may have guessed, not many things on Earth are made of a single element. Rather, you can think of elements as the building blocks of matter. Most kinds of matter are compounds. A **compound** is a kind of matter made up of two or more elements that are joined together.

A planet of elements ▼

Elements and compounds make up a large class of matter that is known as **substances**.

Let's look at a common compound—salt. The kind of salt that you sprinkle on your food is made up of two elements: sodium and chlorine (klôr'ēn). Look at the picture of salt grains as seen through a magnifying glass. Each grain looks like a tiny cube.

As Small as It Gets

Suppose you were to cut a grain of salt in half. You would then have two smaller grains of salt. If you continued to cut the smaller pieces in half, you would finally end up with a tiny piece of salt made up of two very tiny particles. What do you think those particles would be? They wouldn't be salt. They would be atoms—one sodium atom and one chlorine atom.

Of course, all of this is make-believe. A single grain of salt is made up of millions of sodium atoms and chlorine atoms. The drawing below shows how the sodium and chlorine atoms are arranged in salt.

▲ Grains of salt

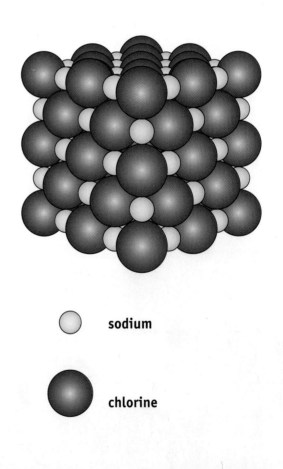

○ sodium

● chlorine

▲ The arrangement of sodium and chlorine atoms shows why salt grains are like cubes.

B34

Describing Compounds

When writing about elements and compounds, scientists often use a shortcut. They use chemical symbols for elements and chemical formulas (fôr′myōo ləz) for compounds. A **chemical formula** is a group of symbols that show the kind and number of each element in a single unit of a compound. For many compounds, but not all, a single unit is called a molecule (mäl′i kyōol).

The drawings show models and formulas for two compounds, water and sugar. Look at the formula for a molecule of water. The number 2 written after the *H* tells you how many hydrogen atoms are in one molecule of water. When only one atom of an element is present, no number is written after its symbol.

Now look at the formula for sugar. What can you learn about this molecule from its formula? ■

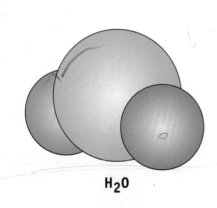

H_2O

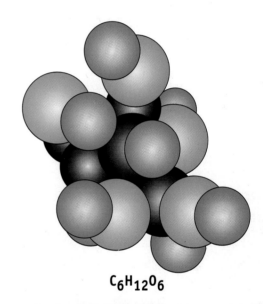

$C_6H_{12}O_6$

▲ As the formula shows, a water molecule is made up of two hydrogen atoms and one oxygen atom.

▲ A single molecule of fructose, the type of sugar found in many fruits, is made up of 24 atoms.

INVESTIGATION 1

1. Name the three states of matter. Give a brief description of each state.

2. Suppose you had a piece of iron and a drop of water. If you kept dividing each substance into smaller and smaller pieces, what would the smallest piece of each substance be like?

How Can Matter Change State?

In many places you can swim in a lake in the summer and skate on it in the winter. It's possible to swim and skate on the same lake because matter changes state. In this investigation you'll learn about changes of state.

Activity

From State to State

What causes ice to change from a solid to a liquid? This activity will help you find out.

MATERIALS
- ice chips
- 2 small plastic dishes
- timer
- *Science Notebook*

Procedure

Hold a small piece of ice in your hand. **Observe** how the ice makes your hand feel and what happens to the ice. **Record** your observations in your *Science Notebook*. Now place one piece of ice on a dish in a sunny spot. Place a second piece of ice on a dish in a shady spot. **Observe** both dishes every few minutes for about 15 minutes. **Record** your observations.

Analyze and Conclude

1. **Compare** the changes you observed in the pieces of ice in the two dishes.

2. **Hypothesize** about the relationship between the way the ice made your hand feel and what happened to the ice in the dishes.

Activity

Liquid From Thin Air

Clouds are made up of tiny drops of liquid water. What kind of change makes these drops appear? You'll have a clue by doing this activity.

MATERIALS
- goggles
- shiny metal can
- paper towel
- ice cubes
- water
- food coloring
- *Science Notebook*

SAFETY
Wear goggles during this activity. Clean up spills immediately.

Procedure

1. Wipe the outside of a can with a paper towel to make sure it's perfectly dry.

2. Place several ice cubes in the can. Carefully add water until the can is full. Gently mix the water with food coloring. If any water spills on or flows over the side of the can, wipe it dry right away.

3. Allow the can of ice water to sit undisturbed. **Observe** it until you see drops of liquid forming on the sides of the container. **Observe** the color of the liquid. Identify this liquid and **record** your observations in your *Science Notebook*.

Step 2

Analyze and Conclude

1. What is the reason for adding color to the water in the can?

2. What is the liquid that formed on the can? **Hypothesize** where it came from. **Compare** your hypothesis with those of other group members.

3. **Describe** any changes of state that you observed during this activity.

Cool It

A refrigerator helps to keep food from spoiling by keeping it cold. Heat always flows from warmer to colder matter. In a refrigerator, heat flows from the food into the cold air around it. The air is kept cold with the help of compounds known as HFCs.

HFCs can exist as either a gas or a liquid, and can easily be changed from one state to another. Look at the drawing to see how a refrigerator works to keep food cold.

After you've seen how the refrigerator works, grab something cold and chill out. Just don't leave the door open too long! ∎

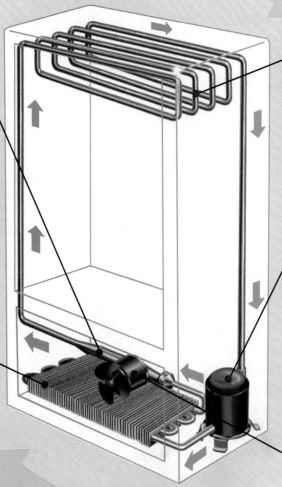

RECEIVER AND VALVE The receiver is a small storage tank. The receiver valve controls the flow of liquid HFC as it leaves the receiver and moves to the evaporator.

EVAPORATOR The evaporator is a section of tubing in the freezer section of the refrigerator. Here heat is absorbed by the liquid HFC as it evaporates, changing from a liquid to a gas.

COMPRESSOR The compressor is an electric pump that forces the HFC gas into the condenser.

CONDENSER In the condenser, the HFC gas releases heat as it condenses, changing back to a liquid. The liquid HFC then moves into the receiver.

FAN The fan blows heat collected by the HFC gas out the back of the refrigerator.

Causing Change

Are you someone who is always "on the go"? Such people are described as being full of energy. On the other hand, when you're sick, you often feel like you have no energy at all. Although we often use the word *energy*, it's hard to explain exactly what energy is.

What Is Energy?

Energy is defined in several different ways. One definition of **energy** is the ability to cause change.

Change often involves movement. It takes energy to make something move. For example, to make your bike move, you push on the pedals. You use energy to move the bike (and yourself) from place to place.

Energy is also needed to change how fast something is moving. Suppose you want to make your bike go faster. You have to use more energy to pedal harder. You even have to use energy to make the bike slow down and stop.

▼ **The riders transfer energy from their bodies to their bikes.**

Energy and Change of State

What does energy have to do with matter? Recall that the particles of matter are constantly moving. If the motion of the particles is changed, a change of state can occur.

You know that matter can change state. A frozen juice bar can change from a solid to a liquid. But you can make more juice bars by putting liquid juice in a freezer.

You have also seen a puddle of water seem to "dry up" and disappear on a warm day. What actually happens is that the water evaporates (ē vap´ə rāts). **Evaporation** is the change of state from a liquid to a gas.

Gaining Energy

All changes of state involve heat energy. As you continue reading, look at the drawings to see how heat energy affects the motion of particles.

❶ When heat is added to a solid, such as ice, the particles in the solid take in the heat energy. They change it into energy of motion and begin moving faster.

❷ As the particles in the solid speed up, they move farther apart. If they gain enough energy, the particles have enough room to slide past each other. The matter begins to melt. **Melting** is the change of state from a solid to a liquid.

❸ If heating continues after all the solid has melted, the particles move still faster and farther apart. Some of the liquid begins to change to a gas called water vapor, causing bubbles to form in the liquid. The bubbles show that the liquid has begun to boil. **Boiling** is the rapid change of state from a liquid to a gas.

❶

❷

4 As long as heat is added to the liquid, it will continue to boil. Bubbles of water vapor will keep forming and escaping into the air until all the liquid changes to a gas.

Losing Energy

Recall holding a piece of ice in your hand in the activity on page B36. The ice made your hand feel cold. What do you think happened to make your hand feel colder? Do you think "cold" left the ice and entered your hand? Wrong!

Your hand felt cold because heat left your hand and was taken in by the ice. Heat energy always moves from warmer to cooler matter. So matter cools down by losing heat— not by gaining "cold."

As you have just learned, when heat is added to matter, the particles that make up the matter speed up

▲ **What happens to water that "boils away"?**

and move farther apart. What do you suppose happens if heat is taken away from matter? Right—the particles of matter slow down and move closer together.

The frost (*left*), fog (*center*), and moisture on a windowpane (*right*) are all examples of condensation.

Let's take another look at water as it changes state—this time in reverse order, starting with water vapor. When heat energy is taken away from water vapor, the particles that make up the gas begin to slow down and move closer together. If the particles lose enough energy, the gas changes to a liquid. **Condensation** (kän dən sā´shən) is the change of state from a gas to a liquid. In the activity on page B37, you observed water vapor, an invisible gas in air, condense on the sides of a can.

Once condensation occurs, suppose that more energy is taken away from the liquid. The particles in the liquid slow down and move closer together. If the particles lose enough energy, the liquid begins to freeze. **Freezing** is the change of state from a liquid to a solid. ■

INVESTIGATION 2

1. What must be done to matter in order to make it change state?

2. Using what you know about changes of state, explain why water is not used as the coolant in a refrigerator instead of HFC.

REFLECT & EVALUATE

WORD POWER

atom
boiling
element
energy
gas
liquid
melting
chemical formula
compound
condensation
evaporation
freezing
solid
substance
chemical symbol
states of matter

On Your Own
Review the terms in the list. Then use as many terms as you can in a paragraph about the three states of matter.

With a Partner
Write each term on one side of an index card and the definition on the other side. Use the cards to quiz your partner.

BUILD YOUR PORTFOLIO

Make a chart that lists the names and symbols for the elements you learned about.

Analyze Information

Study the drawing of the water molecule. Then describe the makeup of a water molecule and write its chemical formula.

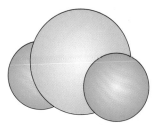

Assess Performance

Design an experiment to study evaporation and condensation. Use the following materials: a plastic jar, plastic wrap, water, a rubber band. If your teacher approves, carry out your experiment and record your observations.

Problem Solving

1. Common table sugar is called sucrose. A molecule of sucrose has the chemical formula $C_{12}H_{22}O_{11}$. What does the chemical formula tell you about a molecule of sucrose?

2. You skated on a pond last week. Today, the ice is gone. Explain how energy was involved in the change of the surface of the pond from solid ice to liquid water. Describe what must happen for the liquid water to change back to ice.

3. Why does frost form on the inside of a window rather than on the outside?

CHAPTER 3

CAUSING CHANGES IN MATTER

Imagine that you have a sore throat and can't swallow your vitamin tablet. How would you solve this problem? You could grind the tablet into a powder and dissolve the powder in fruit juice. In this chapter you'll think about other ways that matter, such as a vitamin tablet, can change.

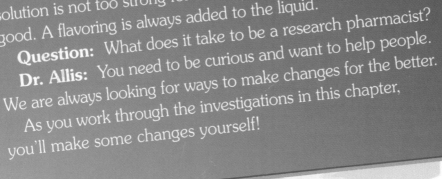

Ask Your Pharmacist

Dr. Beatrice Allis is a research pharmacist (fär′mə sist). She works for a company that makes vitamins. Here is what she told us.

Question: How do you make the liquid vitamins that are given to babies? Do you simply grind a vitamin tablet and add water?

Dr. Allis: It's not that simple. You need to be sure that the solution is not too strong for a baby. It also wouldn't taste very good. A flavoring is always added to the liquid.

Question: What does it take to be a research pharmacist?

Dr. Allis: You need to be curious and want to help people. We are always looking for ways to make changes for the better.

As you work through the investigations in this chapter, you'll make some changes yourself!

INVESTIGATION 1

INVESTIGATION 2

◀ Dr. Beatrice Allis, research pharmacist

INVESTIGATION 1

WHAT ARE PHYSICAL CHANGES?

Does a change in temperature, size, or shape of a material change the kind of matter it is made of? Does mixing materials together change them? In Investigation 1 you'll find out how matter can be changed without changing the kind of matter it is.

Activity

Go With the Flow

Have you ever tried to pour ketchup from a bottle you've just taken from the refrigerator? If so, you know it seems to take forever for the ketchup to flow. Can a change in the temperature of a liquid make a difference in how fast the liquid will flow? Find out!

MATERIALS

- goggles
- grease pencil
- 2 clear plastic cups
- clock or watch with second hand
- plastic bottle containing cold liquid
- paper towel
- *Science Notebook*

SAFETY

Clean up any spills immediately.

Procedure

1. Use a grease pencil to label one plastic cup *A* and another *B*.

2. Have one group member keep time for 10 seconds while another member pours cold liquid from a bottle into cup *A*.

Step 2

3. Stand the bottle with its remaining liquid in a warm place and leave it there for 15 minutes.

4. While the liquid in the bottle warms up, **talk with your group.** Together **predict** which cup, *A* or *B*, will have more liquid in it if you pour the warmed liquid into cup *B* for 10 seconds. **Record** your prediction in your *Science Notebook*.

5. Have one member keep time for 10 seconds while another member pours the warmed liquid into cup *B*.

6. Place the two cups side by side. **Compare** the amount of liquid in each. **Record** your results.

Step 3

Analyze and Conclude

1. In step 6, which cup contained more liquid?

2. How did your result compare with your prediction?

3. Did the cold liquid flow faster, or slower, than the warm liquid? How do you know?

4. **Infer** how temperature affects the way particles in matter move. How do your observations of the liquid support your inference?

UNIT PROJECT LINK

Ask your teacher for some disappearing ink you can use to create mystery answers for your science museum. For each Matter Mystery you have displayed in the museum, write the answer or explanation on a card in this ink. (The ink will become invisible when it dries.) Challenge your classmates or visitors to answer your Matter Mysteries. When everyone is ready, ask your teacher to make the answers on the cards visible.

Activity

Different Look, Same Stuff

Does changing the size of something change the kind of matter it's made of? In this activity you'll find out.

Procedure

1. Work with your group to change two sheets of paper in as many safe ways as you can think of. (No burning, please.) **Observe** what the paper looks like before and after you change it. **Record** your observations in your *Science Notebook*.

2. Repeat step 1, using modeling clay. Repeat again using a paper clip.

3. Place a paper towel and a piece of chalk on one pan of a balance. **Measure** and **record** the mass of the two objects.

4. Remove the chalk and paper towel from the pan. Wrap the chalk in the paper towel. Using a rock, gently pound on the wrapped chalk, grinding it into powder.

5. **Measure** and **record** the mass of the towel and chalk.

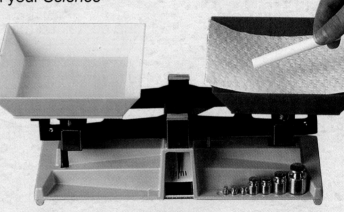

Step 3

Analyze and Conclude

1. Briefly **describe** how you changed the paper, the clay, and the paper clip.

2. **Compare** the mass recorded in step 3 with the mass recorded in step 5.

3. Did crushing the chalk affect its mass? How do you know?

Activity

All Mixed Up

Does mixing different kinds of matter together cause a physical change? Find out in this activity!

Procedure

1. In your *Science Notebook*, **make a chart** like this.

Jar	Items Mixed Together	Appearance of Mixture	How Items Were Separated
A			
B			

2. Place some marbles, paper clips, and buttons in jar *A.* Add a spoonful of sand and a spoonful of copper pellets to jar *B.* Add a spoonful of sand and a spoonful of sawdust to jar *C.*

3. Cover each jar and shake to mix the contents.

4. **Observe** each jar and complete the second and third columns of your chart.

5. With your group, **hypothesize** ways to use materials from the list to separate each mixture into its different parts. **Test** your ideas and **record** in your chart the methods you used.

Analyze and Conclude

1. How did the size of the materials in each mixture affect the way you separated each mixture?

2. **Infer** whether mixing the different kinds of matter together changed the materials. How can you check your inferences?

Step 2

B49

A Change for the Better?

We live in a world of change. Seasons change as the months pass. People change as they grow older. Even rocks are changed by the action of water, wind, and ice—a slow change we're not likely to notice.

A Change in Size and Shape

If you break a stick, you end up with two pieces instead of one.

Breaking a stick is a physical change. A **physical change** is a change in the size, shape, or state of matter with no new matter being formed.

No new matter is formed when you break a stick. Each piece of the stick looks, feels, and acts like wood, and is, in fact, still wood.

When you reshape modeling clay, as you did in the activity on page B48, you cause a physical change. The reshaped clay is still clay. It still has all the properties of clay.

Temperature and Change

A change in temperature can cause a physical change in matter. Recall how a change in temperature changed the speed at which a liquid flowed in the activity on pages B46 and B47.

Changes in temperature can also cause the size, or volume, of an object to change. Recall that volume is the amount of space matter takes up. Most matter expands, or increases in

◀ **How are the two pieces of wood like the stick they came from? How are they different?**

B50

▲ When heated, the metal cap expands more than the glass jar. How does this help you remove the cap from the jar?

volume, when it's heated. When heat is taken away, most matter contracts, or decreases in volume. But water expands as it freezes and contracts as it melts.

A Change in State

Temperature change can also cause another kind of change—a change in state. You know that matter can exist as a solid, liquid, or gas. And you know that matter can change from one state to another. The melting of ice is an example of a change in state.

A change in state is a physical change, although it may be hard to understand why. After all, ice doesn't look like water, or feel like water, or act like water.

The reason a change in state is a physical change is because the kind of matter doesn't change. Ice and liquid water are both water. Even when water evaporates and changes to an invisible gas, it's *still* water. ■

◀ You know that melting is a physical change, because liquid ice cream tastes just the same as the solid kind.

B51

Magnificent Mixtures

Look at all the different vegetables shown in the picture. Suppose you cut up these vegetables, put the pieces in a big bowl, and jumbled them all together. What would you have? A cook might call it a salad. A scientist would probably call it a mixture.

What's a Mixture?

A **mixture** is matter made up of two or more different substances. (Recall that a substance is an element or a compound.) When you mix two or more substances together, you produce a physical change. For example, a salad is different from each of the vegetables in it.

However, mixing substances together doesn't change the physical properties of the substances. A tomato is still a tomato, and a cucumber is still a cucumber,

Some mixtures, like this salad, can be separated by picking out the parts. ▶

even when they're mixed together. If you wish, you can separate a mixture into its individual substances. With a salad, that's easy. You just pick out the different vegetables. As you learned in the activity on page B49, some mixtures are harder to separate than others. That's because of the sizes of the particles. The smaller the particles, the harder it is to separate them.

Another Kind of Mixture

Have you ever added sugar to a liquid and watched the sugar "disappear"? If you taste the liquid, you know the sugar didn't really disappear. It just became invisible.

▲ **Most rocks are mixtures of substances called minerals** (min′ər əlz)**.**

The mixture of sugar and water is an example of a solution. A **solution** is a mixture in which particles of different substances are mixed evenly throughout. One of the most common solutions in nature is sea water. Sea water is a mixture of water and several different salts. ■

SCIENCE IN LITERATURE

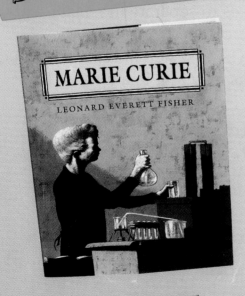

MARIE CURIE
by Leonard Everett Fisher
Macmillan, 1994

Marie Curie was faced with a scientific challenge. Could she separate the matter that she had named radium from a lump of materials? If she could, other scientists would agree that she had discovered a new kind of matter. After four years of work, Marie had a piece of radium no bigger than the point on a pencil. But it was enough for her to experiment with.

Find out what kind of person could work so long to solve a scientific problem. Read about the many times Marie Curie was "first" in her life as a scientist in *Marie Curie* by Leonard Everett Fisher.

RESOURCE

Oil– A Valuable Mixture

▲ **Products made from petroleum**

You may know that oil from the ground is used to make many kinds of fuels. But did you know that oil is also used in making hundreds of products, including plastics, fabrics, and the asphalt (as'fôlt) used on roads and driveways?

It's Too Crude

The material that comes out of an oil well is a dark liquid called crude oil, or petroleum (pə trō'lē əm). Crude oil is a mixture of many substances called hydrocarbons (hī drō-kär'bənz). The name comes from the elements *hydrogen* and *carbon*, which make up hydrocarbons.

Like iron ore, crude oil is not useful as it comes from the ground. It must be refined, or separated into its useful parts. The separating of the mixture is done in tall structures

Huge pumps bring crude oil to the surface from deep underground. ▶

many stories high. These structures are called fractionating (frak'shən-āt iŋ) towers. Refer to the diagram on page B55 as you read about how crude oil is refined.

Changing the State of Crude

Each of the hydrocarbons in crude oil changes state at a different temperature. Chemists use these differences to separate the mixture of hydrocarbons.

The first step in separating crude oil is to heat it in a furnace to a

B54

temperature of 400°C (750°F). At this temperature, the hydrocarbons are in the gas state. This mixture of gases passes from the furnace into the fractionating tower, where it cools.

In the Tower

In the tower, the hydrocarbons made up of the largest molecules are the first to change back into a liquid. This change takes place near the bottom of the tower. The remaining gases cool as they rise in the tower. All but the fuel gases change back into liquids at different heights, depending on the sizes of their molecules.

As the hydrocarbons change state, the liquids leave the tower through pipes. Then the different liquids and gases are collected in huge tanks. ■

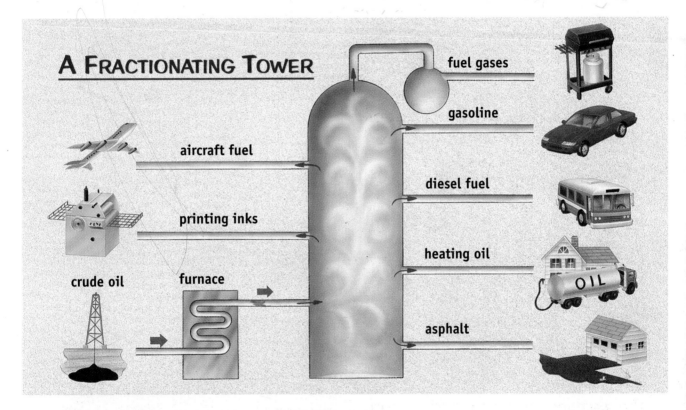

A FRACTIONATING TOWER

fuel gases
gasoline
aircraft fuel
diesel fuel
printing inks
heating oil
crude oil
furnace
asphalt

INVESTIGATION 1

1. When sugar dissolves in water, the sugar disappears. Why is this a physical change? Give examples of three other physical changes.

2. Imagine you had a liquid mixture of three different substances. Each substance changes to a solid at a different temperature. How could you use this information to separate the mixture?

WHAT ARE CHEMICAL CHANGES?

You've seen that a sample of matter can change without changing the kind of matter it's made up of. But matter can change in other ways, too. In Investigation 2 you'll explore how one kind of matter can be changed into another kind of matter.

Activity

Different Look, Different Stuff

Is a rusty nail the same as a shiny new nail? Is rust the same as iron, or are they completely different kinds of matter? Find out how one kind of matter can be changed into another kind of matter.

Procedure

1. Use a plastic spoon to add a spoonful of baking soda to a narrow jar. Carefully add vinegar to the jar until it is about one-quarter full. **Observe** the contents of the jar. **Record** your observations in your *Science Notebook*.

MATERIALS

- goggles
- plastic spoon
- baking soda
- 2 narrow plastic jars
- vinegar
- liquid *A*
- liquid *B*
- timer
- small plastic dish
- water
- steel wool
- 2 large wide-mouth plastic jars
- paper towel
- *Science Notebook*

SAFETY ///////

Wear goggles during this activity. Clean up spills immediately. Be careful when handling steel wool.

B56

2. **Observe** liquid A and liquid B. Carefully pour both liquids into a clean narrow jar. **Observe** the mixture for 5 minutes. **Record** your observations.

Step 2

3. Fill a small dish with water. Place one piece of steel wool next to the dish of water. Place a wide-mouth jar, mouth down, over the dish of water and over the piece of steel wool that is near it, as shown.

4. Place a second jar mouth down over a second piece of steel wool.

Step 3

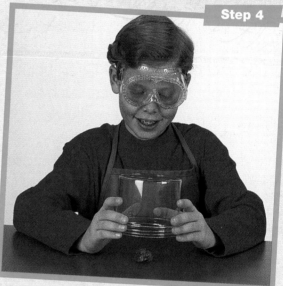

Step 4

5. Leave the jars undisturbed overnight. The next day, **observe** the two pieces of steel wool and **record** your observations.

Analyze and Conclude

1. How are the changes you observed in steps 1, 2, and 5 alike?

2. Make an **inference** about what mixed with the steel wool to cause it to change. Explain why you think as you do.

3. How are the changes you observed in this activity like the changes you observed in the activities on pages B46 and B47, B48, and B49? How are they different?

Changed for Good

Many physical changes can be undone. If you change the shape of a piece of clay, you can change it back. If liquid water freezes, the ice can be melted to get the liquid back.

Some physical changes, such as ripping up paper, can't really be "undone." However, you always have the same *kind* of matter before and after the change.

Something New

Many changes in matter are changes that can't be undone. For example, you can't turn a pile of ashes back into a log. Why? Because ashes are a different kind of matter

than the wood they came from. When it's burned, a log changes into other kinds of matter. Any change in matter that results in one or more different kinds of matter forming is called a **chemical change**.

Recall that the physical properties of matter can be used to describe matter—what it looks like, smells like, and feels like. The physical properties of a material change when a physical change takes place. For example, sawdust doesn't look or feel much like a piece of wood.

Matter can also be described by its chemical properties. The **chemical properties** of matter describe how

The destruction of this building involves both chemical and physical changes. ▼

▲ The rusting of iron is a familiar example of a chemical change. You know it's a chemical change because iron and rust have different physical and chemical properties.

that matter reacts with other matter. You observed the chemical properties of two liquids when they were mixed together in the activity on pages B56 and B57.

Slow Change

Look at the cars in the two pictures on this page. It's hard to believe that the car on the right once looked like the one on the left. What happened to it? What kind of change in matter do you think this is?

As you observed in the activity on pages B56 and B57, damp iron combines with some substance in air to produce a new substance—rust. The scientific name for rust is *iron oxide*. From the name of this compound, can you guess what substance in the air combines with iron to form rust?

The combining of iron and oxygen to form rust is a chemical reaction (rē ak'shən). A **chemical reaction** is the process in which one or more substances are changed into one or more different substances.

Rapid Change

Some chemical changes, like the rusting of metal, take place slowly.

▲ The burning of a fuel, such as wood, is similar to the rusting of iron. When a fuel burns, it combines very rapidly with oxygen in the air.

Others take place very rapidly and can be violent and dangerous. The exploding of dynamite or the burning of a fuel, such as wood, are examples of such changes.

You Can't Get Rid of Matter

Think of all the different ways that matter can be changed. You can grind a solid into powder. You can mix several different kinds of matter together and unmix them again. You can make one kind of matter seem to disappear by dissolving it in another kind of matter. You can evaporate matter. You can burn it. But there's one thing you can't do to matter—you can't destroy it. The total amount of matter on Earth doesn't change. ■

INVESTIGATE FURTHER!

EXPERIMENT

Repeat the activity on pages B56 and B57. This time, coat one piece of steel wool with vegetable oil. Place this piece of steel wool under the large jar along with the dish of water (step 3). Compare the results of this activity with those of the original activity. Explain any differences in these results.

Get the Picture?

How does the film in a camera work? Many chemical changes are needed to get from a roll of film in a camera to a handful of photographs. The film for taking black-and-white photographs is coated with a thin layer that contains two compounds—silver chloride (klôr′īd) and silver bromide (brō′mīd). These compounds change when light strikes them.

Taking the Picture

Think of some subject you want to take a picture of. Some parts of the subject will be darker than others. For example, shadows will be darker than brightly lighted areas. Black objects will be darker than white ones. So your camera receives different amounts of light from these bright and dark areas.

When you click your camera, light from the subject passes through the camera lens and strikes the film. The light causes the silver compounds on the film to change. This change can't be seen until the film is developed.

Developing the Film

The parts of the film that receive bright light turn very dark. The parts of the film that receive only weak light turn gray. The parts that receive no light remain unchanged.

The film is developed by treating it with a solution. The picture, or image, that forms on the developed film is a "reverse" picture, called a negative (neg′ə tiv). Bright parts are dark and dark parts are light on the negative.

Get the Picture?

To get a picture, the negative is placed on photographic paper. Like the film, the photographic paper also contains a coating of silver compounds. When light strikes the paper, a black-and-white image of your subject is produced. The paper is then developed into a black-and-white photograph. The drawings below show the main steps in making a photograph. Get the picture?

1

Light from the subject passes through the camera lens and strikes the film.

2

After being developed, the film is a negative. Light parts are dark, and dark parts are light.

3
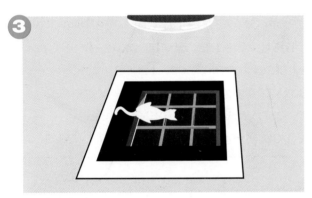
To make a print, the negative is placed on a piece of photographic paper. Light is shined through the negative onto the paper.

4

When the photographic paper is developed, a black-and-white print remains. The print looks exactly like the subject.

INVESTIGATION 2

1. How is the burning of paper like the rusting of iron? How are the two changes different?

2. First you sharpen a pencil. Then you throw the pencil shavings in the fireplace and burn them. Describe the different ways the wood changes.

REFLECT & EVALUATE

chemical change
chemical properties
chemical reaction
mixture
physical change
solution

 **On Your Own**
Review the terms in the list. Then use as many terms as you can to write a summary of the chapter.

With a Partner
Mix up the letters of each term in the list. Provide a clue for each term and challenge your partner to unscramble the terms.

BUILD YOUR PORTFOLIO

Make a poster that shows common physical and chemical changes. Illustrate your poster with pictures cut from magazines or drawings you make yourself. Write captions to explain the changes shown in each drawing or photograph.

Analyze Information

Study the photographs of an egg before and after being cooked. Describe the physical and chemical changes that occurred.

Assess Performance

Plan an experiment to find out whether other common materials react with oxygen in the same way steel wool does. Test a variety of materials. After your teacher has reviewed your plan, carry out your experiment. Compare your results with those of others.

Problem Solving

1. How is the melting of an ice cube similar to the grinding of chalk into a powder? How are the two changes different?

2. A carpenter installs a cast-iron railing for your front steps. Why is it a good idea to paint the railing as soon as possible?

3. Suppose you had a mixture of sand and sugar. Suggest a method for separating this mixture into its parts.

Throughout this unit you've investigated questions related to properties of matter. How will you use what you've learned and share that information with others? Here are some ideas.

Hold a Big Event
to Share Your Unit Project

Set up your displays of Matter Mysteries and the cards with the invisible explanations of the mysteries. Invite your parents and friends to view the displays in your science museum. Create one final display—yourself! Have each member of your group pretend to be a different kind of matter. Each person should prepare a card describing his or her properties in invisible ink. Have your guests try to guess what kind of matter each person represents. As a finale, have your teacher reveal what's written on the cards.

Research

Oxygen in air and rainwater causes changes in many objects. The rusting of iron is an example of this process, which is called oxidation. Read about oxidation in an encyclopedia or science textbook. Then for one week, look for examples of oxidation taking place around you. Record all your observations.

Take Action

In your research, did you see anything around your home or school that was spoiled or damaged by oxidation? Get permission from your teacher to talk with your school principal. Point out the problems and recommend ways that damage by oxidation might be repaired or prevented. If possible, organize a group to correct or prevent oxidation. For example, you might scrape and paint a rusted iron fence.

UNIT C

ANIMALS

Theme: Systems

GET READY TO

OBSERVE & QUESTION

How do behaviors help animals meet their needs?

Animals are all around you, and they are fun to observe. Careful observation will show you how behaviors help animals meet their needs.

EXPERIMENT & HYPOTHESIZE

How do vertebrates differ?

What affects how fast fish "breathe"? This activity and other hands-on activities will help you investigate how animals with backbones differ.

INVESTIGATE!

RESEARCH & ANALYZE

As you investigate, find out more from these books.

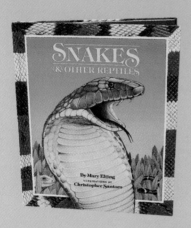

- **Snakes and Other Reptiles** by Mary Elting (Simon & Schuster, 1987). Do you like to eat? In this book you'll find out about an animal that can live for two years without eating.

- **Bugs: Stingers, Suckers, Sweeties, Swingers** by Liz Greenbacker (Franklin Watts, 1993). Are you into bugs? In this book you may find out more about bugs than you care to know!

WORK TOGETHER & SHARE IDEAS

How can you keep track of your observations of local animals?

As you study animals in this unit, you'll work together to identify and make observations about animals that live in your area. Your goal is to publish a Field Guide to Local Animals that can be used by visitors. Look for the Unit Project Links for ideas about how to construct your field guide.

C3

CHAPTER 1

ANIMALS MEET THEIR NEEDS

How smart are the dogs you know? Would the cats you know win a cleverness contest? Animals have the ability to learn new things. Animals learn how to meet their own needs, and they can also learn new ways of behaving.

Helping Paws

Ellen Torop at Canine Companions for Independence trains dogs to help disabled people. She can teach these "helping dogs" to follow about 60 commands. Thousands of disabled people depend on these well-trained animals. The helping dogs carry out simple, but important, tasks, such as turning lights on and off. They can push elevator buttons and carry items for disabled persons. Some dogs have even learned to push and pull wheelchairs.

Some of the animals are trained as "hearing dogs." They work with people who have hearing problems. Hearing dogs have learned how to alert their owners to important sounds, such as ringing telephones, smoke alarms, and doorbells.

In this chapter you'll find out more about all kinds of animals and about things they learn to do.

Coming Up

◄ Ellen Torop's student learns to take a telephone to a disabled person.

WHAT BASIC NEEDS DO ANIMALS SHARE?

Have you ever seen a swimming duck tip forward, dunking its head and neck underwater? The duck is looking for food. Food is just one of the things that all animals need. What other needs do animals have in common? You'll find out in Investigation 1.

Activity

MATERIALS
• *Science Notebook*

Needs in Common

Scientists are trained to make careful observations. In this activity see what you can find out about the needs of animals through careful observation.

Procedure

1. In your *Science Notebook*, **make a chart** like the one shown. **Identify** the animals shown in the pictures on pages C6 and C7. In your chart, **record** the names of the animals.

Animal	Need

2. **Infer** what need each animal is trying to meet. Then **record** your inference in your chart.

Analyze and Conclude

1. How many different needs did you identify? Do some needs seem more important than others? Explain your answer.

2. Do all animals seem to share the same basic needs? **Predict** how or where each animal shown might meet its other basic needs. **Compare** your predictions with those of other group members. Explain why you made each prediction.

UNIT PROJECT LINK

Work with your group to start planning your field guide. Which animals might you include in your field guide? What information about each animal would you be sure to record? Make a list that names and describes local animals. You might use your state's Department of Natural Resources as a source of information. Libraries often have books about animals that live in the area. Put the information you gather in your field guide.

The ABCs of Animal Needs

If you had to take care of a pet dog, cat, and bird, how would you remember what each one needs? It wouldn't be very difficult. All three animals share a basic need for food and water.

Animals in the wild need food and water too. What other basic needs do animals share? In the activity on pages C6 and C7, you discovered some needs of animals. Besides food and water, you found out that animals also need shelter to survive.

A hippopotamus spends much of its time in water. What does a hippopotamus eat? ▼

C8

▲ A killer whale eats seabirds, fish, turtles, and seals.

▲ A leopard with its meal

All animals need a suitable environment (en vī′rən mənt). An animal's **environment** is everything, both living and nonliving, that surrounds and affects the animal. To survive in its environment, an animal needs to keep its body temperature within a certain range. This range varies, depending on the type of animal. In an environment that is suitable for an animal, that animal can meet all of its basic needs.

Different animals eat different kinds of food. In the spring and summer, a rabbit feasts on plants such as dandelions and chickweed. But in the winter it settles for bark, roots, and dry leaves. A hippopotamus wanders out of the water to enjoy a meal of grass. A killer whale fills its stomach with fish, squid, penguins, and even seals. A leopard hunts other animals and then eats them high up in the trees.

First, Some Food

All animals need food to grow, stay healthy, and survive. A mole dies after only a few hours without food! Other animals can wait an entire day for their next meal. Some animals, like snakes, can go for weeks without a meal.

A mole eats mainly worms and insects. ▶

C9

Some Water, Please

Animals need more than just food to survive. They also need water. Many animals drink water every day from water holes, ponds, lakes, rivers, and streams. A budgerigar (buj'ər i gär), an Australian parakeet, can go a long time without taking a drink. But when it's time for that drink, the bird will probably flock together with tens of thousands of other budgerigars at one water hole.

A few animals hardly ever, or even never, drink! A kangaroo rat rarely drinks. It gets its water from the seeds and cactus pulp that it eats. An Australian koala *never* needs to drink. It gets the water it needs by eating eucalyptus (yo͞o kə lip'təs) leaves.

A koala eating leaves ▶

▲ Budgerigars at a water hole

Home Sweet Home

Animals need shelter for protection from enemies and harsh weather. For example, the nest in which a baby bird hatches provides shelter for the bird. Young elf owls are kept safe in an old woodpecker hole in a cactus. And a mouse can find shelter in a hole in the ground. Animals with hard coverings, such as turtles, carry their shelter with them.

▲ **Elf owl in a cactus**

▲ **The waved albatross shades its bare legs, cooling its entire body.**

Not Too Cold, Not Too Hot

An animal also needs to keep its body temperature within a certain range. Your body temperature is about 37°C (98.6°F). If your temperature goes up only three or four degrees, you have a high fever! Most birds have a higher body temperature than yours—between 40°C (104°F) and 42°C (108°F).

Many animals live in places where the temperature can drop very low or climb very high. Some animals have a body temperature that changes with the temperature of the surroundings. These animals often have behaviors that help them keep their body temperature within a certain range. Other animals have a body temperature that stays within a range even while the temperature of the surroundings changes. ■

weaverbird

Animals of the African Savanna

wildebeest

gazelle

wart hog

Wildebeests (wil'də bēsts) munch on grasses. Some drink from a water hole. Female lions hunting together catch a fast gazelle (gə zel'). And a group of mongooses perch on a large termite mound made out of soil. These are some animals of the African savanna (sə van'ə). Like all other animals, they need food, water, and shelter.

A **savanna** is a grassland found in tropical climates. It's a wide-open area that is covered with grasses but has only a few trees and bushes. Savannas cover almost one half of Africa. They are also found in India, South America, and Australia.

Food and Water in the Savanna

Like animals everywhere, animals of the African savanna need food. Zebras, wildebeests, and gazelles eat different parts of the grasses. The zebras feed on the tops of the grasses. Then wildebeests move into the area and feed on the middle parts. Later, gazelles chomp on the remaining bottom parts.

Giraffes eat the leaves of acacia (ə kā'shə) and baobab (bā'ō bab) trees. Secretary birds eat animals such as snakes and insects. Crocodiles in the water attack and eat wildebeests and other large animals as the animals try to cross rivers.

Savannas of the World

savannas

C12

giraffe

zebra

rock hyrax

secretary bird

mongooose

Animals of the savanna also need water. Many of them drink from the same water hole. Some drink there once a day. Others only go there once in a while. Animals may also drink water from nearby rivers.

Savanna Shelters

Animals of the savanna need shelter, too. Rock hyraxes (hī'rak sēz) live in holes in small hills of rocks called *kopjes* (käp'ēs). A wart hog's shelter is a large hole in an old termite mound. Weaverbirds make nests of woven grasses that hang from tree branches. The opening to such nests is on the bottom. This design makes it more difficult for enemies to reach the birds inside.

Animals of all the world's savannas share the same basic needs. And although the animals all need the same things to survive, they must meet these needs in different ways. ■

INVESTIGATION 1

1. Baby birds have just hatched in a nest outside your window. What basic needs do the young birds have?

2. Write about an imaginary animal. Describe the type of environment in which it lives. Explain how it meets each of its basic needs. You might include drawings to help your explanations.

INVESTIGATION 2

HOW DO BODY PARTS HELP ANIMALS MEET THEIR NEEDS?

What do teeth have in common with a bird's beak? Both kinds of body parts are used by animals to get food. In Investigation 2 you'll discover some of the many ways in which animals use body parts to meet their basic needs.

Activity

Feather Feats

Body coverings are one of the body parts that help animals meet their needs. A bird's body is covered with two basic types of feathers. What purpose does each type serve? Find out!

MATERIALS

- wing or tail feathers
- down feathers
- hand lens
- *Science Notebook*

SAFETY

Wash your hands when you have finished this activity.

Procedure

1. **Observe** a wing feather or tail feather under a hand lens. In your *Science Notebook*, **make a drawing** of what you see.

Tail feather ▼

barbs

central shaft

▲ **Down feather**

2. Work with group members to **identify** the central shaft and the barbs on your feather. Use the picture on page C14 for help. Gently pull some of the barbs apart. **Record** your observations.

3. Pull the feather through your fingers as shown. **Observe** and **record** what happens.

4. Repeat steps 1 and 3, but this time examine a down feather.

5. Wave the wing or tail feather through the air. Then do the same with the down feather. **Observe** how the two types of feathers push the air around them. **Record** your observations.

Analyze and Conclude

1. In what ways are the two types of feathers alike? What differences did you observe?

2. **Infer** which type of feather would help a bird fly. **Infer** which type of feather would help a bird keep warm. Discuss your inferences with other members of your group. Explain your thinking.

INVESTIGATE FURTHER!

RESEARCH

Find out how body coverings other than feathers help animals meet basic needs. You might research an unusual body covering, such as the spines on a hedgehog, described in the book *Mammal* by Steve Parker. Or you might investigate the fur on seals or the moist body coverings of worms and salamanders. Prepare a brief report on your findings.

Activity

Color Me, Color My World

The body coverings of animals are many different colors. How does an insect's color help it survive? Try this activity and find out!

MATERIALS
- large green cloth
- pipe cleaners, 50 red, 50 blue, 50 green, and 50 yellow
- timer
- *Science Notebook*

Procedure

1. Imagine that you're a bird looking for insects in a field. A green cloth represents the grass. Pipe cleaners represent insects of different colors.

2. **Talk with your group. Predict** which color "insect" will be hardest to find when the pipe cleaners are placed on the cloth. **Record** your prediction in your *Science Notebook*.

3. Spread the cloth out on the floor. Mix up the pipe cleaners and then put them on the cloth, as shown.

4. Collect as many insects as you can in 15 seconds. The pipe cleaners must be picked up one at a time. A group member using a timer should tell you when to start and stop.

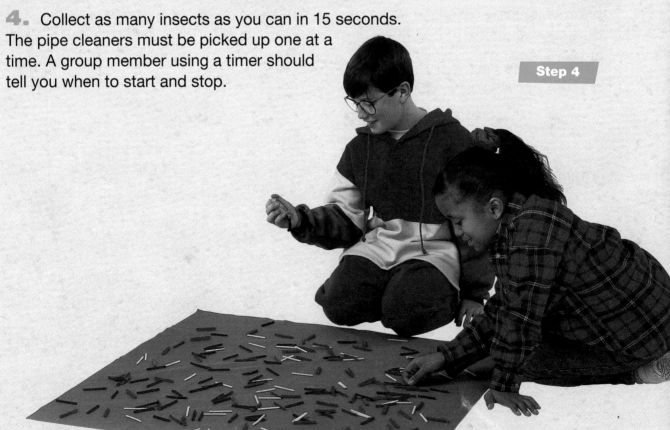

Step 4

C16

5. **Make a chart** like the one shown. Count the number of pipe cleaners of each color you picked up. In your chart, **record** the data as Trial 1.

NUMBER OF PIPE CLEANERS				
Trial	Red	Blue	Green	Yellow

6. Repeat steps 3 and 4. Again count the number of pipe cleaners of each color you picked up. **Record** the data in your chart as Trial 2.

7. **Compare** your results with the results of other groups.

Analyze and Conclude

1. Look at the data from both of your trials and your classmates' trials. **Infer** which color pipe cleaner was the most difficult to find. **Compare** your prediction with your results.

2. Suppose the grass turns yellow in the winter. **Infer** which color insect has the best chance to avoid being eaten by a bird. Explain why you think as you do.

INVESTIGATE FURTHER!

EXPERIMENT

With your group, set up an experiment like the one in this activity to test your inference for question 2 of Analyze and Conclude. Record your results and share your findings with your classmates.

Parts That Help the Most

Have you ever wondered how penguins, birds that can't fly, use their wings? Or if elephants use their very large ears just for hearing? These body parts help the animals meet their needs.

Different kinds of animals have different parts that help them get food and water, make shelters, and even warm up and cool down. These helpful parts are adaptations (ad əp-tā′shənz). **Adaptations** are different ways of acting or parts of living things that help them survive in a certain environment.

Finding Food

Animals have parts that help them get the food they need. A penguin's strong wings don't work for flying. But they're terrific for paddling underwater. A penguin can chase after fish and squid at speeds of up to 32 km/h (20 mph).

A brown bear has adaptations for catching and eating its food. It has short, strong legs and large feet with long, heavy claws. The brown bear uses these claws and its strong jaws and sharp teeth to catch and kill its prey—the animals that it hunts.

A brown bear catching dinner in its mouth ▼

An alligator snapping turtle has an adaptation that tricks its prey. The turtle swims at the bottom of a river with its mouth wide open. At the end of its tongue is a pink flap that looks like a delicious worm. When a fish swimming by tries to eat the worm—chomp! The turtle eats the fish.

A long, tough snout and sharp tusks are the body parts a wart hog uses to dig up food from the ground. The wart hog eats earthworms and moles as well as the roots and bulbs of plants.

▲ An alligator snapping turtle, waiting underwater for food

Taking a Drink

Animals also have parts that are adaptations for getting water. An elephant can use its tusks to drill into dry water holes to get to hidden water below the ground. Then it uses its long trunk to lift the water up to its mouth.

▲ A wart hog searching for food

An elephant can use its tusks to get food and water. ▼

An elephant uses its tusks, which can be as long as 3 m (10 ft), to splinter the outside of trees so that it can get to the soft inner pulp. It also uses its tusks to pry plants, such as yams, from the ground.

Animals get some water from their food. A vampire bat's food is the blood of another animal. To get the blood, the bat sticks its sharp teeth into the skin of its prey.

Some adaptations keep animals from losing water. At low tide at the seashore, a clam uses its foot to dig its way into the damp sand. This helps keep the clam from drying out.

Many animals, such as dogs, use their long tongues to scoop up water into their mouths. A bird takes a drink by dipping its beak into the water and then raising its head so that the water trickles down its throat. Have you ever stuck your tongue out to catch raindrops? One type of bird, the swift, catches rain- drops in its open beak while flying through the air.

Keep Warm or Cool Down

Animals have parts that keep their body temperatures from going too high or too low. Think about the bird feathers you observed in the activity on pages C14 and C15. The fluffy down feathers help keep a bird warm.

An emperor penguin, which lives in the cold Antarctic, has a layer of fat below its skin. Its down feathers are covered by a layer of overlapping contour feathers. The contour feath- ers are coated with waterproof oil. The layers of its body covering keep the penguin warm as it dives for food in icy waters.

The emperor penguin is adapted for living in a cold climate. ▼

▲ A swift uses its beak to get water while flying.

An African elephant and a fennec fox have similar body parts for cooling off. Both animals have large spread-out ears. Blood passing through the ears gives off heat to the air, cooling down the entire animal.

A polar bear has thick fur, which appears white but is actually clear. The clear fur allows the Sun's rays to reach the bear's dark skin, which absorbs the Sun's warmth. The coat's thickness also prevents heat loss.

A polar bear's fur helps keep the animal warm. ▼

▲ The ears of a fennec fox help keep the animal cool.

A fruit bat doesn't have big ears to help it cool down, but its big wings do the job. The bat usually hangs upside down. It flutters its wings to cool its body.

Having Shelter

Many animals have adaptations that help the animals get shelter. Some animals have parts that serve as shelters. Snails have hard shells and armadillos have hard outer coverings.

◀ **The wings of a fruit bat help control its temperature.**

SCIENCE IN LITERATURE

SNAKES AND OTHER REPTILES
by Mary Elting
Simon & Schuster, 1987

Did you know that

- Egg-eating snakes can swallow an egg bigger than their heads, crush it, and then burp up the shell?

- The Gila monster, a lizard, can live up to two years without eating?

- Only one kind of turtle—the box turtle—can pull its head, limbs, and tail all the way inside its shell and then close the shell tight?

Specialized body parts allow these animals to perform such amazing feats. Find out about these and other adaptations of reptiles when you read *Snakes and Other Reptiles* by Mary Elting.

Some animals have adaptations for making shelters. Pocket gophers have large front teeth, sharp claws, and flexible bodies that help them dig underground tunnels.

Next time you notice an animal with some interesting body parts, think about how the parts might help the animal meet its needs. Look for parts that help the animal get food or water, keep its body temperature just right, or get shelter. ■

▲ What body parts help this pocket gopher get shelter?

▲ An armadillo's covering is its shelter.

INVESTIGATION 2

THINK IT WRITE IT

1. Write a description of your favorite animal. Describe different body parts, such as teeth, claws, a tail, scales, and feathers. Explain how each part helps your favorite animal survive.

2. A bat hangs upside down and flutters its wings. How does fluttering its wings help a bat meet a certain need?

HOW DO BEHAVIORS HELP ANIMALS MEET THEIR NEEDS?

Behavior is the way an animal acts or responds to its environment. Some behaviors are inborn. Others are learned. Now you can discover how behaviors help animals meet their needs.

Activity

Tap, Tap, Tap

In this activity you'll test whether you can change the behavior of goldfish as they learn that food is on the way.

Procedure

1. With your group, **observe** how goldfish move in their tank. In your *Science Notebook*, make a list of the different behaviors of the fish.

2. Talk with your group and **predict** how the behavior of the goldfish might change if you try to attract them by making a sound.

Step 1

C24

3. **Test your prediction.** Use a pencil to tap ten times on a wall of the fish tank. **Record** what you observe. Look for any changes in the behavior of the fish.

4. Sprinkle some fish food on the surface of the water at one end of the fish tank. At the same time, have another student tap the wall of the fish tank at that end. **Record** the behavior of the fish.

5. Repeat step 4 each day for two weeks. **Record** what you observe.

6. At the end of two weeks, tap on the wall of the fish tank ten times, but do *not* put any food in the water. **Observe** and **record** the behavior of the goldfish.

Step 4

Analyze and Conclude

1. With your group, **compare** what you observed during step 3 with what you observed in step 6. How did the behavior of the goldfish change?

2. **Hypothesize** about how a sense of hearing might help fish survive. **Compare** your hypothesis with hypotheses of other group members. Explain why you made the hypothesis you did.

UNIT PROJECT LINK

Think about each of the animals you have decided to include in your field guide. What special adaptations do the animals have to help them survive? What behaviors help them survive? Think of interesting ways to add these important facts to your field guide descriptions.

The Dance of the Bees

You point your finger at a plate of cookies on a table. Your friends follow you to the table to eat the sweet snack. You were able to lead your friends to the food by your behavior. Can other animals do the same? The honeybee is an example of an animal that can signal others of its kind when it finds food. But it doesn't point a finger—it does a dance!

Honeybees are **social animals**. That is, they live in groups and work together to meet their needs. In order to work together, social animals must have behaviors that give information to other group members.

Honeybees gather nectar (nek′tər), a sweet liquid from flowers. The bees use the nectar to make honey, which they store in their hive in wax cells called a honeycomb. The honey is food for the bees. Worker bees fly alone in search of flowers. When a worker bee finds flowers, it returns to the beehive and tells the other bees where the flowers are. Then all the bees can fly to the flowers and help gather nectar.

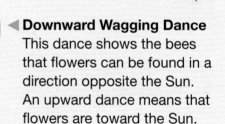

Downward Wagging Dance
This dance shows the bees that flowers can be found in a direction opposite the Sun. An upward dance means that flowers are toward the Sun.

The worker bee can't draw a map. Instead, it delivers its message by dancing on the upright surface of the honeycomb inside the hive.

The bee can perform two kinds of dances—a round dance and a wagging dance, in which the bee wags its body. The faster the wagging dance, the closer the flowers are to the hive. The drawings here show how the behavior of a bee can communicate information to other bees.

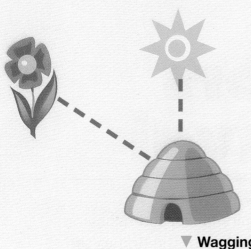

Wagging Dance Done on an Angle A dance done on an angle shows that flowers can be found toward or away from the Sun at that angle.

Round Dance This dance tells the other bees that the flowers are nearby.

A honeybee gathering nectar ▶

Behaviors for Survival

You go to a park and see a dog and its owner playing with a ball. When you walk over to pet the dog, the owner tells the dog to sit. The dog sits. The owner tells the dog to lie down. But just as the dog starts to lie down, a squirrel runs past. The dog leaps up and runs after the squirrel. You have just observed some interesting **behaviors**, or ways living things act or respond to their environment.

Animals sometimes respond in ways that are instinctive. **Instinctive behaviors** are behaviors that living things are born with. Other behaviors, called **learned behaviors**, develop after birth. They are learned. When the dog in the park sits at the command of its owner, it

is performing a learned behavior. The owner taught the dog to sit when told. But the dog's owner didn't teach it to chase squirrels! Running after a squirrel is an instinctive behavior of dogs.

Playful Practice

Both kinds of behavior—learned and instinctive—help animals survive. A young wolf is born with deer-chasing behavior. But the wolf pup must learn how to catch the deer for food. As a pup, a wolf learns this behavior by chasing and jumping on other wolf pups and its parents. It also learns by watching other wolves catch deer.

Wolf pups pounce and playfully bite each other.

Time to Eat

Different kinds of animals have different behaviors for getting food. Some spiders have the instinctive behavior of spinning a silk web to catch prey. When an unlucky bee gets stuck in a spider's web, the spider bites the bee to paralyze it. The spider then wraps the bee in silk, preventing it from escaping.

A spider spins a web that catches prey.

A young herring gull signals its parent that it wants food. The young gull taps its beak on the dark spot at the end of its parent's beak.

A mother crocodile holds baby crocodiles in her mouth.

Keeping Safe

Animals have behaviors that help them protect themselves or their young. A mother crocodile has an unusual instinctive behavior for protecting her young. When there is danger, the crocodile keeps her young safe by holding them in her mouth and throat. When the danger is past, the crocodile spits out her young!

A newborn rattlesnake doesn't need help from a parent. It can defend itself. A young rattlesnake instinctively coils and strikes at danger, just as its parent does.

The Right Temperature

Animals also have behaviors for keeping their temperatures within a certain range. Turtles and lizards bask in the sun to warm up. When their body temperatures get too high, they move to cooler shady places. ■

Birds and many other animals shiver when they're cold. This behavior warms up their bodies.

A dog pants with its tongue hanging out to lower its body temperature when it's hot.

INVESTIGATION 3

THINK IT WRITE IT

1. A dog lies down and rolls over at the command of its owner. What kind of behaviors are these? Explain your answer.

2. List three different kinds of animals. For each animal, describe one behavior that helps it meet a basic need.

REFLECT & EVALUATE

WORD POWER

adaptations
behaviors
environment
instinctive behaviors
learned behaviors
savanna
social animals

On Your Own
Write a definition for each term in the list.

With a Partner
Mix up the letters of each term in the list. Provide a clue for each term and challenge your partner to unscramble the terms.

BUILD YOUR PORTFOLIO

Make a drawing of an African savanna and some of the animals that live there. Show the animals meeting different basic needs. Under each kind of animal, write the need it's trying to meet.

Analyze Information

Study the photograph. Describe how the armadillo is meeting one of its basic needs.

Assess Performance

Observe some goldfish to see how they meet some of their needs. Identify the basic needs of the goldfish. Notice the body parts and behaviors that help the goldfish meet those needs. Think about how some of the adaptations might help them if they were swimming in a pond rather than in a fish tank.

Problem Solving

1. Describe four basic needs of animals. What might happen to some animals if it did not rain in their environment for several months?

2. You take an imaginary trip to an African savanna. You see many different kinds of animals. What are some of the things the animals of the savanna use for food?

3. On a cold day you see a bird sitting with its feathers fluffed out. It's shivering. What need is the bird trying to meet? What adaptations does the bird have to help it meet that need?

CHAPTER 2

ALL KINDS OF ANIMALS

What's your favorite animal? Are there other animals that are similar to it? In this chapter you'll learn about many kinds of animals. As you explore, think about ways that animals are similar and about things that make them different.

Homes for Macaws

You may have seen a macaw (mə kô') at the zoo, a pet store, or in someone's home. These large parrots live in the tropical rain forests of South America. Macaws nest in trees more than 31 m (100 ft) off the ground.

Eduardo Nycander is a field biologist. He studies wild macaws at a research station in the Amazon forest of Peru. He has found that macaws have a hard time finding hollow tree trunks that can serve as suitable places to build nests.

Eduardo Nycander now works at providing macaws with plastic nests. The nests are hollow tubes about 35.6 cm (14 in.) wide and 2.4 m (8 ft) long. Nycander climbs high above the ground and straps the nests to the tree trunks. The birds love them! The nests look and feel like hollow tree trunks. What would you ask Eduardo Nycander about his work?

Coming Up

◄ Eduardo Nycander checks on a macaw chick 31 m (100 ft) above the ground.

INVESTIGATION 1

HOW CAN LIVING THINGS BE CLASSIFIED?

Suppose you made a list of all the living things that you could think of. How would you put them into groups to make it easy to study them? In this investigation, find out how scientists classify living things.

Activity

MATERIALS
• *Science Notebook*

Studying Backbones

What supports the different parts of your body? What do you have for support that a jellyfish and a worm don't? You'll find out in this activity.

Procedure

Raise one arm and try to reach as far down the center of your back as you can. Now slowly run your fingertips up your back until you reach your neck. Feel for "knobs" sticking out along the way. These are the separate bones that make up your backbone. By touching these bones, **infer** their size and shape. **Record** your inference in your *Science Notebook*. **Make a drawing** to show what you think your backbone looks like.

Analyze and Conclude

Hypothesize about the ways that a backbone helps support your body.

Activity
Animals Are Different

Which animal is a cat more like—a catfish or a dog? How would you decide? In this activity you'll make observations that could be used to classify animals.

MATERIALS
- hand lens
- 3 animals for observation
- *Science Notebook*

SAFETY /////

Do not touch the animals unless you have your teacher's permission.

Procedure

1. Your teacher will give your group some animals to observe. As you **observe** the animals, look for likenesses and differences. In your *Science Notebook*, **record** the ways you think these living things are alike and the ways they are different.

2. **Make a chart** like the one shown. Add as many different characteristics as you can think of. **Record** your observations under the column for each animal.

Characteristics	Animal 1	Animal 2	Animal 3
How It Moves			
Type of Body Covering			
Number of Legs/Description			
Number of Eyes			
Number of Ears			
Where It Might Live			

3. You may want to use a hand lens to **observe** some animals more closely. **Record** any further observations you make. **Infer** where each animal might live and **record** your inference.

Step 3

Analyze and Conclude

1. Are there any characteristics that all the animals share? If so, what are they?

2. **Infer** how each animal's body parts help it survive.

3. **Infer** which of the animals might have a backbone. Give reasons for your inferences.

Variety of Life on Earth

How many kinds of living things could there be on Earth—hundreds? thousands? The answer is millions! Millions of kinds of **organisms** (ôr′gə niz əmz), or living things, exist on Earth.

Living things can be found in oceans, forests, deserts, mountains, soil, air—almost everywhere on Earth. And incredibly, all organisms can be classified, or grouped, into five large groups, called kingdoms.

Organisms placed in the same kingdom share certain characteristics, or features. Scientists use the different characteristics of living things to classify them. The number of cells, the basic units that make up all organisms, is just one characteristic used to classify living things. Other characteristics include life processes, such as how an organism gets food or reproduces. Study the table and the pictures on the next page to see the general characteristics shared by living things in each kingdom.

How many kinds of living things can you find in this picture? ▼

The Five Kingdoms

Kingdom	Examples	Characteristics
Animal	horse, dog, bird, fish, spider, worm, starfish, coral	• many-celled • most have structures for moving from place to place • feed on other organisms • reproduce by eggs or live birth
Plant	pine tree, cactus, tulip, tomato, ivy, maple tree	• many-celled • no structures for moving from place to place • make their own food • reproduce by seeds or spores
Fungus	yeast, slime mold, mushroom, mold	• many-celled; some one-celled • most don't have structures for moving from place to place • absorb food from other organisms
Protist	amoeba, paramecium, diatom, algae	• most one-celled; some many-celled • can make their own food or feed on other organisms • some have structures for moving from place to place
Moneran	bacteria	• very simple cells • some make their own food; some feed on other organisms • some have structures for moving from place to place

ANIMAL KINGDOM   The clownfish and the orangutan look very different from one another. But they are both members of the animal kingdom. Like most kinds of animals, they move from place to place, often in search of food.

orangutan

clownfish

PLANT KINGDOM   The largest members of the plant kingdom are trees. Trees, like other plants, use the Sun's energy to make food in their leaves. An oak tree can produce over a million leaves in a single year!

oak tree

FUNGUS KINGDOM   You might think these mushrooms look like plants, but they're not. They belong to a different kingdom—the fungus kingdom. Unlike plants, mushrooms can't make their own food. Most mushrooms get their food from the dead plant material on which they grow.

mushroom

PROTIST KINGDOM   A paramecium is a member of the protist kingdom. Like most other protists, the paramecium is made up of one cell and so is microscopic. Some protists have structures for moving from place to place. The paramecium has hairlike parts that pull it through the water.

paramecium

different view of a paramecium

MONERAN KINGDOM   Bacteria belong to the moneran (mə-nir'ən) kingdom. Unlike other monerans, blue-green bacteria make their own food. All monerans are made up of one cell.

blue-green bacteria

bacteria that form a chain

Classifying Past and Present

For over 3,000 years, scientists have looked for features that would relate living things to one another. From about 350 B.C. to the mid-1900s, most scientists were content to classify organisms into just two groups—plants and animals.

But as science has advanced over the years, so have ideas about classifying organisms. The time line tells about a few of the people throughout history who have invented classification systems.

Georges Cuvier classifies everything that can move from place to place on its own as a member of the animal kingdom.

1812

Aristotle, a scientist and teacher in ancient Greece, invents a system that places living things in two groups—plants and animals.

350 B.C.

1750s

Carolus Linnaeus, a Swedish scientist, develops a system for naming organisms that is still used today. He is known as the Father of Modern Classification.

Leon Roddy, an African American scientist, classifies more than 6,000 spiders and becomes a world expert on this group of animals.

1960s

1988

Lynn Margulis, an American scientist, suggests a protoctist (prə tōk′tist) kingdom to replace the protist kingdom. This larger kingdom includes the protists as well as many-celled organisms that don't fit in the other four kingdoms. This system is not yet widely accepted.

1959

Robert Whittaker, an American professor of biology, introduces the five-kingdom classification system that is widely used today.

UNIT PROJECT LINK

Think about ways you can classify the animals you plan to put in your field guide. How might you organize the descriptions within your guide? Think of ways that might help the reader find information quickly.

Classification of Animals

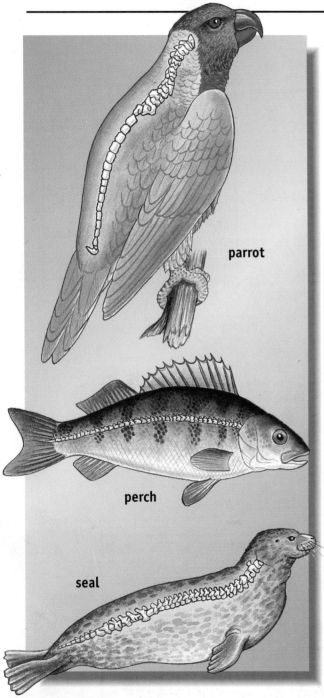

parrot

perch

seal

▲ **Examples of vertebrates**

Each organism in the animal kingdom moves on its own, is large enough to be seen without a microscope, gets its own food, and produces young. These few characteristics are common to all animals. In the activity on page C35, you noticed that different kinds of animals can have different characteristics. For this reason, scientists have further classified animals into smaller groups within the animal kingdom.

Who Has a Backbone?

Animals that have backbones make up one group. In the activity that you did on page C34, you felt the knobs of your backbone. Each bone that makes up the backbone is called a **vertebra**. Animals that have backbones are called **vertebrates** (vʉr′tə brits).

Vertebrates include many different kinds of animals. They can be found just about anywhere—in oceans, rivers, forests, mountains, and deserts. Horses, hippos, cats, birds, snakes, lizards, frogs, and fish are all vertebrates. All vertebrates have one thing in common—a backbone.

Life Without a Backbone

The members of many different animal groups don't have backbones. Animals that don't have backbones are called **invertebrates**. In fact, 97 percent of the animal kingdom is made up of invertebrates! They include some of the smallest animals, such as spiders, mites, and insects. Some invertebrates can be found in ponds, oceans, and other water environments where they can move about easily. Others have no trouble moving about on land or in the air.

Insects and some other invertebrates have exoskeletons (eks ō-skel′ə tənz). An **exoskeleton** is a hard outer covering that protects an animal's body and gives it support.

The animals within each of the major groups of the animal kingdom have many different characteristics. These major animal groups, then, are classified into even smaller groups, based on characteristics the animals within them share. ■

centipede

snail

▲ **Examples of invertebrates**

INVESTIGATION 1

1. An organism has no structures for moving from place to place. It makes its own food, and it reproduces by seeds. In what kingdom would you place this organism? Explain your answer.

2. As you pet a dog along its back, you feel hard knobs under its skin. What are you feeling? Based on this feature, into what group of animals would you classify the dog? Explain your answer.

HOW DO VERTEBRATES DIFFER?

A backbone, two eyes, and one mouth are some characteristics shared by a snake, a cat, and a human. But you probably can name many more ways in which snakes, cats, and people are different. In Investigation 2 you'll explore how vertebrates can be different from one another.

Activity

Cold Fish

How is the way a fish breathes different from the way you breathe? What change might make a fish breathe faster or slower? In this activity you'll find out!

Procedure

1. In your *Science Notebook*, **make a chart** like the one shown. Your teacher will give your group a plastic jar with a goldfish in it. Use a thermometer to **measure** the temperature of the water. **Record** the temperature in your chart.

2. **Observe** two flaps behind the fish's eyes. Under the flaps are **gills**, which help the fish "breathe." The flaps open and close once with each breath. **Count** and **record** the number of breaths that the fish takes in one minute.

	Water Temperature	Breathing Rate
First reading		
Two minutes after ice cubes were added		

3. **Predict** how the number of times the flaps open and close in one minute will change if ice cubes are added to the water. **Record** your prediction. Gently place two or three ice cubes in the water in the jar.

4. Wait two minutes. Then again **measure** the temperature of the water. **Count** the number of times the flaps open and close in one minute. **Record** your observations. Remove the ice from the water.

Analyze and Conclude

1. How does the temperature of the water affect how the fish breathes? **Compare** your results with your prediction.

2. Think about what happens when you go outside in very cold weather. Does your breathing rate change when you go from warm air into cold air? How are you different from a fish, in terms of breathing?

INVESTIGATE FURTHER!

EXPERIMENT

Predict what would happen to the breathing rate of the fish if warmer water was added to the jar. Explain your prediction. With the help of your teacher, test your prediction. Remove 250 mL of water from the jar. Add the same amount of water, with a temperature of 15°C, to that remaining in the jar. Record the temperature and count the breaths per minute. Compare your findings with your prediction and with the breathing rates you recorded for your earlier activity. Share your findings with your classmates.

Fascinating Frogs

 GLOBAL views

If you like exploring out-of-doors, you may have met a frog face to face. Many youngsters have no fear of chasing after tree frogs and spring peepers to get a closer look. These little creatures with bulging eyes are amphibians, and they are found all over the world. As in any family, there are some pretty unusual relatives in this group. You can meet some of them on these pages.

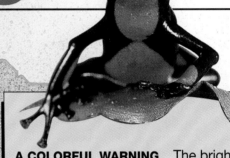

A COLORFUL WARNING   The bright colors of the South American poison dart frog are a warning. The poison of these frogs can kill!

A BACKPACKING FROG
Marsupial (mär sōō′pē əl) frogs of South America carry their eggs in the skin on their backs. When the hatched tadpoles grow legs, the mother sends them off.

A FEROCIOUS FROG   The large horned frog lives in South America as well as Central America. A horned frog will eat almost anything that moves, including small mammals and even other horned frogs!

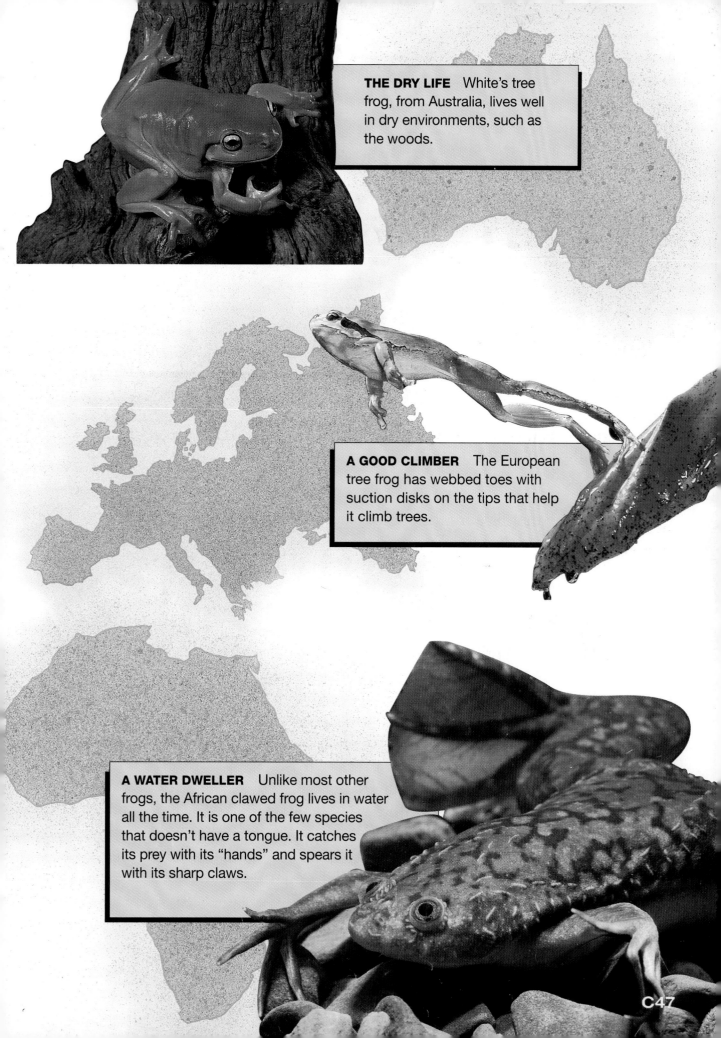

THE DRY LIFE   White's tree frog, from Australia, lives well in dry environments, such as the woods.

A GOOD CLIMBER   The European tree frog has webbed toes with suction disks on the tips that help it climb trees.

A WATER DWELLER   Unlike most other frogs, the African clawed frog lives in water all the time. It is one of the few species that doesn't have a tongue. It catches its prey with its "hands" and spears it with its sharp claws.

Swim, Leap, and Slither

Has anyone ever told you that you're one in a million? Actually, as a vertebrate, you're one in several thousand. Vertebrates can be classified into smaller groups by characteristics that they have in common. Fish, amphibians (am fib'ē ənz), and reptiles are three of these groups.

Fish Tales

Did you know that fish are the largest group of vertebrates? There are more than 30,000 different kinds of fish in all. They come in many sizes and shapes, from the tiny minnow to the great white shark.

Many vertebrates that live in water are classified as **fish**. Most fish have body temperatures that vary with the temperature of the environment.

Most fish also have fins that help them steer and balance in the water. **Gills** are feathery parts on the side of a fish's head. Water flows over the gills and allows the fish to "breathe" underwater. Many fish are covered with scales. Scales, which are hard, help protect fish.

Fish are vertebrates that live in water. ▶

Slippery Amphibians

There are almost 4,000 varieties of frogs, toads, salamanders, and other amphibians. An **amphibian** is a vertebrate that usually lives in water after hatching from an egg but as an adult can live on land. The body temperature of an amphibian varies with the temperature of its surroundings. On land, amphibians live in wet environments. Some amphibians have smooth, moist skin, which makes them look and feel slippery.

Amphibians hatch from jelly-coated eggs. Their young usually do not look anything like the parents. Young amphibians start life with gills and breathe like fish. They even have tails that help them swim.

As they get older, amphibians grow legs and lose their gills. Adult amphibians breathe air with lungs. Frogs and toads lose their tails as adults, but salamanders keep theirs.

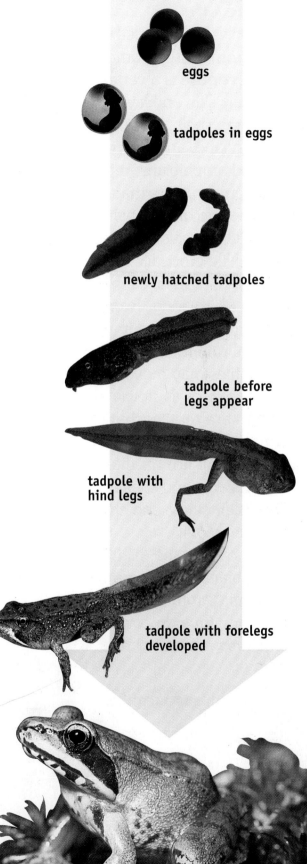

eggs

tadpoles in eggs

newly hatched tadpoles

tadpole before legs appear

tadpole with hind legs

tadpole with forelegs developed

adult frog

Variety Is the Spice of Reptile Life

Reptiles have some features that differ from those of amphibians and fish. A **reptile** is a vertebrate that has dry, scaly skin and lays eggs that have a leathery shell. All reptiles lay their eggs on land, and all breathe air. Like fish and amphibians, reptiles have body temperatures that vary with the temperature of the environment.

Reptiles include animals as large as the Nile crocodile, 5.5 m (18 ft) long, and as small as the bog turtle, 10 cm (4 in.) long. Reptiles live in hot, dry deserts and in warm, wet tropical rain forests.

Reptiles may move as quickly as a rattlesnake or as slowly as a tortoise. Snakes are reptiles that slither. Some turtles swim underwater. Reptiles may or may not have tails or even legs. Lizards and snakes are able to shed their skins, and chameleons can change colors!

As you can see, fish, reptiles, and amphibians have some very different features. But these vertebrates all have one thing in common. That is, of course, a backbone! ■

▲ **Jackson's chameleon**

A crocodile is a reptile. ▶

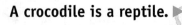

Fly, Dive, and Gallop

Besides fish, amphibians, and reptiles, there are two other groups of vertebrates with some very different characteristics. These are the birds and the mammals.

To Fly Like a Bird

There are about 9,000 types of birds on Earth. **Birds** are vertebrates that have wings and are covered with feathers. Birds lay hard-shelled eggs, which hatch in their nests. Birds range in size from a hummingbird, no bigger than your finger, to an ostrich, taller than an adult human.

A bird's skeleton is very light in weight. Its bones are hollow, which helps to make the bird light enough to fly through the air. The fastest of all birds is the white-throated spinetail swift. This little bird can fly over 160 km/h (100 mph)!

No matter their size, their color, or where they live, all birds have feathers covering their bodies. No other group of animals has this feature.

A scarlet macaw ▼

◄ **A bird's hollow bone**

▲ **A close-up view of a macaw's feathers**

▲ A whale baby can drink 11 L (3 gal) of milk in less than five minutes!

Our Group, the Mammals

Do you remember your first meal? It was milk, and it probably made you stop crying. **Mammals** are vertebrates that have hair and feed milk to their young. The young of most mammals grow inside the mother. When they have developed enough, the young are born live.

You may not have realized that mammals include a wide range of animals. Apes, lions, hippos, elephants, kangaroos, squirrels, cats, pigs, bats, horses, rabbits, and even whales are all mammals. They're mammals because they all have hair or fur, give birth to live young, and feed milk to their young.

A squirrel is a mammal that can live in a city. ▼

UNIT PROJECT LINK

Create a plan to publish your field guide to local animals. Think of different ways to present your facts, such as in a booklet, in a bulletin-board display, or on audiotape.

Most mammals have furry coats. Hair or fur traps a layer of air near the body, which helps the mammal stay warm. Humans don't have as much hair as other mammals. So wearing clothes helps us stay warm.

There are many different kinds of mammals in the world around you. The next time you watch a squirrel scramble up a tree or find a raccoon in your trash, remember that they're mammals, just as you are! ■

▲ **The timber wolf pup will get a thicker coat of fur as it grows.**

INVESTIGATION 2

1. Name the five groups of vertebrates. List the characteristics that are special to each group.

2. A salmon, a penguin, and a whale can all swim. In what other ways are these three animals alike? How are they different?

HOW DO THE GROUPS OF INVERTEBRATES DIFFER?

You learned that many animals don't have a backbone supporting their body. How are these animals without backbones grouped? Find out in this investigation.

Activity
Worming Their Way Home

Earthworms have no backbone and no eyes. How do you think these animals find their way around? How do they know when they are in their "home" environment? After doing this activity, you'll know how.

Procedure

1. Mark off four sections inside a cardboard box. Label the sections 1 through 4, as shown.

2. Place each material in a different section of the box, as shown in the diagram.

3. Remove the earthworm from its container and gently place it in section 1 of the box. With your group, **predict** which numbered section the worm will move toward. **Record** your prediction in your *Science Notebook*.

	Step 1
1 newspaper	2 dry soil
3 damp soil	4 sand

Step 4

4. Using a hand lens, **observe** the location of the worm each minute for ten minutes. Also **observe** how it uses its body parts to move. **Record** your observations.

5. When you finish observing the worm, gently place it back in its container.

Analyze and Conclude

1. Into which sections did the worm move during the ten minutes? Which materials are in those sections? Where did the worm spend the most time? the least time?

2. **Describe** how the worm used its body parts to move.

3. **Compare** your results with your predictions. **Infer** the kind of environment earthworms like best.

INVESTIGATE FURTHER!

RESEARCH

Some people are using earthworms to recycle trash. Find out how worms are able to turn trash like paper into a useful material called compost.

Nothing in Common

Some tumble along the ocean floor. Others glide through the water. Some burrow into the soil. Others fly through the air. The groups of animals without backbones are very different from one another. From spikes and soft bodies to claws and hard shells, you'll see how different some of these groups are.

Sponges

In the ocean you might mistake some animals for plants. Sponges are one group of invertebrates that look like plants because they stay fixed in one place—on a rock, for example. Sponges are animals that have bodies full of holes and skeletons made of spiky fibers.

If a sponge can't move around, how does it catch a meal? Water flows through the holes of a sponge. Small pieces of food in the moving water become trapped in the sponge.

◀ These animals, called sponges, look like plants. The holes in a sponge (*inset*) trap food for the animal.

Corals, Hydras, and Jellyfish

Corals may also look like plants, but they belong to another group of invertebrates. The animals in this group have soft, tubelike bodies with a single opening surrounded by arm-like parts called tentacles. At night, corals feed by catching tiny animals in their tentacles.

Sea anemones (ə nem'ə nēz) and hydras also belong to this group. Sea anemones have tentacles that may look like the petals of a flower. But unlike flowers, sea anemones can move from place to place, gliding or tumbling along the ocean floor. Hydras are much smaller animals, with lengths of about

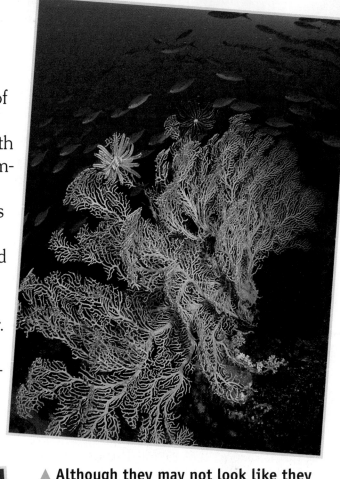

▲ Although they may not look like they belong, corals are members of the animal kingdom.

1 cm (0.4 in.). Like the larger animals in their group, hydras use their tentacles to trap food.

Jellyfish are part of the group that includes corals, sea anemones, and hydras. If you've ever gone to a beach, you may have seen jellyfish floating in the water or washed up on the sand. As a jellyfish drifts through the ocean, it catches shrimp, fish, and other animals in its tentacles.

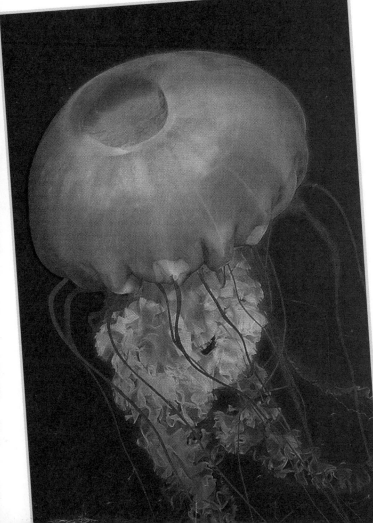

◀ Jellyfish shoot tiny poison darts from their tentacles to paralyze or kill their prey.

▲ Flatworm

▲ Roundworms

Worms of Different Shapes

Worms are tube-shaped invertebrates. They can be found in both land and water environments. Worms are classified into groups by their body designs.

Flatworms are a group of worms that have heads and tails, and flattened bodies. A tapeworm is a flatworm that can live inside the body of other animals—even humans!

Roundworms are another group of worms. As you might guess, these worms have rounded bodies. They live in damp places and can also live inside humans and other animals. Both flatworms and roundworms can make people and other animals sick.

Another worm group, the segmented worms, includes the earthworm. When you did the activity on pages C54 and C55, you may have noticed that an earthworm's body is divided into segments, or sections. All earthworms and other worms in this group have bodies made up of segments.

In the earthworm activity you may also have discovered that the earthworm prefers burrowing through moist soil. In such a dark, damp environment, the earthworm can move easily and can keep from drying out.

Starfish and Sea Urchins

A starfish is an odd-looking underwater animal. It belongs to a group of invertebrates that have many tiny tube feet and body parts arranged around a central area. The starfish shown has five arms and no head! The hard, spiny covering of the starfish gives the animal protection.

The sea urchin belongs to the same group as the starfish. A sea urchin's body is covered with long spines. Like a starfish, it moves around on tiny tube feet.

This large starfish is attacking a clam. ▶

▲ **Featherduster worm, a segmented worm that lives in the ocean**

Shells Outside or Inside

The mollusks make up another group of invertebrates. A mollusk has a hard shell, a rough tongue, and a muscular foot. A snail is a mollusk with a single hard shell protecting its soft body. A clam has two shells joined together by a hinge.

Squids and octopuses also belong to this group. But their hard shells are small and *inside* their bodies.

Lobsters to Butterflies

Arthropods are a group of invertebrates with jointed legs and hard exoskeletons that

protect the arthropods. There are nearly 1 million known kinds of arthropods!

As an arthropod grows, it **molts**, or sheds its old exoskeleton. Then the animal grows a new, larger exoskeleton that allows its body to continue growing. A lobster is an arthropod with a thick exoskeleton.

◄ **An octopus is a mollusk.**

Insects make up the largest subgroup in the arthropod group and include the only invertebrates that can fly. Insects have bodies divided into three parts, and six legs arranged in three pairs. Some insects have two pairs of wings.

Like other arthropods, spiders have jointed legs. But spiders are *not* insects. Spiders have eight legs—two more legs than insects. They also have jaws and fangs!

Centipedes and millipedes are also arthropods. But they too are not insects. Centipedes can have up to 175 pairs of legs. They can use their many legs to run from enemies.

▲ **Dragonfly, an insect with two pairs of wings**

Millipedes can have up to 240 pairs of legs! But unlike centipedes, they don't use their legs to run from enemies. Instead, millipedes roll up their bodies when they sense danger approaching. ■

SCIENCE IN LITERATURE

BUGS: STINGERS, SUCKERS, SWEETIES, SWINGERS
by Liz Greenbacker
Franklin Watts, 1993

Of the 1 million kinds of arthropods, 900,000 are insects! With so many kinds, it shouldn't surprise you that scientists have divided the insects into many groups. For example, there are over 3,000 different kinds of mosquitoes! In *Bugs: Stingers, Suckers, Sweeties, Swingers* by Liz Greenbacker, you can find out how insects are classified and where to find them.

You'll also find out that insects do more than annoy humans. Although some destroy crops and others bite or sting people, many kinds of insects are useful to humans.

Lifesaving
Leeches

STS
SCIENCE
TECHNOLOGY
& SOCIETY

It may be brown, black, or covered with colored spots and stripes. It has 32 body segments and can grow as long as 45 cm (18 in.). What is it? It's a leech, an animal that belongs to the same group as an earthworm.

A Bloodsucking Cure

Like the earthworm, the leech is an invertebrate with a segmented body. But unlike an earthworm, a leech has a mouth like a suction cup. And a leech has pointed teeth that it uses to attach itself to another animal. Leeches feed on the blood of other animals. A leech can suck a blood meal of up to ten times its own weight.

Doctors of the 1800s often used leeches to cure everything from headaches to serious diseases. Doctors attached leeches to patients, believing that the leeches would remove diseases or evil spirits from a patient's blood.

In the 1900s, new medicines came into use. And leeches were no longer used as part of the cure.

▲ Leeches, or bloodsuckers, attach themselves with their suction-cuplike mouths.

◀ In the past, people used leeches to cure almost any illness.

C61

▲ **Researchers in a Berkeley, California, laboratory study leeches.**

New Uses for Leeches

Today, researchers are once again focusing on leeches to treat illnesses. These creatures may play a role in new cures—but in a different way from their role in the past.

If a leech attached itself to you, you might not notice it for a while. The leech has a chemical in its saliva that would numb your wound.

Leech saliva contains other chemicals that scientists are studying. As the leech takes its meal of blood, chemicals in its saliva prevent the blood from clotting, or clumping. This allows the blood to continue to flow into the leech. Normally, clotting stops bleeding.

But clotting can also be a problem for people. When blood clots form inside the heart or brain, a person can have a heart attack or a stroke. Both can lead to death. Scientists hope that the chemicals in leech saliva that stop blood from clotting will help prevent or break up such clots.

Scientists are also studying leeches to learn how nerves work. Damaged nerves in a leech can regrow. New findings may help scientists better understand human nerves. In the future, leeches may once again become part of some cures. ■

INVESTIGATION 3

1. Name eight groups of invertebrates. List the characteristics that are special to each group.

2. Insects have been called the most successful group of animals. What are some characteristics of insects that have helped them to live so successfully on Earth?

REFLECT & EVALUATE

WORD POWER

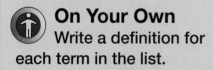

amphibian
bird
exoskeleton
fish
gills
invertebrate
mammal
molt
organism
reptile
vertebra
vertebrate

On Your Own
Write a definition for each term in the list.

With a Partner
Mix up the letters of each term in the list. Provide a clue for each term and challenge your partner to unscramble the terms.

BUILD YOUR PORTFOLIO

Make a poster to show how animals are classified. Include all the animal groups you learned about.

Analyze Information

Study the photograph. Then use it to explain in which group of the animal kingdom you would place this organism.

Assess Performance

Develop a chart similar to the one on page C35 to distinguish between the five groups of vertebrates. Then choose five animals to test your chart.

Problem Solving

1. How do you think the invention of the microscope affected how scientists classified organisms?

2. The body temperature of amphibians and reptiles varies with the temperature of their environment. How is this a disadvantage for these animals?

3. Explain how a jellyfish, a worm, and a dragonfly are alike. Then tell something about the group to which each animal belongs.

Throughout this unit you've investigated questions related to animals. How will you use what you've learned and share that information with others? Here are some ideas.

Hold a Big Event
to Share Your Unit Project

With your classmates, plan an Animal Safari Day to try out your Field Guide to Local Animals. Plan routes for different field trips. Invite family and friends. Then on Animal Safari Day, trade guides with another group. Use the borrowed guide to identify animals you observe on your field trip. Make a list of the animals and compare it with the lists of other groups.

Experiment

Place an earthworm on a damp paper towel in a pan. Determine which is the head end of the earthworm. (Hint: Earthworms usually crawl forward.) Find out how earthworms respond to touch and to light. Share your observations with classmates.

Research

Choose an activity, problem, or person in this unit to research. You might choose an animal and investigate its needs. Or you might discover more about a scientist. Carolus Linnaeus, for example, promoted the use of Latin names for living things. Share what you find with your classmates.

Take Action

Make a plan to observe how the needs of animals are met. You might visit a zoo or adopt a local animal to observe. Make a booklet that contains your observations.

UNIT D

MAGNETISM AND ELECTRICITY

Theme: Models

GET READY TO

OBSERVE & QUESTION

What is static electricity?

You can't see electricity, but you often see its effects. Lightning is one of these effects. What are some others?

EXPERIMENT & HYPOTHESIZE

What are magnets?

What do you think would happen if you moved one magnet near another? Testing one magnet with another magnet will help you investigate the properties of all magnets.

INVESTIGATE!

RESEARCH & ANALYZE

As you investigate, find out more from these books.

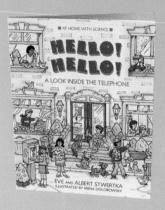

- ***Hello! Hello! A Look Inside the Telephone*** by Eve and Albert Stwertka. (Julian Messner, 1991). How are different kinds of magnets and electric circuits used in telephones? How do cordless phones work? What does the future hold for telephones? This book will help you answer these and other questions about telephones.

- ***Magnets: Mind-boggling Experiments You Can Turn Into Science Fair Projects*** by Janice VanCleave. (John Wiley & Sons, 1993). How do magnets work? Why do they behave as they do? Use this book to find out.

WORK TOGETHER & SHARE IDEAS

How can you invent magnetic and electrical devices that are fun or useful?

Working together, you'll have a chance to use the knowledge you develop about magnets and electric circuits to create games, toys, and machines. Then you can share your new knowledge with others.

MAGNETISM

Where do you find magnets? Perhaps your refrigerator door at home has small magnets that are holding up papers. You may have seen pictures of a giant magnet lifting tons of junked cars in the air. How do these magnets work?

Putting Magnets to Work

The rear doors of an ambulance open. Quickly, Pat is rolled into the hospital. There are bandages around her head and arm. Her injuries are the result of a car accident. Pat's head hurts. The doctors need to make sure there are no serious injuries to her head and spine.

After doctors quickly check her over, Pat is taken to the <u>M</u>agnetic <u>R</u>esonance <u>I</u>maging (MRI) center. MRI uses powerful magnets to produce computer pictures of parts inside the body.

Dr. Ray Cobb, a radiologist, gives Pat the MRI. A radiologist is trained to understand MRI pictures. The MRI pictures help Dr. Cobb identify injuries to muscles and tissues. He can even find problems with blood circulation. In this chapter you'll find out about other ways that magnets help people.

Coming Up

◄ Dr. Ray Cobb uses MRI to identify injuries.

INVESTIGATION 1

WHAT ARE MAGNETS?

Go on a magnet hunt—real or imaginary—around your home. Start at the refrigerator, but keep in mind that many magnets are out of sight. Just what is a magnet and what can it do? In Investigation 1 you'll find out.

Activity

Make a Magnet

Discover how to make your own magnet. Then use your magnet to find out what kinds of objects a magnet pulls on, or sticks to.

MATERIALS
- bag of small objects
- magnet
- nail
- *Science Notebook*

SAFETY
Be careful when handling the nail.

Procedure

1. Open the bag of small objects and spread them on a table. Have all your group members collect other small objects from their pockets and around the classroom. Include things made of many different materials.

2. In your *Science Notebook,* **make a chart** like the one shown to record your observations.

Attracted By or Sticks to Magnet		
Object	Prediction	Actual

Step 3

3. Talk with your group and together **predict** which objects will stick to a magnet. **Record** your predictions in your chart. Then move a magnet close to each object. **Record** your observations in your chart.

4. **Make a chart** like the one you made in step 2. **Predict** whether a nail will attract any of the objects. Then move a nail close to each object. **Record** your observations.

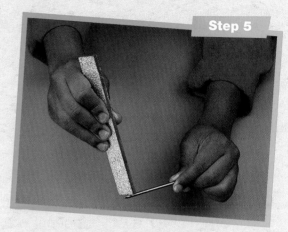

Step 5

5. Stroke the nail with the end of the magnet 20 times. *Stroke in one direction only*.

6. Repeat step 4 using the stroked nail. Make a set of predictions about the stroked nail. **Record** your predictions and, after testing the objects, **record** your observations.

Analyze and Conclude

1. How did your predictions about which objects would be attracted to a magnet compare with your results?

2. How did your predictions about the nail before you stroked it with a magnet compare with your results?

3. Explain your observations about the nail after you stroked it with a magnet. **Hypothesize** how stroking the nail with the magnet affects the nail.

4. What can you **infer** about the objects that were attracted by the magnet and the stroked nail?

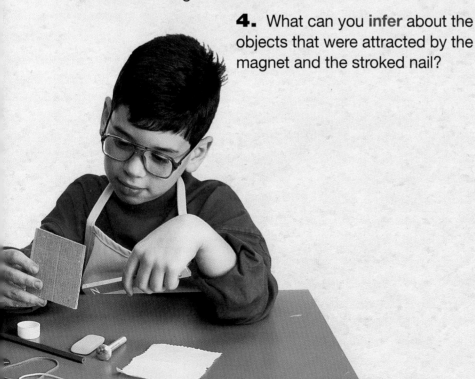

INVESTIGATE FURTHER!

EXPERIMENT

Hold the nail that you stroked with a magnet near a pile of paper clips. If nothing happens, stroke the nail with the magnet 20 times. How many paper clips does the nail pick up?

Suppose you stroke the nail with the magnet 30 times and then 40 times. Will the nail be able to pick up more paper clips? Find out. Make a chart of your results.

Activity

A Magnet's Ends

Both ends of a magnet have "pull." But are both ends of a magnet alike in every way? Find out in this activity.

MATERIALS
- string
- 2 bar magnets
- meterstick
- 2 chairs
- *Science Notebook*

Procedure

1. Tie a string to a bar magnet on which one end is marked *N* and the other is marked *S*. Tie the string to a meterstick placed between two chairs, as shown.

2. **Predict** what will happen if you move the end of another bar magnet marked *N* and *S* close to the hanging magnet. Think about the ways you might arrange the ends of the magnets. **Record** each arrangement and what you **predict** for each arrangement in your *Science Notebook*.

3. **Make a plan** with your group to test your predictions. Then **test** your plan and **record** your observations.

Step 2

4. Now **test** a bar magnet on which one end is marked *X* and the other end is marked *Y*. Hold one end and then the other end of this magnet near one end of the hanging magnet. Decide which end, *X* or *Y*, you can **infer** is really *N* and which is really *S*. **Record** your inference and state your evidence. Remove the tape. **Record** whether your inference was correct.

Analyze and Conclude

1. The *N* on the end of a magnet marks its north-seeking pole, or north pole. The *S* on the other end of a magnet marks its south-seeking pole, or south pole. From your observations, what can you conclude about which poles attract, or pull toward each other?

2. What can you conclude about which poles repel, or push away from, each other?

UNIT PROJECT LINK

As you go through this unit, you'll invent games, fun devices, and machines. You'll use magnets or electricity in all your inventions. Your first challenge is to invent a magic trick that makes use of magnets. Think about a trick that works because the force of a magnet can be "felt" through various materials. Build a model of your magic trick. Include instructions for others to follow.

Activity
Pulling Through

A magnet can have a lot of force, or pull. In this activity you'll find out more about how that force works.

MATERIALS
- string
- bar magnet
- meterstick
- 2 chairs
- paper clip
- assorted materials
- *Science Notebook*

Procedure

1. Tie a string around a bar magnet. Hang the magnet from a meterstick between two chairs.

2. Place a paper clip on the palm of your hand. Then move your hand under the magnet until the magnet is just close enough to attract the paper clip.

Force of Magnet Through Materials		
Material	Prediction	Result

3. **Talk with your group** and together **predict** whether the magnet can attract the paper clip through materials such as paper, aluminum foil, cloth, plastic, and steel. In your *Science Notebook*, **make a chart** like the one shown to record your predictions and observations.

4. Plan a way to find out whether the magnet's force can act through different materials. **Test** your plan. If it doesn't work, try something else. **Record** your observations in your chart.

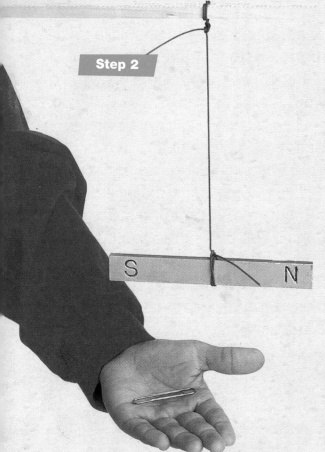

Step 2

S N

Analyze and Conclude

1. **Compare** your predictions about the force of a magnet through different materials with your observations.

2. From your observations, **infer** whether the force of a magnet can pass through different materials.

Properties of Magnets

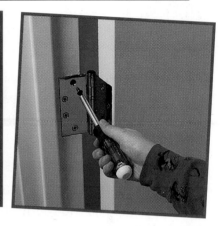

▲ **How is a magnet being used in each picture?**

What's an easy way to clean up a mixture of metal paper clips and rubber bands spilled on the floor? If you drag a magnet over the floor, the paper clips, but not the rubber bands, will stick to the magnet. Why does this happen?

The Pull of Magnets

When you did the activity on pages D6 and D7, you saw how a magnet affects some materials. A **magnet** is an object that attracts, or pulls on, certain materials, mainly

The steel figures of this toy can be arranged in various ways on a magnet. ▼

iron and steel. A magnet's property of attracting these materials is called **magnetism** (mag′nə tiz əm).

Paper clips are made of steel, which contains iron. That's why you could pick them up with a magnet. Rubber bands contain no iron or other materials that a magnet attracts.

The photographs above show some uses of magnets around the home. The part of the can opener that lifts the steel lid of the can is a magnet. Using a magnet to pick up pins keeps fingers from being pricked. A magnetic screwdriver makes it easier to hold screws in place.

D11

Two Kinds of Magnets

Commercial magnets made in a factory are permanent magnets. A permanent magnet is not easy to make, but it keeps its magnetism for a long time. It may be made from steel that contains both iron and other metals.

Some objects—for example, iron nails—are easy to make into magnets. As you saw in the activity on pages D6 and D7, you only have to stroke a nail with a permanent magnet to magnetize the nail. But magnets made in this way are temporary magnets. A temporary magnet is one that doesn't keep its magnetism for very long.

▲ **Are the magnets on this refrigerator door likely to be temporary or permanent?**

SCIENCE IN LITERATURE

MAGNETS: MIND-BOGGLING EXPERIMENTS YOU CAN TURN INTO SCIENCE FAIR PROJECTS
By Janice VanCleave
John Wiley & Sons, 1993

Magnets—they seem simple, don't they? Maybe there's more to magnets than you think. Janice VanCleave is a science teacher who thinks magnets are fascinating. She has written a book of activities that can be done with magnets and other easy-to-find materials.

In her book *Magnets: Mind-boggling Experiments You Can Turn Into Science Fair Projects*, VanCleave includes lots of interesting facts about magnets. Are you planning to enter a science fair? Do you want to present a science experiment to your class? This book has plenty of great tips for both activities.

▲ The south poles or north poles of two magnets repel each other.

▲ The south pole of one magnet attracts the north pole of another magnet.

North and South Poles

When a magnet is hung so that it can move freely, one end of it always points toward the north. This is the magnet's north-seeking pole, or **north pole**. If one end points north, you know what direction the other end points toward. It points south. This is the magnet's south-seeking pole, or **south pole**.

What happens if you move the north pole of one magnet near the north pole of another? If both magnets are free to move, they move farther apart. And what happens if you bring the north pole of one magnet near the south pole of another? The two magnets move closer together and the north and south poles may stick to each other.

Here is a rule to remember about how magnets behave. Like poles of magnets repel, or push away from, each other. Unlike poles of magnets attract, or pull toward, each other. In the activity on pages D8 and D9, you could identify the poles of a magnet by the way the magnet moved. ■

Maglev Trains

Can a train fly? The maglev train does, in a way. If you visit Germany or Japan, you might ride on a maglev. It may look as if this train runs on a track, but it doesn't. The maglev train floats about 1 cm (0.4 in.) *above* the track!

It Flies and It's Fast

The maglev's full name tells something about how it works. *Maglev* is short for "magnetic levitation" (lev ə-tā′shən). *Levitation* means "rising into the air." The maglev uses magnetic force to rise into the air.

Friction, or rubbing, between the wheels of railroad cars and tracks slows down ordinary trains. Because the maglev doesn't touch its track, there's no friction. This means that it can go really fast, up to 500 km/h (310 mph)!

An ordinary train goes "clackety-clack" on the rails—but not the maglev. Speeding on air makes the ride superfast. It also makes the ride very smooth and quiet.

A maglev train in Germany ▼

▲ Maglevs are lifted into the air by magnetic forces. There are powerful magnets on both the train and on the rails.

Magnets attached to the train run below the rail.

Magnets on the rail pull on magnets on the train.

It's Clean

Most buses and cars run by burning oil or gasoline. So do most trains. When oil and gasoline burn, they pollute the air. That means those vehicles make the air dirty by giving off harmful substances.

Power plants that produce electricity burn fuels that also pollute the air. The maglev runs on electricity. But the train itself doesn't produce pollution in the air around it. You could call the maglev an environmentally friendly train. ■

INVESTIGATION 1

1. Suppose a rock sample from Mars is brought to Earth. Pieces of the rock can be picked up by a magnet. What metal may be present in the rock?

2. Two doughnut-shaped magnets are placed on a pencil. One of the magnets floats above the other one. What makes this happen?

INVESTIGATION 2

WHAT ARE MAGNETIC FORCE FIELDS?

You can't see, hear, or smell a magnetic force field. But bring a magnet near an object made of iron, and you can *feel* the force. In Investigation 2 you'll explore the patterns of magnetic force fields.

Activity

Getting Directions

Earth has a magnetic force field around it. In this activity you'll make a magnet and use it to detect directions from Earth's magnetic field.

MATERIALS
- goggles
- bar magnet
- needle with blunt end
- plastic-foam ball
- small bowl
- water
- *Science Notebook*

SAFETY

Wear goggles during this activity. Clean up any spills immediately.

Procedure

1. Magnetize a needle by stroking it many times with one end of a bar magnet. Stroke the needle in the same direction each time.

2. Stick the needle through the center of a plastic-foam ball, as shown.

Step 2

3. Half-fill a bowl with water. Carefully place the foam ball and needle on the water. **Observe** what happens. **Record** your observations in your *Science Notebook*.

4. Wait until the foam ball is still. **Talk with your group** and together **predict** what will happen if you move the bar magnet near the bowl. **Test** your prediction and **record** your observations.

5. Take away the bar magnet. Give the bowl a quarter turn. Make sure that the foam ball is free to move. Keep turning until you complete a full circle. **Record** your observations.

Analyze and Conclude

1. Find out from your teacher which direction is north. In which direction did the needle point?

2. **Compare** your prediction with your observation of what happened when you moved a bar magnet near the bowl.

3. A compass always points in a north-south direction. From your observations, **infer** whether or not you have made a compass. Give reasons for your inference.

INVESTIGATE FURTHER!

RESEARCH

When you magnetize an object, the particles that make up the object become tiny magnets called domains. In a library, find out more about magnetic domains. One book you might read is *Magnets: Mind-boggling Experiments You Can Turn Into Science Fair Projects* by Janice VanCleave. Write a report and illustrate it with a drawing of magnetic domains.

Activity

Picture a Magnet's Force

Even though you can't see a magnet's force, you can make a picture of it. In this activity you'll find out how.

MATERIALS
- goggles
- gloves
- bar magnet
- newspaper
- 2 sheets of stiff white cardboard
- iron filings in jar with a sprinkler top
- horseshoe magnet
- *Science Notebook*

SAFETY

Wear goggles during this activity.
Wear gloves when handling iron filings.

Procedure

1. Place a bar magnet on a sheet of newspaper. Put a sheet of white cardboard on top of the magnet.

2. Hold a jar of iron filings over the cardboard. Carefully sprinkle iron filings on the cardboard over the magnet.

3. Tap the cardboard gently. Look for a pattern of lines of iron filings. In your *Science Notebook*, **draw** the pattern the lines form.

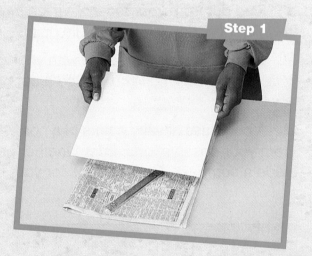

Step 1

4. Put a clean sheet of cardboard over a horseshoe magnet. **Talk with your group** and together **predict** the pattern that will form if you sprinkle iron filings on the cardboard. Then **make a drawing** to show your prediction.

5. **Test** your prediction. Then **draw** what you see.

Analyze and Conclude

1. **Compare** your predictions with your observations of the patterns of the iron fillings.

2. The lines made by the iron filings are called **lines of force**. The space in which the lines of force form is a **magnetic field**. A pattern formed by the lines is a picture of the magnetic field. What do the magnetic fields you observed tell you about where the magnetic force is greatest?

Force Fields

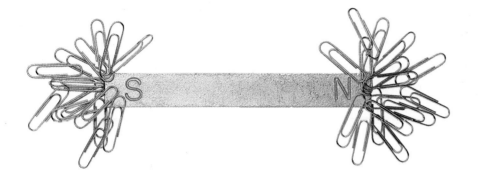

◀ **A magnet is strongest at its poles.**

What happens if you dip a bar magnet into a pile of paper clips and then hold the magnet up? Look at the picture. A lot of clips stick to the magnet. Notice where the clips stick—at the magnet's two poles. Why does this happen?

Lines of Force

In the activity on page D18, you made pictures of the force fields of bar and horseshoe magnets. When iron filings are sprinkled on cardboard over a magnet, the iron filings line up in a pattern. The pattern of filings shows how the force field spreads between the poles of the magnet and around it. The filings are thickest and closest together where the force is strongest.

These lines made by the iron filings are called **lines of force**. The picture below shows a bar magnet that was sprinkled with iron filings. Actually, it's the same magnet that was used with paper clips in the picture above. Notice how the lines of force are heaviest at the poles, where the magnet also picked up the paper clips.

Pattern formed by lines of force of a bar magnet ▶

A Magnet's Force Field

The space in which the force of a magnet can act is called a **magnetic field**. You can't see a magnetic field. But you have seen some evidence that it exists.

For example, suppose you want to use a magnet to pick up a paper clip. You know that you have to move the clip and the magnet close enough together for the magnet to attract the clip. That's because a magnet attracts only those paper clips—or other objects that contain iron—that come into its magnetic field.

You have seen how to use iron filings to make pictures of the lines of force around a magnet. The lines of force you can see on flat cardboard make it seem that the magnetic field is also flat. But is the field really flat?

The magnetic field actually spreads out in all directions throughout the space around the magnet.

Comparing Force Fields

You've found out about several properties of magnets.

- A magnet attracts objects made of iron.
- The force of a magnet is greatest at its poles.
- Like poles of two magnets repel each other.
- Unlike poles of two magnets attract each other.

How are the force fields of magnets related to those properties? Use the pictures on the next page to find out. As you look at each picture, read the description below it.

▲ The pattern of the iron filings around the magnet in this jar of oil show how a magnetic field spreads out all around a magnet.

INVESTIGATE FURTHER!

EXPERIMENT

Make a permanent display of one or more patterns made by magnets as shown in the pictures on page D21. Use the procedure in the activity on page D18 to make the patterns you choose. Then put on goggles and spray white vinegar over the filings. Let them stand overnight. Brush off the rusted filings and observe what remains. Write captions for your pictures and put the pictures on display.

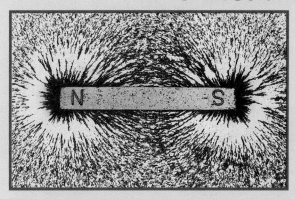

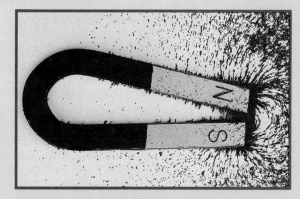

▲ This picture shows the magnetic field of a bar magnet. With your finger, trace the lines of force as they come out of the north pole, curve around the magnet, and enter the south pole.

▲ This picture shows the magnetic field of a horseshoe magnet. Notice how the strongest lines are closer together than they are for the bar magnet. Infer why this is so.

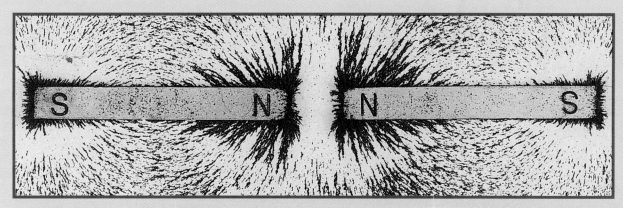

▲ The north poles of these two magnets are facing each other. What do you observe about the lines of force between the two magnets? If you hold two magnets with their north poles together like this, what will you feel?

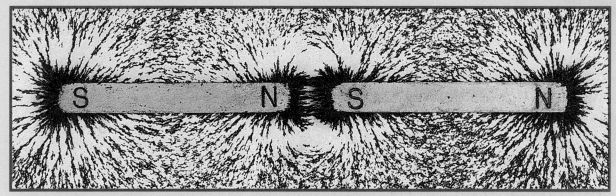

▲ The north pole of the magnet on the left is facing the south pole of the magnet on the right. Notice that the lines of force seem to move straight from one magnet to the other. If you hold two magnets like this, what will you feel?

Earth as a Magnet

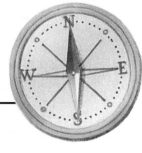

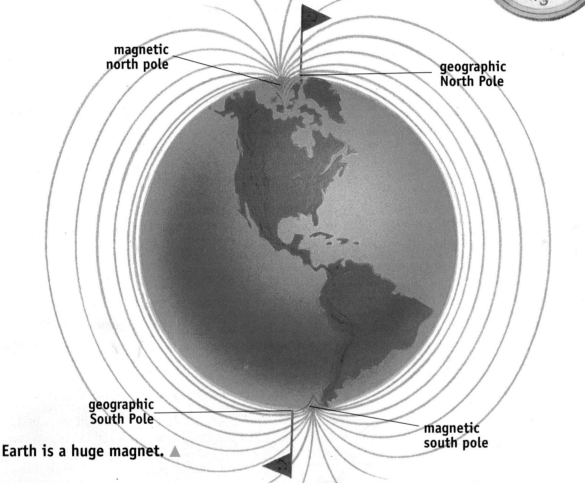

magnetic
north pole

geographic
North Pole

geographic
South Pole

magnetic
south pole

Earth is a huge magnet. ▲

Today scientists know that Earth is a giant magnet. However, long before scientists knew anything about Earth's magnetism, they knew about lodestone (lōd'stōn).

Lodestone is a naturally magnetic rock found at or near Earth's surface. The first lodestone was discovered by a sheepherder in Turkey more than 2,000 years ago. The stone attracted iron nails in his shoes. Almost 1,000 years later, the Greeks discovered that when hung from a string, lodestone always lined itself up in a north-south direction. The same end of the lodestone always pointed toward the north.

A Stone Leads the Way

Chinese sailors found a practical use for this property of lodestone. They floated a small piece of lodestone on some straw in a bowl of water. Since one end of the stone always pointed toward the north, the sailors always knew in which direction they were sailing.

Does the device used by the Chinese sailors sound familiar? In the activity on pages D16 and D17, you made a similar device with a magnetized needle and a foam ball. The device is a simple compass. A **compass** is a magnetized needle that is allowed to swing freely.

Earth's Magnetism

Since the discovery of lodestones, scientists have learned that Earth's center is made up mostly of iron. They know that the spinning of Earth on its axis has magnetized this iron, turning Earth into a giant magnet. But they can't explain it.

Like all magnets, the "Earth magnet" has poles and is surrounded by a magnetic field. This field has lines of force like those you saw in the activity on page D18. Magnets are affected by Earth's magnetic field. The north-seeking pole of a magnet is attracted to Earth's magnetic north pole. This attraction is what makes a compass work.

Why Two Sets of Poles?

As the drawing on page D22 shows, Earth has two sets of poles—geographic and magnetic. The geographic poles mark the ends of the imaginary line around which Earth rotates.

When the first explorers set out for the North Pole, they expected their compass to lead them to the geographic North Pole. But it didn't.

A lodestone ▼

▲ **This ancient Chinese compass is a spoon that turns so that its handle points south.**

▲ **An aurora in the northern sky**

Their compass led the explorers to a spot more than 1,600 km (1,000 mi) from the geographic North Pole. This spot marks the location of Earth's magnetic north pole.

Magnetism Lights Up the Sky

At certain times of the year, people living in regions near the poles get to see the northern or southern lights. During these times, the sky above the poles lights up in a display of brilliant colors.

These displays, called auroras (ô-rôr′əz), are produced when particles of matter from space are captured by Earth's magnetic field. Why are these displays brightest near Earth's magnetic poles? ■

INVESTIGATION 2

1. When a circular magnet is dipped into a pile of paper clips, about the same number of clips stick to the top as to the bottom. What does this tell you about the magnetic field of that magnet?

2. How could you make a compass with a magnetized nail, a string, a plastic jar with a lid, and some tape?

WORD POWER

compass
lines of force
lodestone
magnet
magnetic field
magnetism
north pole
south pole

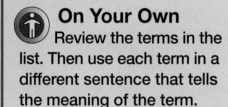 On Your Own
Review the terms in the list. Then use each term in a different sentence that tells the meaning of the term.

With a Partner
Write a clue for each term in the list. Then challenge your partner to write the correct term for each clue.

PORTFOLIO

Use a magnet to test ten metal objects to find out which ones are attracted to a magnet. Record your findings on a poster.

Analyze Information

Study the photograph. Describe whether the magnetic poles that are closest together are *like* or *unlike*. In your own words, explain how you can determine this information.

Assess Performance

Plan an experiment to find out how the number of times a needle is stroked with a magnet affects the length of time the needle remains magnetized. After your teacher has reviewed your plan, carry out the experiment. Compare your results with those of others.

Problem Solving

1. Imagine that you are lost in the woods. You do not have a compass, but you do have a bar magnet and some string. How can you use the magnet and string to find your way?

2. You find a rock that you think may be lodestone. What would be a simple way to determine if the rock is lodestone or just a plain rock?

3. You have two magnets—one strong and one weak. How could you use paper clips to find out which magnet is stronger?

CHAPTER 2
ELECTRICAL ENERGY

What does a comic-book artist show by drawing a zigzag line? How can you tell that a character in a cartoon is having a bright idea? Think of some other signs and symbols that stand for electrical energy in action.

A Flash of Artistry

Artist David Archer creates pictures with an electric paintbrush. This device produces lightninglike arcs of electricity. Archer uses a wand to direct the arcs so that they hit large blobs of wet paint. The paint forms cloudy shapes on large glass plates. The artist calls these shapes art storms.

Most often, David Archer paints pictures of planets and other bodies in space as he imagines them. His work has appeared in magazines and even in the movies. You may have seen some of this artist's works on a television science fiction show.

To run his electric paintbrush, David Archer uses household electricity. In this chapter you'll find out more about why electricity is such hot stuff!

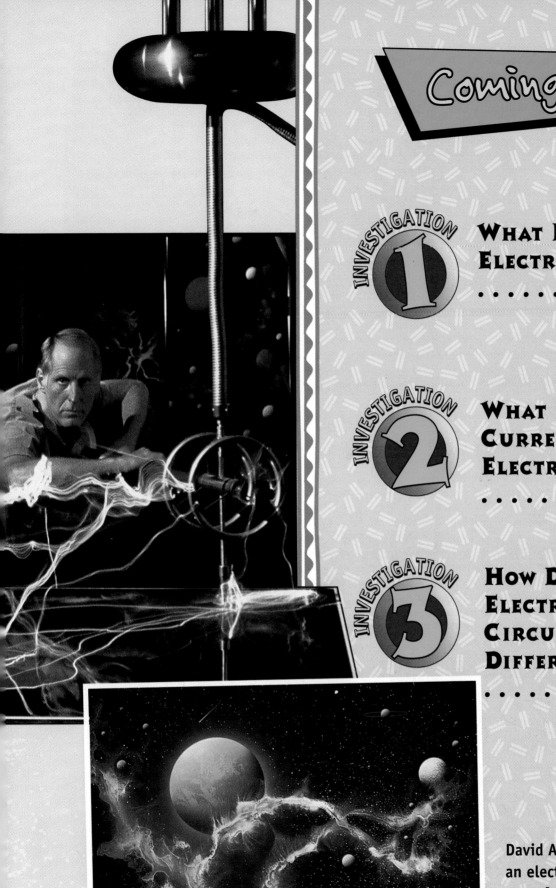

David Archer (*top*) uses an electric paintbrush; one of Archer's paintings (*bottom*).

WHAT IS STATIC ELECTRICITY?

Your clean hair clings to your comb. A shirt you take out of the dryer has socks stuck to it. As you pull up a blanket on a chilly night, you see sparks and feel a slight shock. In Investigation 1 you'll find out how all these events are related.

Activity

Charge!

Sometimes a balloon will stick to another balloon; other times it won't. Try this activity and see if you can figure out why.

MATERIALS

- 2 balloons
- 2 strings (30 cm each)
- metric tape measure
- wool cloth
- plastic wrap
- *Science Notebook*

Procedure

1. Have two members of your group blow up balloons. Tie each balloon tightly with a string.

2. Have two other group members hold the strings so that the balloons hang about 10 cm apart. What happens to the movement of the balloons? **Record** your observations in your *Science Notebook.*

Step 1

3. Rub each balloon with a wool cloth. **Predict** what will happen now if you repeat step 2. **Talk with your group** and then **record** your prediction. Then repeat step 2.

4. Repeat step 3, but this time rub each balloon with plastic wrap instead.

5. With your group, **predict** what will happen when a balloon rubbed with wool is brought near a balloon rubbed with plastic wrap. **Test** your prediction and **record** your observations.

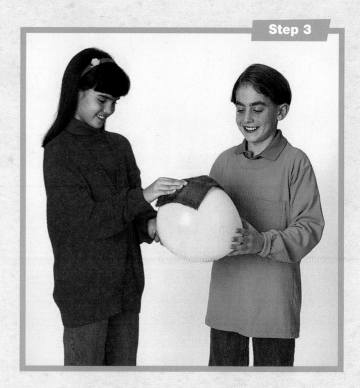

Analyze and Conclude

1. Rubbing a balloon with wool or plastic wrap gives the balloon an electric charge. From observing the behavior of the balloons, **infer** whether there is more than one kind of electric charge. Explain how you made your inference.

2. **Compare** your prediction about the balloons with your observations after they were rubbed with the wool cloth.

3. **Compare** your prediction about the balloons with your observations after they were rubbed with the plastic wrap.

4. Like charges repel, or push away from, each other. Unlike charges attract, or pull toward, each other. How do your results support these statements?

INVESTIGATE FURTHER!

EXPERIMENT

How does a charged balloon interact with objects that have not been charged? Bring a charged balloon close to some puffed-cereal grains. Then bring a charged balloon near a wall. What can you conclude about the effect of a charged balloon on uncharged objects?

Static Electricity

You're combing your clean, dry hair. Strands of your hair fly away from each other. At the same time, the strands also stick to your comb. In the activity on pages D28 and D29, balloons you rubbed with wool cloth or plastic wrap attracted or repelled each other. Why does rubbing materials together cause these effects?

Hair, combs, balloons, wool, and plastic are kinds of matter. All matter is made up of tiny particles. Some of these particles carry bits of electricity called **electric charges**.

Positive and Negative Charges

An electric charge can be positive or negative. A plus sign (+) stands for a positive charge, and a minus sign (−) stands for a negative charge. A neutral object has the same number of positive charges as negative charges.

If negative charges move from one neutral object to another, the first object then has an overall positive charge and the second one has an overall negative charge. The pictures show balloons becoming charged.

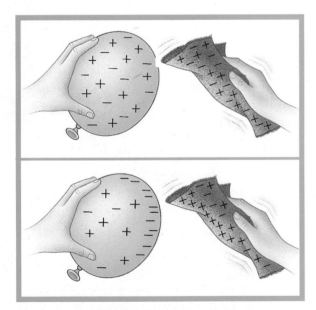

▲ Rubbing a balloon with wool (*top*) gives a negative charge to the balloon (*bottom*). What is the charge on the wool?

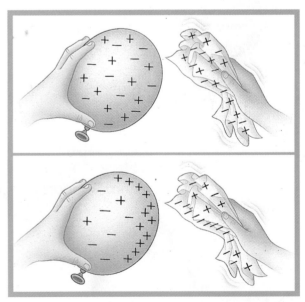

▲ Rubbing a balloon with plastic (*top*) gives a positive charge to the balloon (*bottom*). What is the charge on the plastic?

D30

The form of energy that comes from charged particles is called electrical (ē lek′tri kəl) energy. Negative electric charges can move from one object to another. When this happens, an electric charge builds up on both objects.

This buildup of electric charges is called **static electricity**. An object charged with static electricity has a buildup of electric charges on its surface. Objects with a buildup of like charges repel, or push away from, each other as shown in the top picture below.

What happens when you comb freshly washed and dried hair with a hard rubber comb? You're rubbing hair, which is one kind of matter, with hard rubber, which is another kind of matter.

If the air is dry enough, negative charges move from the hair to the comb, giving the comb an overall negative charge. Since the hair loses negative charges, it now has an overall positive charge. As the bottom picture of the balloons shows, objects having unlike charges attract, or pull toward, each other.

Why do separate strands of the girl's hair repel each other? Why does the comb attract each strand of hair? ▼

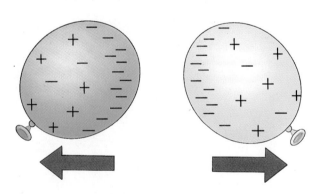

▲ A balloon that has a negative charge repels another one that has a negative charge.

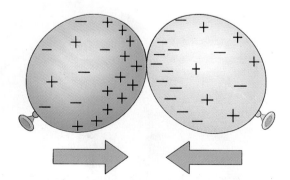

▲ A balloon that has a positive charge attracts one that has a negative charge.

You're taking the laundry out of the dryer, and your socks are stuck to your shirt. This is a case of static cling. Why does this happen?

As the dryer whirls, the clothes rub together. When different materials rub together, negative charges move from some materials to others. So the clothes become charged with static electricity. Your wool socks may have a positive charge and your cotton shirt a negative charge. So they attract one another.

When cotton is rubbed with wool, negative charges move from the wool onto the cotton. The cotton then has more negative charges than positive charges. And the wool has more positive charges than negative charges. So both socks and shirt become charged with static electricity.

Attracting Neutral Objects

If you charge a balloon by rubbing it on wool, the balloon may stick to a wall. But the wall is neutral. In the

Why is static cling called "static"? ▼

▲ **What evidence is there that the charge on the balloon is the opposite of the charge on the wall?**

activity on pages D28 and D29, the balloons that stuck together were both charged. Why does a charged balloon stick to a neutral wall?

The rubbed balloon collects extra negative charges that repel the negative charges in the wall. As a result, that part of the wall has extra positive charges that attract the negative charges of the balloon.

Shock, Spark, and Crackle

Do you want to shock a friend? Walk across a rug; then touch your friend's hand. Your friend may get a mild electric shock. There's a catch, though. You'll feel the shock, too.

You may even see a spark and hear a slight crackling sound.

What causes the shock, the spark, and the crackle? You rub your shoes against the rug. Negative charges move from the rug onto your shoes. The charges move from your shoes onto your body. Your body is now charged with static electricity.

Charges that build up in this way don't stay on the charged object. Sooner or later the charges move away. They may jump into the air or onto another object. When static electric charges jump off a charged object, an **electric discharge** takes place. ■

In an electric discharge, negative electric charges move from a charged object to another object. ▼

INVESTIGATE FURTHER!

RESEARCH

Benjamin Franklin lived in Philadelphia in the eighteenth century. He was a statesman, scientist, and an inventor. Franklin had the idea that lightning is a kind of electricity. He did a famous experiment to prove this idea. He also invented the lightning rod. In a library, find out about Franklin's experiment and invention. One book you might read is *What's the Big Idea, Ben Franklin?* by Jean Fritz.

Lightning

▲ **A lightning flash is so bright that it's visible from a great distance.**

Zap! Boom! Lightning flashes across the sky. Then thunder cracks. The wind is strong and rain starts pouring down—it's a thunderstorm. You may know that lightning causes thunder. But what causes lightning?

During a thunderstorm, positive charges can build up at the top of a cloud. Negative electric charges build up at the bottom of the cloud.

These negative charges at the bottom of a cloud repel negative charges in the ground below. This leaves the ground, and objects on the ground, with positive electric charges.

When negative charges jump between the cloud and the ground, there's a giant electric discharge, or spark. This spark is lightning.

1 Negative charges on a cloud cause positive charges to build up on the ground and the tree.

2 Lightning strikes when negative charges jump from the cloud to the ground or to the tree.

Lightning Safety

Lightning often strikes the tallest object on the ground. Often this object is a tree, so you should never stand under a tree during a lightning storm. Also, don't play in an open field or swim. Take shelter in a building or an enclosed car.

A lightning rod is a metal rod about 20 cm (8 in.) long. It is attached to the highest point of a building or tower. Heavy wires connect the rod to the ground. When lightning strikes the rod, electric charges move through the wires safely to Earth. ■

▲ **How can you stay safe if you're outdoors when lightning starts?**

INVESTIGATION 1

1. How might you use a balloon with a negative charge to find out whether the charge on another balloon is positive or negative?

2. Imagine you've just come inside on a cold, dry day. As you pull off your sweater, it sticks to your shirt and then you hear a crackling sound. What causes these effects?

WHAT IS CURRENT ELECTRICITY?

In Investigation 1 you saw that electric charges can move from place to place. In Investigation 2 find out how this flow of electricity can be controlled.

Activity

On or Off?

You usually take for granted that flipping on a light switch will turn on a light. What else has to happen for the light to go on? Find out in this activity.

MATERIALS
- dry cell (size D) in holder
- light bulb in holder
- 3 insulated wires (stripped on ends)
- thick cardboard
- 2 brass paper fasteners
- paper clip
- *Science Notebook*

Procedure

1. Place all the materials listed above on your desk. With your group, **hypothesize** ways you can connect some of the parts to make the bulb light. **Record** a list of these ways in your *Science Notebook*.

Step 1

2. **Test** each idea that is on your group's list. **Draw** each arrangement you try. Circle the ones that make the bulb light.

3. When the bulb lighted, you had made an **electric circuit** (sur'kit). This is a path through which electricity can flow.

4. Use the inset picture as a guide to arrange a paper clip, two brass fasteners, and two wires on a piece of thick cardboard.

Step 4

5. You have made a switch, which you can use to turn the bulb on or off. **Predict** how you can connect the switch to the circuit. **Record** and **test** your prediction. **Make a drawing** that shows how the parts are connected when the switch works.

Analyze and Conclude

1. **Compare** your predictions about lighting the bulb—with and without the switch—with your results.

2. An electric circuit through which electricity moves is called a closed circuit. When you disconnect a part of a closed circuit, the circuit is called an open circuit. When you flip a switch to turn on a light, are you opening a circuit, or closing it? Explain your answer.

INVESTIGATE FURTHER!

RESEARCH

What are some different types of switches? How do the switches on electric devices and on the wall work in your home? Why do some switches click and others not click when you turn them on or off? Use resources in a library to find the answers.

Activity

Stop or Go?

Does electricity flow easily through all materials? Test some materials to find out.

Procedure

1. With your group, use a wire to connect a light-bulb holder to a dry-cell holder. Attach a second wire to the light-bulb holder only. Attach a third wire to the dry-cell holder only. *Do not allow the two wires that are attached to the dry cell to touch.*

2. Predict what will happen if you touch the free ends of the wires together, as shown. **Record** your prediction in your *Science Notebook*. **Test** your prediction and **record** your results.

Step 2

D38

3. A material that allows electricity to flow through it is called a **conductor** (kən duk'tər). **Infer** whether the wires in your circuit are conductors. **Record** your inference in your *Science Notebook*.

4. A material that does not allow electricity to flow through it easily is called an **insulator** (in'sə lāt ər). **Make a chart** like the one shown. **Predict** which objects in the Materials list are conductors and which are insulators. **Record** your predictions in the chart. Then **test** them and **record** your results.

Step 4

CONDUCTOR OR INSULATOR		
Object or Material	Prediction	Result

Analyze and Conclude

1. **Compare** your predictions about which materials electricity would flow through with your results.

2. Which of the objects or materials that you tested are conductors? How do you know?

3. Which of the objects or materials that you tested are insulators? How do you know?

UNIT PROJECT LINK

Invent a way to use the opening and closing of circuits to make a quiz board. Work with your group to write a set of questions and answers. Then decide how to place dry cells, wires, and light bulbs. Test your invention on members of other groups in your class.

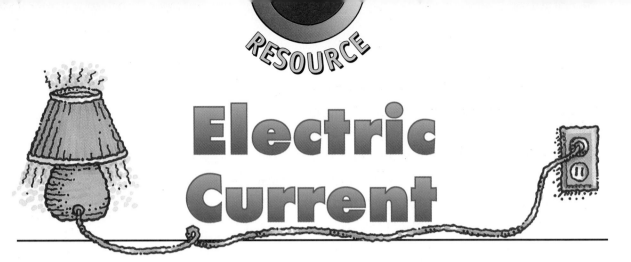

Electric Current

You press a switch and your flashlight lights or your radio plays music. Electrical energy powers your flashlight and radio. You depend on electricity in hundreds of other ways, too. The picture below shows some ways that electricity works for the members of one family.

Charges in Currents

In Investigation 1 you found out about static electric charges. The charges collect on objects and may jump quickly between objects. But these charges can't be used to run electric devices. For electric charges to be useful, they have to flow.

How might the people do these things without electricity? ▼

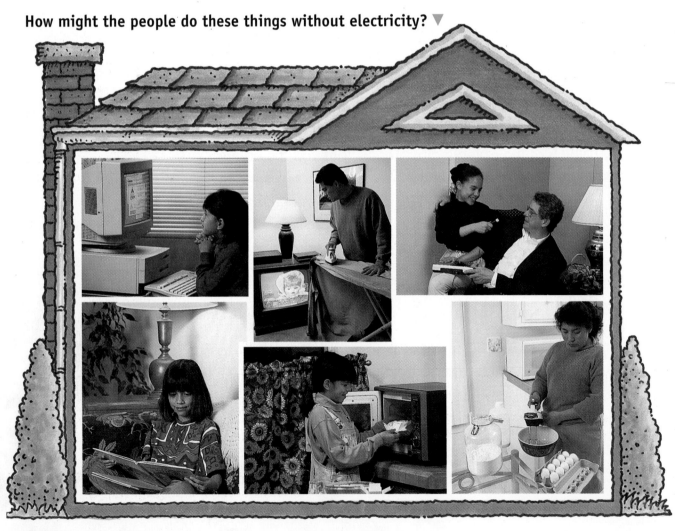

In the more useful form of electricity, electric charges flow steadily, like currents of water in a stream. An **electric current** is a continuous flow of negative charges. Think back to the activity on pages D36 and D37, in which you put together an electric circuit. An **electric circuit** is a path along which negative charges can flow.

A simple electric circuit starts with a source of electric charges, such as a dry cell. A wire connects the source to a light bulb or other device. Another wire connects the bulb or other device back to the source of negative charges.

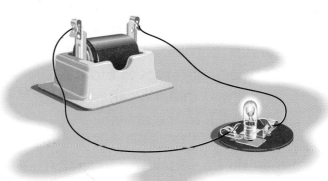

▲ Trace the path of electric charges in this circuit. Start and end at the dry cell. Why does the bulb light?

Open and Closed Circuits

When a circuit is closed, or complete, there is no break in the pathway of negative charges. The charges can flow through a closed circuit. In a closed circuit containing a light bulb, the bulb lights.

When a circuit is open, or incomplete, there's a break in the pathway. Charges can't flow through an open circuit. If you disconnect a wire in a simple circuit, the bulb can't light.

A **switch** is a device that opens or closes a circuit. When you turn a switch to *on*, you close a circuit. When you turn a switch to *off*, you open a circuit. If you add a switch to a circuit, you don't have to disconnect a wire to open the circuit.

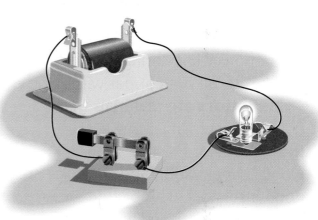

▲ This circuit contains a closed switch. Trace the path of the charges through this circuit. Why does the bulb light?

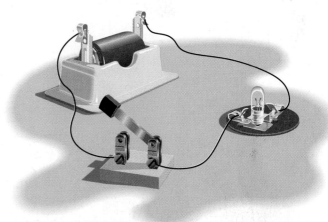

▲ How is this circuit the same as the one in the middle picture? How is it different? Why doesn't the bulb light?

Conductors and Insulators

Have you ever tried running through water? It's hard work, isn't it? Running through air is a lot easier. Electricity also moves more easily through some materials than others.

Think back to the activity on pages D38 and D39. There you tested materials for their ability to conduct electricity. Materials that allow electricity to pass through them most easily are called **conductors**. Most metals are good conductors of electricity. Copper is a metal that is used in wires in electrical cords. The wires in the power lines bringing electricity to your house are copper wires, too.

Insulators are materials that don't let electricity move easily through them. Plastics, rubber, wood, paper, cloth, and ceramics are good insulators. The picture shows how a conductor and an insulator are used in an electrical cord.

How a Flashlight Works

What happens inside a flashlight when you turn it on or off? When you turn the switch to *on*, you close the circuit and the bulb lights. When you turn the switch to *off*, you open the circuit, so the light in the bulb goes out. Suppose you take the flashlight apart. The picture shows what's inside one kind of flashlight and how it works.

insulator

conductor

◀ Electricity flows through copper wires that are coated with plastic. The electric charges can't get through the plastic covering because the plastic is an insulator.

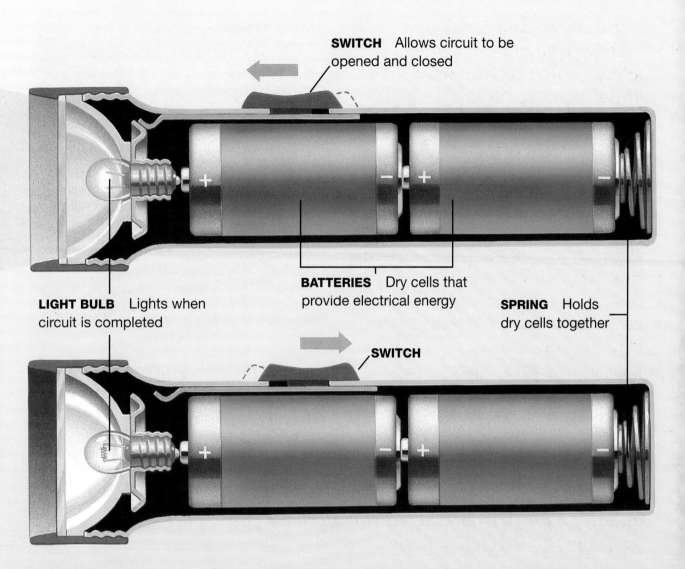

SWITCH Allows circuit to be opened and closed

LIGHT BULB Lights when circuit is completed

BATTERIES Dry cells that provide electrical energy

SPRING Holds dry cells together

SWITCH

▲ When the flashlight is on, electric current flows from the batteries through the spring, along the metal case of the flashlight to the metal strip attached to the switch, to the bulb holder, through the light bulb, and back to the batteries.

INVESTIGATION 2

1. A dry cell, a light bulb, and some wires are connected in a circuit, and the bulb lights. Which part of the circuit is the source of electrical energy? Is the circuit open or closed?

2. In one activity you made a switch. Would the switch work if you used aluminum foil instead of a paper clip? Explain your answer.

HOW DO ELECTRIC CIRCUITS DIFFER?

Suppose you want to put up a string of lights for a party, but one bulb is missing from the string. Is this a problem? It depends on how the lights are wired. In this investigation, find out the different ways lights can be wired.

Activity

One Type of Circuit

In the activity on pages D36 and D37, you made an electric circuit. In this activity you'll examine an electric circuit more closely.

MATERIALS

- dry cell (size D) in holder
- 3 insulated wires (stripped on ends)
- 2 light bulbs in holders
- colored pencil
- *Science Notebook*

Procedure

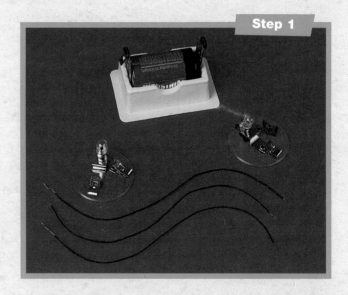

Step 1

1. On your desk, place a dry cell, three wires, and two light bulbs.

2. Find a way to make both bulbs light. **Talk with your group** and together **predict** a way to use the materials to light both bulbs at once. In your *Science Notebook*, **draw** a diagram that shows the arrangement of materials for your group's prediction.

3. Work with your group to **test** your prediction. You may change the connections until both bulbs light. Then **draw** a diagram of your complete circuit.

Step 3

4. When both bulbs are lighted, **predict** what will happen if you take one bulb out of its holder. **Record** your prediction. **Test** your prediction and **record** your observations.

Analyze and Conclude

1. The circuit you constructed is called a series circuit. In a **series circuit** there is only one path for an electric current. Place your finger on the dry cell in your drawing. Then, with your finger, follow the path of electric current through the circuit. Use a colored pencil to show this path on your drawing.

2. Think back to the circuit you made in the activity on pages D36 and D37. Was the circuit you put together a series circuit? Explain your answer.

3. Some strings of lights used for decoration are connected in a series circuit. If one light bulb burns out, **infer** what happens to the other bulbs. Why does this happen?

INVESTIGATE FURTHER!

EXPERIMENT

Make a series circuit with two dry cells. Current moves away from the negative (−) end and into the positive (+) end of a dry cell. Draw a diagram showing how you would connect another dry cell in your series circuit. Predict the effect of a second dry cell in your circuit and then test your prediction.

Activity

Another Type of Circuit

Can you wire a circuit so that one bulb stays lighted when another is missing? Try out your ideas in this activity.

Procedure

1. On your desk, place a dry cell, four wires, and two light bulbs.

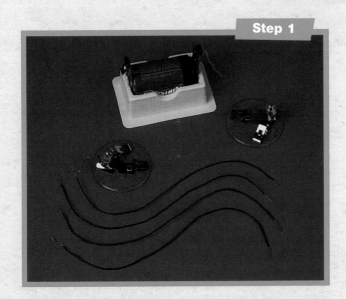

Step 1

2. In the activity on pages D44 and D45, you connected two bulbs in a series circuit. Now you'll connect both bulbs in a different kind of circuit. This circuit will use four wires instead of three. **Talk with your group** and together plan a way to connect the materials. In your *Science Notebook*, **draw** a diagram of your group's plan.

3. **Predict** how the materials will look when connected so that both bulbs light. Work with your group to **test** your prediction. If you need to, change the connections until both bulbs light. Then **record** your observations.

Step 3

4. When both bulbs are lighted, draw a diagram of your complete circuit. Then work with your group to **pre-dict** what will happen to the other bulb if you take one bulb out of its holder. **Record** your prediction and explain why you predicted as you did. Then work with your group to **test** your prediction. **Record** your observations.

Analyze and Conclude

1. The circuit you constructed is a parallel (par′ə lel) circuit. In a **parallel circuit** there is more than one path for an electric current. Starting at the dry cell in your drawing, use your finger to trace each path in your cir-cuit that a current can follow. Use a different colored pencil for each path in your drawing.

2. Suppose you could choose between a set of lights wired in a series circuit and a set wired in a parallel cir-cuit. Which would you choose? Why?

The Light Bulb

HOW IT Works

What everyday object turns electrical energy into light? It's a light bulb, of course. Light bulbs come in lots of sizes, shapes, and colors.

There are bulbs for ceiling fixtures and for table lamps. There are bulbs for street lights, for headlights, and even for growing plants.

Many light bulbs are incandescent (in kən des'ənt) bulbs. Look at the diagram of this type of bulb. As electric current passes through the **filament** (fil'ə mənt), the filament gets so hot that some of the heat changes into light.

Now look at the fluorescent (floo-ə res'ənt) bulb. In this bulb, ultraviolet light is changed into white light.

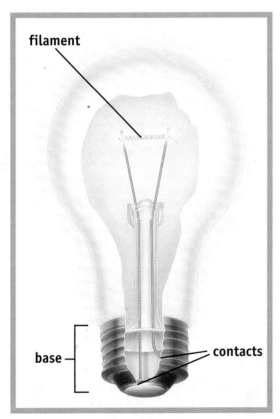

filament

base —
— contacts

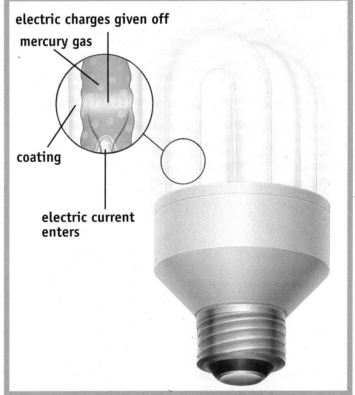

electric charges given off
mercury gas
coating
electric current enters

▲ **INCANDESCENT BULB** The filament is a long, thin wire coil made of the metal tungsten (tuŋ'stən). It glows when electricity passes through it. The contacts at the base conduct electricity.

▲ **FLUORESCENT BULB** As electricity enters the bulb, electric charges bump into mercury gas. The gas gives off ultraviolet light. This light strikes the coating, which gives off white light.

INVESTIGATE FURTHER!

TAKE ACTION

Survey your home for incandescent bulbs. Find out from the electric company that serves your town which incandescent bulbs you can replace with fluorescent bulbs. Ask how much money your family can save by replacing incandescent bulbs. With the permission of adults at home, replace these incandescent bulbs with fluorescent ones.

▲ **Thomas Edison (top) and Lewis Latimer (bottom) are shown with an early incandescent light bulb.**

Bulbs and Energy

In incandescent bulbs, electrical energy changes to heat and light. These bulbs produce much more heat than light, so they get very hot. All the heat that these bulbs produce is wasted energy.

In fluorescent bulbs, electricity is used to change one type of light to another. These bulbs produce much less heat than incandescent bulbs do. Fluorescent bulbs are good for the environment because they don't waste energy.

Invention of the Light Bulb

Thomas Edison, who headed a team of scientists called the Edison Pioneers, invented the light bulb. Edison's first bulb used a filament made of scorched thread. But this bulb was costly and didn't last long.

Lewis Latimer was a member of the Edison Pioneers. Latimer made a greatly improved bulb that used a carbon filament. This bulb cost less and lasted longer than Edison's bulb. The carbon was later replaced by tungsten, which is used in bulbs today. ∎

Series and Parallel Circuits

You've seen how electricity flows along paths called circuits. You can compare a circuit's path to a path in a maze. In the two mazes shown below, you start at point A, go through some paths, and come back to A. You can turn right or left, but you must move only in the direction of the arrows.

In the first maze there is only one path you can follow. You can move from A to B and then through C to get back to A. In the second maze there are two paths you can follow to make a round trip. Use your finger to trace these paths.

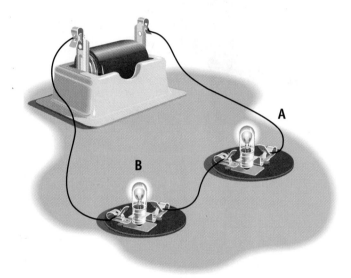

▲ Trace the path of current through this series circuit.

Just One Path

In the activity on pages D44 and D45, you made a series circuit. A **series circuit** is one that has only a single path for current to follow. In a series circuit, all of the parts are connected one after the other in a single loop, or path, as shown in the drawing above.

In this circuit, charges flow from the dry cell through bulb A and bulb B and back to the dry cell. If either bulb is removed from the circuit, the current stops.

▼ Mazes that are like two kinds of circuits

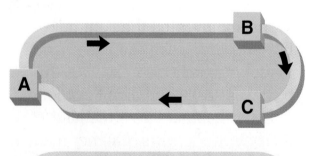

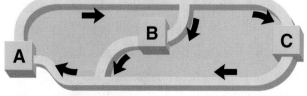

More Than One Path

In the activity on pages D46 and D47, you made a parallel circuit. A **parallel circuit** is one that has more than one path for an electric current to follow, as shown.

In path 1, negative charges can flow from the dry cell through bulb *A* and back to the dry cell. In path 2, negative charges can flow from the dry cell through bulb *B* and back to the dry cell.

When both bulbs are in place, current will follow both paths, and both bulbs will be lighted. However, if either bulb is removed, current will still follow the path through the other bulb, which will remain lighted. ■

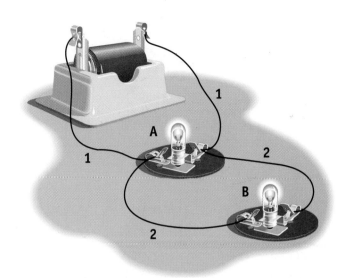

▲ **There are two paths a current can follow in this parallel circuit.**

SCIENCE IN LITERATURE

**HELLO! HELLO!
A LOOK INSIDE THE TELEPHONE**
by Eve and Albert Stwertka
Illustrated by Mena Dolobowsky
Julian Messner, 1991

What do roller skates have to do with telephone circuits? You'll find the answer in *Hello! Hello! A Look Inside the Telephone* by Eve and Albert Stwertka. Read pages 24–30 to find out how telephone wires were hooked up into circuits about 100 years ago. Then read how telephone circuits work today.

Did you ever consider what life would be like without telephones? Read pages 4–10 to find out how people communicated before the telephone was invented. Then make a list of all the ways your life would be different without telephones. Oh, no! No more pizza deliveries!

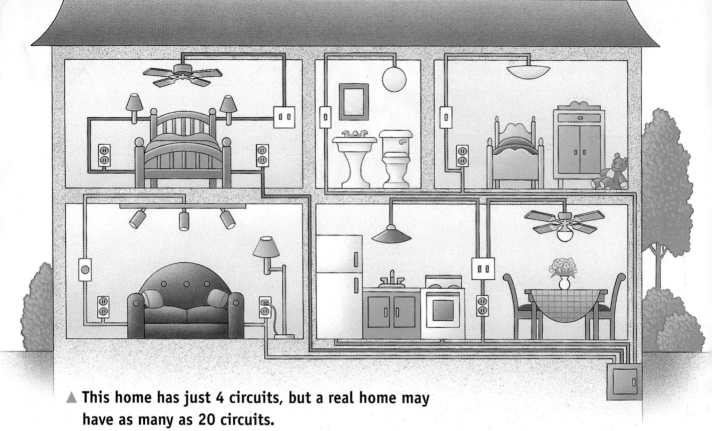

▲ This home has just 4 circuits, but a real home may have as many as 20 circuits.

How Homes Are Wired

All of the lights and electric appliances in your home are linked in circuits. Lamps, toaster ovens, stereo systems, hair dryers, and refrigerators are parts of the circuits. The circuits in home wiring are parallel, not series. Why?

Different circuits control electrical outlets in different parts of a home. Each of these circuits is connected to an outside source of electric current.

One circuit in the house shown above controls all of the outlets in the kitchen. Can you trace another circuit that includes the outlets in a child's bedroom?

Every home circuit has a fuse or a circuit breaker. These devices protect homes by opening overloaded circuits that are overheated. A **fuse** opens a circuit by melting and breaking. A **circuit breaker** is a switch that opens a circuit by turning off. ■

INVESTIGATION 3

1. Explain why you can open a series circuit, but not a parallel circuit, by removing one bulb.

2. Suppose you want to make a parallel circuit with two light bulbs, a dry cell, and two switches. Draw the way you would connect the parts so that each switch can turn off one bulb at a time.

REFLECT & EVALUATE

WORD POWER

circuit breaker	fuse
conductors	insulators
filament	switch
electric circuit	
electric current	
electric discharge	
electric charges	
parallel circuit	
static electricity	
series circuit	

 On Your Own
Review the terms in the list. Then divide them into three lists to show how they are related.

 With a Partner
Make up a quiz, using all the terms in the list. Challenge your partner to complete the quiz.

PORTFOLIO

Make a drawing to show how you would set up four light bulbs in a series circuit. Include a dry cell and a switch. Use arrows to show the path of the current.

Analyze Information

Study the drawing. Then explain why the drawing is incorrect.

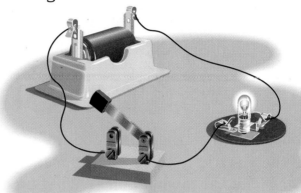

Assess Performance

Design an experiment to determine if ten common materials are conductors. Predict whether each material will act as a conductor and explain your prediction. After your teacher has reviewed your plan, carry out the test.

Problem Solving

1. Sam ran across the living room to answer the door. When he grasped the doorknob, he received a shock. Why did Sam get a shock from touching the doorknob?

2. Imagine that all of the outlets in a room are part of the same circuit. Why is it better to have the outlets wired in a parallel circuit than in a series circuit?

3. How do circuit breakers and fuses protect a home?

CHAPTER 3

ELECTRICITY
AT WORK

You can turn on the TV set and the picture appears. Where does the electricity come from to make this happen? How does electricity get to your home? What produces this electricity? In this chapter you'll find out the answers to these questions as you explore the story of electricity.

Electrifying Work

Y ou hunt for a flashlight. Someone else lights a candle. It shines like a tiny beacon in the darkness. An electric power line has snapped, leaving thousands of homes and businesses without electricity. Whom do you call? Call Kim Goode and the line crew!

Kim Goode is a line worker for an electric utility company. She climbs utility poles and makes repairs on transformers, switches, and wires.

Goode and her co-workers often receive calls to go out in stormy weather to quickly restore electricity to powerless homes. This is dangerous work. Sometimes fallen electric wires still have electricity flowing through them. Sometimes the wind shifts suddenly, almost knocking the line worker off the pole. Kim Goode's training and skill keep her safe as she does her important work.

Coming Up

◀ Kim Goode repairs electric power lines.

WHAT ARE SOME SOURCES OF ELECTRIC CURRENT?

You've seen that electricity can flow through wires. A dry cell provided a source of energy for that current. In this investigation you'll find out about some other sources of electrical energy.

Activity

Detect a Current

A detective detects, or finds out things. In order to find out about sources of electricity, you'll need a current detector.

MATERIALS

- insulated wire (stripped on ends, 50 cm)
- metric tape measure
- compass
- transparent tape
- dry cell (size D) in holder
- *Science Notebook*

Procedure

Starting from the middle of a 50-cm wire, wrap 10 cm of wire around a compass. Turn the compass so that the wire forms an **X** with the compass needle. Tape the wire in place. You've made a current detector. Connect one end of the wire to a dry cell. **Talk with your group** and **predict** what will happen when you connect the free end of the wire to the dry cell. **Test your prediction** and **record** your observations in your *Science Notebook*.

Analyze and Conclude

1. What happens when a current flows through the wire?

2. **Infer** what causes any changes you observe.

Activity

A Magnetic Source

Use your current detector to find another source of electric current.

MATERIALS
- insulated wire (stripped on ends, 3 m)
- cardboard tube
- current detector from activity on page D56
- bar magnet
- *Science Notebook*

Procedure

1. Wind 3 m of wire into a coil around a cardboard tube, as shown. Then set the current detector you made in the activity on page D56 on your desk.

Step 1

2. **Talk with your group** and **predict** the effect of the coil on the detector. **Record** your prediction in your *Science Notebook*. **Plan** how to test your prediction and then carry out your plan. **Record** your observations.

3. Connect your detector to the coil. Hold a bar magnet in the cardboard tube, as shown. Move the magnet back and forth quickly inside the tube. Have a group member **observe** the current detector. Note what happens while you're moving the magnet and when you stop moving the magnet. **Talk with your group** about your observations and then **record** them.

Step 3

4. Repeat step 3, but hold the magnet still and move the tube back and forth. **Record** your observations.

Analyze and Conclude

1. **Infer** what caused the electric current in this activity. What observations support your inference?

2. The device you made with a wire coil and a magnet is called a **generator** (jen′ər āt ər). How might a generator be used to make an electric current?

Activity
A Fruity Source

You might say about a lemon, "Wow! That's sour!" But after this activity, you may say, "Wow! That's electric!"

MATERIALS

- lemon with two slits cut in it
- paper towel
- zinc strip with hole at one end
- copper strip with hole at one end
- current detector from activity on page D56
- *Science Notebook*

Procedure

1. Your teacher will give you a lemon with two slits cut in it. Place the lemon on a paper towel on your desk.

2. Push a zinc strip into one slit in the lemon. Push a copper strip into the other slit. Make sure that the two metal strips do not touch and that the holes are showing.

Step 2

3. Set the current detector you made in the activity on page D56 on your desk. Connect one end of the detector wire to the hole in the zinc strip.

4. You know how an electric current affects your current detector. **Talk with your group** and **predict** what will happen if you connect the current detector to the copper strip. **Record** your prediction in your *Science Notebook*.

5. Connect the free end of the current detector wire to the hole in the copper strip, as shown. Check again to be sure that the two metal strips don't touch. **Record** your observations.

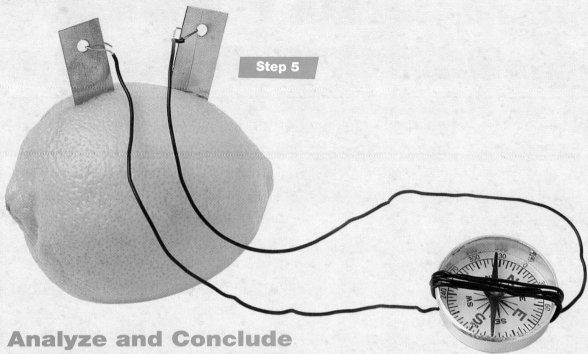

Step 5

Analyze and Conclude

1. Trace the path of electric current in the wires, starting with one of the metal strips. How can you tell that the circuit is closed?

2. Zinc and copper metal strips stuck into a lemon and connected in a closed circuit make an electric cell. In an **electric cell**, chemical energy changes form. **Infer** what form of energy the chemical energy changes into.

3. What did you observe that supports your inference?

INVESTIGATE FURTHER!

EXPERIMENT

You can make an electric cell that uses a folded paper towel soaked in salt water instead of a lemon. Use a penny and a nickel instead of zinc and copper. What other parts will you need? Plan a way to connect these parts in a circuit similar to the one in the activity with the lemon. Draw your setup. After your teacher has reviewed your plan, test it.

Producing Electric Current

Where do you get energy to kick a soccer ball? You get energy from food. Suppose you eat a peanut butter sandwich. The sandwich—and everything else you eat—has chemical energy stored in it. Your body changes that chemical energy into energy of motion.

Electricity From Magnetism

Energy of motion can change to electrical energy. In the activity on page D57, moving a magnet inside a wire coil produced an electric current in the wire. Moving a wire coil in a magnetic field will also produce a current.

A device in which a wire coil and a magnet are used to produce electricity is called a **generator**. A generator changes energy of motion into electrical energy.

Getting a Strong Current

The magnet you used in the activity was not very strong. And you did not use very many turns of wire. With a current detector you can detect a current produced by such a generator. But the current isn't even

strong enough to light a bulb. How can a stronger current be made?

The stronger the magnet in a generator, the stronger the current. Adding more turns of wire to the coil also strengthens the current. So, you could make your generator stronger by using a strong magnet and many coils of wire.

Giant generators produce the electricity that comes to the electrical outlets in your home and school. These generators also produce the electricity that lights cities, powers machinery, and works in other ways. The generators have powerful magnets and huge coils of wire.

Where does the energy of motion that turns large generators come from? The energy may come from a power plant that uses coal or nuclear fuel to heat water. The heated water makes steam, which turns the generator. Or the energy may come from water falling over a dam such as the one shown on the next page. Sometimes the energy comes from wind turning the blades of a windmill.

Hoover Dam stands in the Black Canyon of the Colorado River. Water falling over the dam provides energy to turn large generators.

▲ Power plant at Hoover Dam

▲ Generators inside power plant at Hoover Dam

Chemicals and Currents

Batteries are another source of useful electrical energy. A battery is made up of one or more smaller parts called **electric cells**. Energy is stored in chemicals used in an electric cell. When all the parts of the cell are connected in a circuit, this stored chemical energy changes into electrical energy.

Wet cells and dry cells are two types of electric cells. In the activity on pages D58 and D59, you made a wet cell. Study the drawing below. It shows a wet cell in which a liquid chemical does what the chemical in lemon juice did in the activity.

In this wet cell, strips of the metals zinc and copper hang in a liquid. Chemical changes in the liquid separate negative electric charges from the zinc strip.

The charges move through the zinc strip, which becomes the negative end of the cell. Next, the charges move through the current detector. The charges then move to the copper strip, which has become

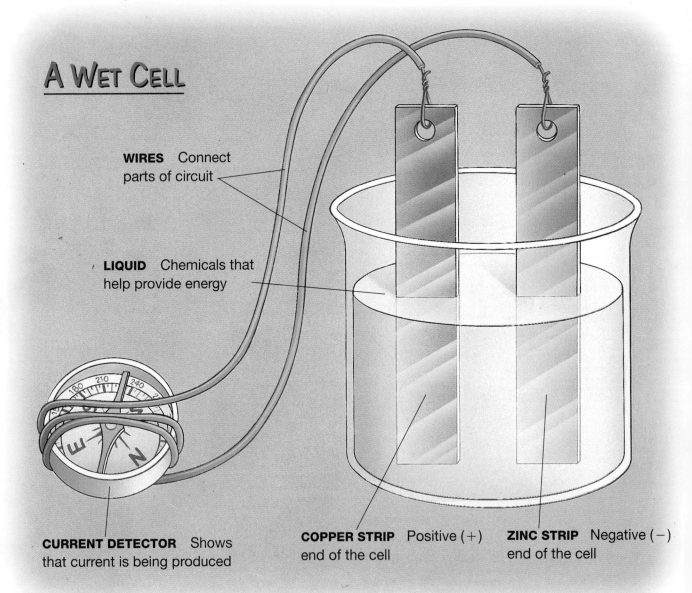

A WET CELL

WIRES Connect parts of circuit

LIQUID Chemicals that help provide energy

CURRENT DETECTOR Shows that current is being produced

COPPER STRIP Positive (+) end of the cell

ZINC STRIP Negative (−) end of the cell

the positive end of the cell. As the charges move back into the liquid, the circuit is completed.

A dry cell, like the one you used in the activity on page D56, is shown below. Trace the path of the charges through the cell and the current detector. A zinc case is the negative end of the cell. A chemical paste inside the case has a carbon rod in its center. The carbon rod is the positive end of the cell. Chemical changes in the paste separate negative electric charges from the zinc case. ■

UNIT PROJECT LINK

Have you seen electric devices that run on solar cells, such as solar calculators or solar hats with propellers? Ask your teacher for a solar cell. Work with your group to design a solar-powered machine. Display your invention.

A DRY CELL

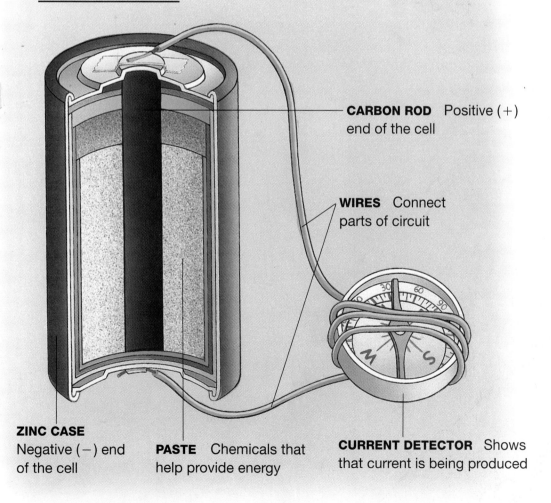

CARBON ROD Positive (+) end of the cell

WIRES Connect parts of circuit

ZINC CASE Negative (−) end of the cell

PASTE Chemicals that help provide energy

CURRENT DETECTOR Shows that current is being produced

From Power Plant to You

Most of the electricity you use is as near as a wall switch or outlet. When you flip a switch or plug in a cord, the electric current is right there. But the generators in the power plant that make this current may be very far away from your home. How does electricity from power plants get to homes, schools, and other places where it's used?

The Force of Electricity

The generators in power plants push the electricity through heavy duty power lines that leave the plant.

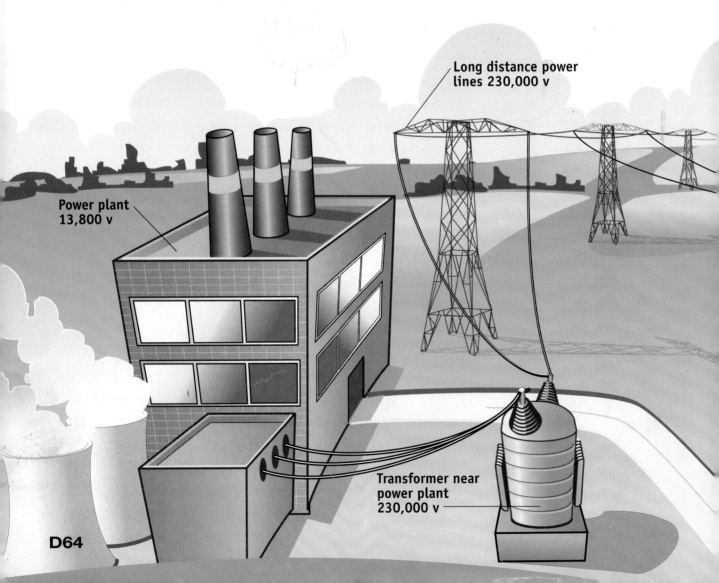

Long distance power lines 230,000 v

Power plant 13,800 v

Transformer near power plant 230,000 v

The force that pushes electricity along wires is called **voltage** (vōl′tij). This force is measured in units called volts.

You can compare voltage to the pressure, or pushing force, of water in a hose. Water can rush from a hose, or flow gently, depending on the pressure. The flow of electricity in a wire can also be strong or weak, depending on the voltage.

Raising and Lowering Voltage

A transformer (trans fôrm′ər) is a device that changes the voltage of a current. The voltage of the current coming from a power plant is too low to send long distances. A transformer raises the voltage for cross-country trips to users.

After current makes a long journey from a power plant, its voltage must be lowered. It is too high for use in homes and in most other buildings. So the current is sent through another transformer. Study the drawing to see how voltages are changed as current travels from a power plant to you and to other users of electricity. ■

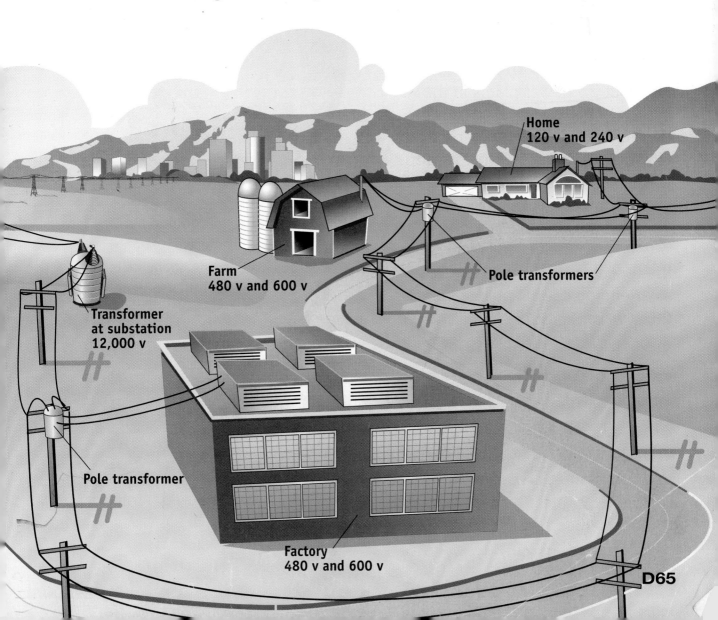

Home
120 v and 240 v

Farm
480 v and 600 v

Pole transformers

Transformer
at substation
12,000 v

Pole transformer

Factory
480 v and 600 v

Electricity From Sunlight

STS
SCIENCE
TECHNOLOGY
& SOCIETY

Did you ever use a solar calculator? **Solar energy**, or the energy of the Sun, powers the calculator. Inside solar calculators are solar cells. A **solar cell** changes sunlight into electrical energy. When sunlight strikes a solar cell, an electric current is produced.

Solar Cells, Clean Energy

About 25 power plants in the United States use solar cells to produce electricity. Solar cells produce electricity in a way that helps keep the environment clean. Burning coal or oil to produce electricity can pollute the air. Using nuclear energy to produce electricity can create wastes that pollute water and land. Using solar energy doesn't pollute in any of these ways.

Look at the photographs to see some uses of solar cells.

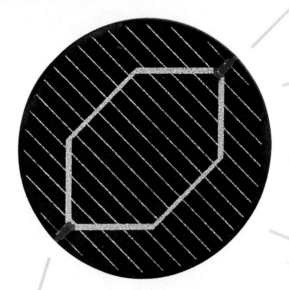

▲ **One solar cell produces a tiny amount of electricity. Because of this, many cells are wired together in panels.**

Solar-powered aiplane ▼

◄ Solar-powered car

◄ Solar-powered watch

Solar-powered garden light ▶

◄ Solar-powered home

INVESTIGATION 1

THINK IT WRITE IT

1. What energy change takes place in a generator? in a battery? in a solar cell?

2. Certain electric devices in the home, such as cordless telephones and video games, have small transformers that plug into the wall. What do the transformers do?

HOW IS ELECTRICITY USEFUL?

Light and sound come from your TV. Heat comes from your toaster oven. A motor spins inside your toy car. In all these examples, electricity is changed into another form of energy to make it useful. Explore some of these energy changes and how to stay safe around electricity.

Activity

Make It Move

How can you use electricity to make something move without touching it? Find out in this activity.

MATERIALS

- insulated wire (stripped on ends, 125 cm)
- metric ruler
- iron nail
- 10 paper clips
- dry cell (size D) in holder
- *Science Notebook*

Procedure

1. **Measure** about 20 cm from one end of a 125-cm length of insulated wire. From that point, wrap 25 turns of the wire around a nail. You will have a length of free wire at both ends of the nail, as shown.

Step 1

2. Make a small pile of paper clips. **Talk with your group** and together **predict** whether the nail will have any effect on the paper clips. **Record** your prediction in your *Science Notebook*. **Test** your prediction and **record** your observations.

3. Attach each end of the wire to a different end of a dry cell, as shown.

4. Predict what will happen if you now bring the tip of the nail toward the paper clips. **Record** your prediction. **Test** your prediction and **record** your observations.

5. Disconnect the wire ends from the dry cell. Wrap 25 more turns of wire around the nail. Leave the nail bare at the end.

6. Repeat steps 3 and 4.

Analyze and Conclude

1. Compare your predictions about the nail and the paper clips with your observations.

2. A magnet made when an electric current is sent through a wire wrapped around iron is an **electromagnet** (ē lek'trō mag nit). **Infer** how adding more turns of wire affects an electromagnet. Give evidence to support your inference.

3. What happens to an electromagnet when the current is turned off? What can you **infer** about electromagnets?

INVESTIGATE FURTHER!

RESEARCH

The discovery of the way magnetism and electricity are related led the way to the invention of electric motors. Who made the first electromagnet? How are both permanent magnets and electromagnets used in a motor? In a library, find out. One book you might read is *Electricity and Magnets* by Barbara Taylor.

Long Distance, Short Time

How do you communicate (kə myōō'ni kāt) with friends over long distances? That is, how do you talk with them or send them messages? Do you talk on the phone? Do you use electronic mail, or E-mail, on a computer? If so, then you use telecommunication (tel' i kə myōō ni-kā'shən). This is using electricity for almost instant communication over a long distance.

Electricity has made telecommunication possible. It all started with the invention of the telegraph in the 1830s. The time line shows highlights of what's happened in the field of telecommunication since the 1830s. What telecommunication devices may be invented in the future?

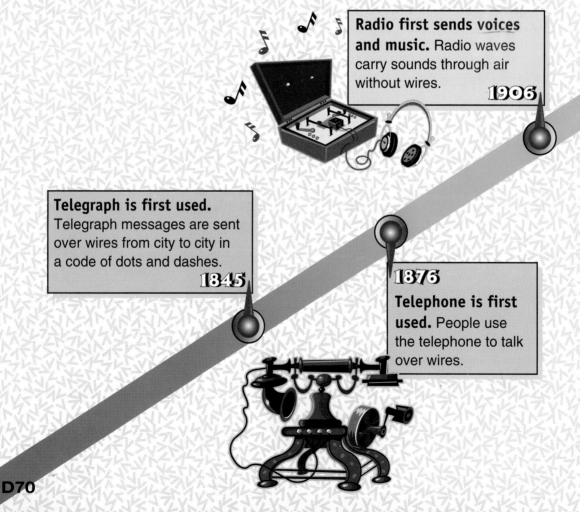

Radio first sends voices and music. Radio waves carry sounds through air without wires. **1906**

Telegraph is first used. Telegraph messages are sent over wires from city to city in a code of dots and dashes. **1845**

1876 Telephone is first used. People use the telephone to talk over wires.

Internet system is in use.
People use Internet to send information from computer to computer. They use this system to communicate almost instantly throughout the world.
1990s

Communications satellite *Telestar* is sent into space.
Satellites carry live television, radio, telephone calls, and computer data all over the world. **1962**

1980s
Cellular (sel'yōō lər) **phones and fax machines are in use.** Cellular phones allow people to talk on the phone as they travel. Facsimile (fak sim'ə lē), also called fax, machines are used to send written messages over telephone lines.

1936
Television programs are broadcast.
Television sends clear pictures and sound.

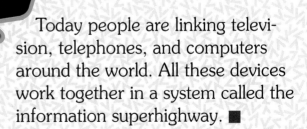

Today people are linking television, telephones, and computers around the world. All these devices work together in a system called the information superhighway. ■

Electric Magnets

Did you ever flip a coin? When the heads side of the coin is up, you can't see the tails side. But you know the tails side is there. In a way, electricity and magnetism are like the two sides of a coin.

In Investigation 1 you found out one way that magnetism and electricity are related. Moving a coil of wire in a magnetic field produces electric current. In this way, magnetism produces electricity.

Electricity and magnetism are also related in another way. In the activity on pages D68 and D69, you made an electromagnet. An **electromagnet** is a magnet made when electric charges move through a coil of wire wrapped around an iron core, or center. In an electromagnet, electricity is used to produce magnetism.

Properties of Electromagnets

Electromagnets are like other magnets in some ways. Like other magnets, they attract materials that contain iron. Electromagnets have a north pole and a south pole. An electromagnet also has a magnetic field, as the drawing above shows.

This electromagnet makes it easy to separate steel from other materials. It's strong enough to lift large amounts of steel at once. The magnet is turned on for lifting the steel. ▶

How are electromagnets different from other magnets? In Chapter 1 you made a temporary magnet. Recall that a temporary magnet slowly loses its magnetism over time. An electromagnet is a different kind of temporary magnet. It acts like a magnet while electric current flows through it. But as soon as you turn off the current, it loses its magnetism. As a result, an electromagnet can be turned on or off.

Using Electromagnets

Imagine that you're in charge of a collection center for recycling. People dump bags of cans made of different metals in one big pile. But the cans made of steel and those made of aluminum have to be sent to different places to be recycled. You have to separate the two kinds of cans. One way to do this job is by using a large electromagnet, as the pictures below show.

After the crane swings away from the pile of mixed materials, the magnet is turned off. Then the steel objects fall into a separate pile. ▶

When you push a doorbell, a circuit closes and the electromagnet pulls on the hammer, which strikes the bell ▶

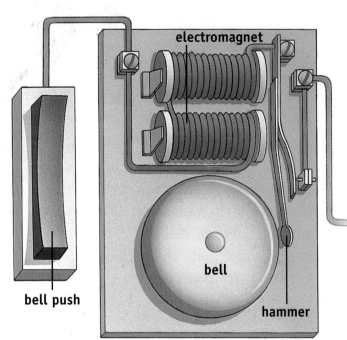

electromagnet

bell push

bell

hammer

Many objects in your home have electromagnets in them. These electromagnets are hidden inside loudspeakers, telephones, VCRs, tape decks, and doorbells. All electric motors contain electromagnets, too. Electric motors drive refrigerators, clocks, hair dryers, vacuum cleaners, and ceiling fans.

Look again at the pictures on page D40 in Chapter 2. Electric motors drive many of the devices shown there, too. What other things in your home—and outside it—can you think of that are run by electric motors? ■

SCIENCE IN LITERATURE

■ AT HOME WITH SCIENCE ■

HELLO! HELLO!

A LOOK INSIDE THE TELEPHONE

EVE AND ALBERT STWERTKA
ILLUSTRATED BY MENA DOLOBOWSKY

HELLO! HELLO!
A LOOK INSIDE THE TELEPHONE
by Eve and Albert Stwertka
Illustrated by Mena Dolobowsky
Julian Messner, 1991

Exactly where is the electromagnet hidden inside a telephone? You'll find the answer on pages 21–23 of *Hello! Hello! A Look Inside the Telephone* by Eve and Albert Stwertka. Not only is there an electromagnet in a telephone, but there's also a permanent magnet there. Find out how the two magnets work together to let you hear the voice of a friend. When you think you understand it, try to explain it to a friend—over the telephone.

A Car That Plugs In

STS
SCIENCE
TECHNOLOGY
& SOCIETY

Do you live in or near a large city? In many cities, air pollution is a serious problem. As you read in Chapter 1, cars that run on gasoline pollute the air around them. Many cars crowded together in a city can make the air unhealthy. Using electric cars may be one way to solve this problem. These cars run on batteries, which don't pollute the air.

Have you ever used a rechargeable dry cell? Electric cars have rechargeable batteries. As you know, batteries are made up of electric cells. Regular dry cells run down in time. The electric cells in the batteries of electric cars also stop working after being used a certain length of time. For this reason, the batteries have to be recharged when they run down.

Electric cars aren't used much today. Why not? Their batteries must be recharged about once every 96 km (60 mi). Their top speed is about 80 km/h (50 mph). And electric cars cost more to own and operate than most gas-powered cars.

In the future, many people may drive electric cars. Why? Gasoline comes from oil, and the need to conserve oil is great. The need to clean up the air in cities is also strong. To meet these needs, people are working on more powerful batteries and other parts for the cars. In time, there will probably be newer and better models of cars that plug in. ■

Instead of filling up at a gas station, the owners of these electric cars plug them into electrical outlets. Electric current from the outlets recharges the batteries. ▶

Safety Around Electricity

STS
SCIENCE
TECHNOLOGY
& SOCIETY

In your activities, you've sent electric currents through wires. But why were the wires safe for you to touch? You may have noticed that your size-D dry cells are marked 1.5 v, which stands for 1.5 volts. A current with such a low voltage has very little energy. But the voltage of the current in the wiring of a house is 110 volts or more. This amount of electrical energy is dangerous. But you can be safe if you follow certain safety rules.

DON'T use any appliance that has a torn cord or a cord that is worn out. If two bare wires of a cord touch each other while the cord is in use, current will go to the crossed wires and back to its source. This is an example of a short circuit. In a short circuit, wires overheat. Overheated wires can cause a fire. ▶

◀ **NEVER** stick your finger or anything else except an electrical plug into an electrical outlet. Be sure any electrical plug you use is in good condition. Also, always hold a cord by its plug when you pull it from an outlet. What do you think is the reason for this rule?

DON'T overload circuits. Plugging too many appliances into one circuit can overload the circuit. Wires in overloaded circuits can become hot enough to start fires. ▶

◀ **STAY AWAY** from anything with a sign that says "High Voltage." Voltages in electric power lines and electric rails are even higher, and more dangerous, than they are in house current.

NEVER touch an electrical cord, appliance, or light switch when you are wet. Unless water is pure, electric current can pass through the water and your body more easily than through an appliance. Any water that's in contact with a person's body is not pure. ▶

Have you ever had a power failure in your home? This can happen if a fuse blows or a circuit breaker switches off. As you read in Chapter 2, page D52, fuses and circuit breakers are safety devices. They open circuits when wires get too hot.

What should be done when a fuse blows or a circuit beaker trips, or switches off? First, it's important to find out the cause. Is there an overloaded circuit? Is there a short circuit somewhere? The cause of the overheating should be corrected. Then an adult in your home should replace the fuse or turn the circuit breaker back on. ■

▲ **A home circuit-breaker box**

▲ **A good fuse**

▲ **A blown fuse**

INVESTIGATION 2

1. What devices can change different kinds of energy into electricity?

2. How would you explain to a group of first-graders why radios used in the bathroom should be battery-powered?

REFLECT & EVALUATE

WORD POWER

electric cell
electromagnet
generator
solar cell
solar energy
voltage

 On Your Own
Review the terms in the list. Then use as many terms as you can in a paragraph about the uses of electricity.

 With a Partner
Make up a quiz using all the terms in the list. Challenge your partner to complete the quiz.

PORTFOLIO

Find out how the power plant that supplies your home with electricity produces the electricity. Make a simple drawing that shows how the electricity gets from the plant to your home. Include two transformers in your drawing.

Analyze Information

Study the photograph. Name the device shown and describe how it works. Explain how the usefulness of the device would change if it could not be turned on and off.

Assess Performance

See how changing the thickness of the iron core of an electromagnet affects the magnet's strength. Follow the procedure you used in the activity on pages D68 and D69, using iron nails of different thicknesses.

Problem Solving

1. A magnet passing through a coil of wire does not produce enough electric current to light a bulb. What are two ways to increase the amount of current?

2. How do you think the energy of the Sun might be used to power a motorcycle?

3. Think of three devices you use that are powered by electricity. How might the jobs they do be done without electricity?

Throughout this unit you have learned about magnetism and electricity. How will you use what you've learned? How will you share that information with others? Here are some ideas.

Hold a Big Event
to Share Your Unit Project

Hold an inventor's fair. Display your group's inventions, demonstrating how each one uses magnetism or electricity. Be sure you can explain how each one works, using the ideas you developed in this unit. Invite other classes, your family, and your friends to come to your event.

Experiment

Make an electromagnet like the one you made on pages D68 and D69. Design an experiment to show the effect on a permanent magnet when the current flows through the wire in the opposite direction from that in the activity. After your teacher has reviewed your plan, carry out your experiment. What do you observe? Use a library to find out how this effect is used in a motor.

Take Action

Call or write to the electric company serving your town and ask for free information on safety around electricity. Work with your group to make a set of posters on electrical safety that you can display in your school.

UNIT E

WEATHER AND CLIMATE

Theme: Constancy and Change

GET READY TO

OBSERVE & QUESTION

What factors affect climate?

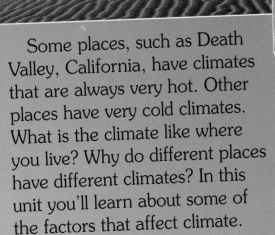

Some places, such as Death Valley, California, have climates that are always very hot. Other places have very cold climates. What is the climate like where you live? Why do different places have different climates? In this unit you'll learn about some of the factors that affect climate.

EXPERIMENT & HYPOTHESIZE

How can you stay safe during dangerous weather?

In this unit you'll learn about tornadoes and other dangerous weather conditions. Make a model of a tornado to learn how this powerful storm moves.

INVESTIGATE!

RESEARCH & ANALYZE

As you investigate, find out more from these books.

- **Lightning and Other Wonders of the Sky** by Q. L. Pearce (Julian Messner, 1989). Read about halos, sundogs, and other wonders of the sky in this book.

- **Professor Fergus Fahrenheit and His Wonderful Weather Machine** by Candace Groth-Fleming (Simon and Schuster Books for Young Readers, 1994). A visitor comes to the town of Dry Gulch, Texas.

- **The Third Planet: Exploring the Earth from Space** by Sally Ride and Tam O'Shaughnessy (Crown Publishers, 1994). See photos from the space shuttle in this book.

WORK TOGETHER & SHARE IDEAS

How can you be a weather forecaster?

Working together, you'll have a chance to apply what you have learned. Construct a classroom weather station that you can use to predict the weather. Look for activities and Unit Project Links to find out how to build weather instruments. Then become a weather forecaster.

CHAPTER 1

THE AIR AROUND US

What do you need air for? You need it to breathe, of course. But is air important for anything else? A good way to start learning about air is to visit a place where there _isn't_ any.

Another Day on the Moon

Good morning. Here's the latest weather report: "Today will be the same as yesterday. No clouds, no rain, no wind—to put it another way, no weather. The sky will be black, with stars visible. By noon, temperatures could reach 127°C (260°F). If you're thinking about taking a moon walk, don't forget your spacesuit—it's going to be hot out there! Tonight, temperatures will drop below −173°C (−280°F).

"If you have just tuned in, here's today's weather report in brief—no surprises. As for the next lunar day, coming your way in about two Earth weeks, the weather will be the same—none."

This "weather report" from the Moon gives you several clues about the importance of air to Earth. As you do the investigations in this chapter, think about life on Earth. What does air have to do with it?

Coming Up

◀ Because the Moon has no air, astronauts must wear spacesuits to protect them and help them breathe.

WHAT IS AIR?

Suppose someone asked you to describe the air. Perhaps you'd say, "Air is something that makes your hair blow on a windy day." But what is that "something"? In Investigation 1 you'll find out.

Activity

An Empty Cup

If you had a cup filled with hot chocolate, would you say that the cup is empty? Of course not. But what if you were to drink all the hot chocolate? Would the cup be empty then? Find out!

MATERIALS
- large clear plastic bowl
- water
- plastic-foam peanut
- clear plastic cup
- clear plastic cup with small hole
- *Science Notebook*

SAFETY
Clean up any spills immediately.

Procedure

1. Fill a clear bowl with water. Float a plastic-foam peanut in it.

2. **Talk with your group** and together **predict** what will happen to the peanut if you cover it with a clear plastic cup and then push the cup under the water to the bottom of the bowl. **Write** your prediction in your *Science Notebook*. **Draw** a picture to show your prediction.

Step 1

Step 4

3. **Test** your prediction. Turn a cup upside down and push it *straight down* over the peanut until the rim of the cup touches the bottom of the bowl. **Record** what happens to the peanut.

4. Repeat step 3, using a clear plastic cup that has a small hole in its side, near the base. **Record** your observations.

Analyze and Conclude

1. **Compare** your results in step 3 with your prediction. What happened to the peanut? Write a **hypothesis** to explain why this happened. Give reasons why you think as you do.

2. What happened to the peanut in step 4? **Hypothesize** why this happened. Based on this hypothesis, **predict** what would happen if you were to cover the hole with a finger or piece of tape and then repeat the experiment.

3. Was the cup empty or not? Explain your answer. What can you **infer** about air from this activity?

INVESTIGATE FURTHER!

EXPERIMENT

Use a straw to blow air into the bottom of the bowl of water you used in this activity. Blow as hard and as steadily as you can. Have a partner observe what happens to the level of the water in the bowl as you blow into the straw. Infer what's causing a change in water level.

Activity

An Ocean of Air

Have you ever gone swimming in the ocean? Can you remember the feeling of water pressing against you? In this activity you'll find out about the ocean that presses against you on dry land!

MATERIALS
- goggles
- thin wooden slats
- newspaper
- scissors
- *Science Notebook*

SAFETY //////
Wear goggles during this activity.

Procedure

1. Lay a wooden slat across your desk so that about one half of it hangs over the edge of the desktop. Use the palm of your hand to strike down on the end of the slat that is hanging over. **Record** what happens in your *Science Notebook*. Then put the slat back in the same position as before.

2. Place a sheet of newspaper over the part of the slat that is on the desk. Strike the slat as you did in step 1. **Record** your observations.

Step 1

Step 2

3. Place a slat on the desk in the same position you placed it in step 1. Cut the newspaper in half. Lay one half of the paper over the part of the slat that is on the desk. With other group members, **predict** what will happen when you strike the slat this time. **Record** your prediction and then test it. Be sure to strike the slat as you did in step 1. **Record** your observations.

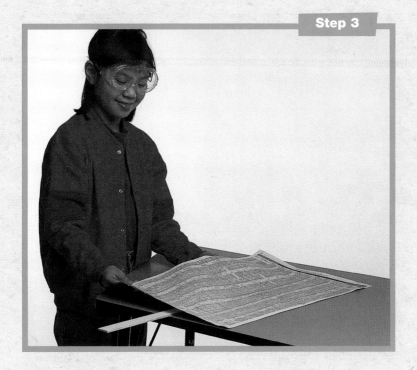

Step 3

Analyze and Conclude

1. **Compare** what you observed in step 1 with what you observed in step 2. **Describe** the difference in your results.

2. **Describe** what happened in step 3. How does it **compare** with your prediction?

3. Think about what was holding down the newspaper when you struck the slat in step 2. **Infer** whether that same "thing" was holding down the half sheet of newspaper in step 3. Do you think this "thing" has weight? Give reasons for your answer.

INVESTIGATE FURTHER!

EXPERIMENT

Something was pressing downward on the newspaper in this activity. Find out if that same something can press in other ways. Blow up a balloon. How does the balloon feel when you press it in different places? Hypothesize what causes the balloon to have the shape it does.

It's Got Us Covered

▲ **Air is matter, just as all of these objects are matter.**

You feel it when a gentle breeze touches your face. You hear it rustling leaves and rattling windows. You see it bend the branches of trees. What is this thing that offers hints of its presence but is tasteless, odorless, and unseen? It's the air.

It's a Mix of Matter

Air is made up of matter. Like objects that you can see, air takes up space and has weight. You discovered that air takes up space in the activity on pages E6 and E7. When you pushed the cup down over the plastic-

foam peanut, the water did not rise to fill the cup. That's because the cup was already filled with air. You saw the effect of the weight of air when you struck the wooden slat covered with newspaper in the activity on pages E8 and E9. The weight of the air held the newspaper down over the slat as you struck it.

Air is a mixture of gases. The gases in air are matter. And like all matter, they are made up of tiny particles that are in constant motion.

The graph shows the mixture of gases that make up air. The largest part of air is composed of **nitrogen** (nī′trə jən). The second most plentiful gas is **oxygen** (äks′i jən). The portion of air that's left is made up of small amounts of other gases, including **carbon dioxide** (kär′bən dī äks′īd) and **water vapor**.

A Life-Support System

Think back to the first page of this chapter. Did you get the idea that the Moon is a lifeless place? Nothing lives or grows on the Moon. There's no air or water. But on Earth, life is everywhere. Nitrogen, oxygen, carbon dioxide, and water vapor make life possible, as the picture shows.

Gases in the air ▼

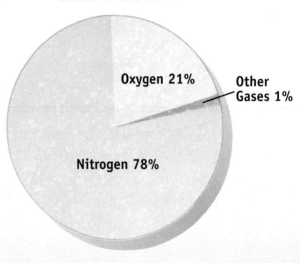

Oxygen 21%

Other Gases 1%

Nitrogen 78%

▼ **The gases in air make life possible.**

Carbon dioxide from the air is used by plants to make food.

Water vapor makes clouds, and therefore rain, possible.

Oxygen is given off to the air when plants make food.

Oxygen from the air is used by animals to release energy from food.

Nitrogen from the air is used by bacteria on plant roots. The bacteria change nitrogen into materials that plants use to grow.

Water and nitrogen-containing materials in the soil are used by plants to make food and to grow.

Earth's Blanket of Air

Imagine that you are riding in the space shuttle. You look down and see patterns of clouds in constant motion above Earth. These clouds are part of a blanket of air that always surrounds Earth. This blanket of air, which is made up of gases, liquids, and some solid matter, is called the **atmosphere**. It reaches from the ground to about 700 km (420 mi) above Earth's surface.

As you can see in the diagram on the next page, the atmosphere is made up of four main layers. But only the lowest layer of the atmosphere can support life. This layer is called the **troposphere** (trō′pō sfir).

The troposphere reaches about 11 km (6.6 mi) above Earth's surface. It is where most of the oxygen, nitrogen, carbon dioxide, and water vapor in the atmosphere are found. It's where you live. It's also where all the things you call weather happen.

Sometimes It's a Wet Blanket

What's the weather like today where you live? Is it wet and chilly? Hot and dry? *Hot, wet, cold, dry, cool, warm, windy, chilly, rainy, foggy, sunny*, and *cloudy* are all words used to talk about weather. Those words are actually ways of describing what's happening in the atmosphere.

SCIENCE IN LITERATURE

LIGHTNING AND OTHER WONDERS OF THE SKY
by Q. L. Pearce
Illustrated by Mary Ann Fraser
Julian Messner, 1989

What made Earth's first atmosphere poisonous? How can the sky look blue if air is colorless? Where can you see an electric light show that fills the night sky? You'll find the amazing answers to these questions in *Lightning and Other Wonders of the Sky* by Q. L. Pearce.

But don't stop there! You can learn more amazing science facts by reading this book.

Thermosphere
In this highest layer of the atmosphere the particles of air may be as far as 10 km (6 mi) apart!

Mesosphere

Stratosphere

Troposphere

You would need a supply of oxygen to help you breathe at the top of Mount Everest.

The particles that make up air are packed close together in the lower part of the troposphere.

Sears Tower

▲ Weather occurs in the troposphere, the lowest layer of Earth's atmosphere.

Weather is the condition of the atmosphere at a certain place and time. It can change from day to day, from hour to hour, and even from minute to minute. Air temperature and the amount of water vapor in the air greatly affect weather. Without the atmosphere, there would be no weather. What place do you know of where there is no weather? ■

What's your favorite kind of weather? ▶

Not Too Warm, Not Too Cold

SCIENCE TECHNOLOGY & SOCIETY

Have you ever visited a gardener's greenhouse? A greenhouse is usually made of glass. The glass lets sunlight in, which warms the ground and other surfaces. As these surfaces warm, they release heat into the air. The glass keeps this heat from escaping. This is similar to the way the inside of a car heats up when sunlight shines through closed windows. The air inside the greenhouse stays warm enough for plants to grow year-round.

Plants are grown in a greenhouse like this one. ▼

Earth's Greenhouse

In some ways, Earth's atmosphere acts like the glass of a greenhouse. It allows the Sun's rays to pass through it and heat Earth's land and water. Some of the heat from the warmed Earth then goes back into the atmosphere. Some of this heat will escape into space. But some of the heat is trapped by water vapor, carbon dioxide, and other gases of Earth's atmosphere.

The gases send some of this heat back toward Earth's surface, as

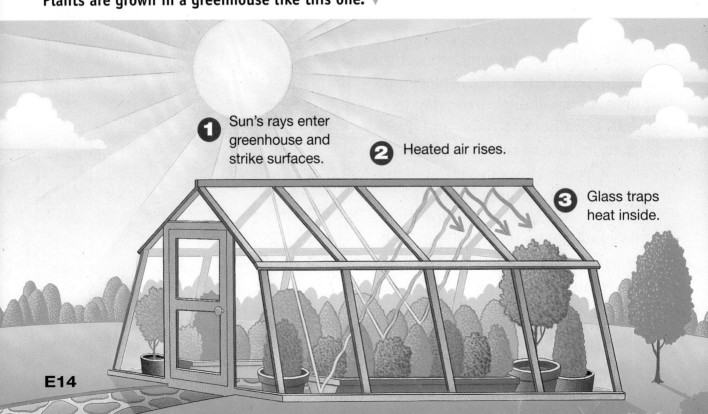

1 Sun's rays enter greenhouse and strike surfaces.

2 Heated air rises.

3 Glass traps heat inside.

shown in the diagram below. So the air in the lower atmosphere stays warm enough for life to exist. This process in which heat from Earth is trapped by the atmosphere is called the **greenhouse effect**.

Look back at the first page of the chapter to find how cold the temperature on the Moon can get. The Moon's surface gets much colder than any place on Earth. Because the Moon has no atmosphere, there is no greenhouse effect there. On Earth the atmosphere keeps the average surface temperature at about 14°C (58°F).

The greenhouse effect on Earth ▼

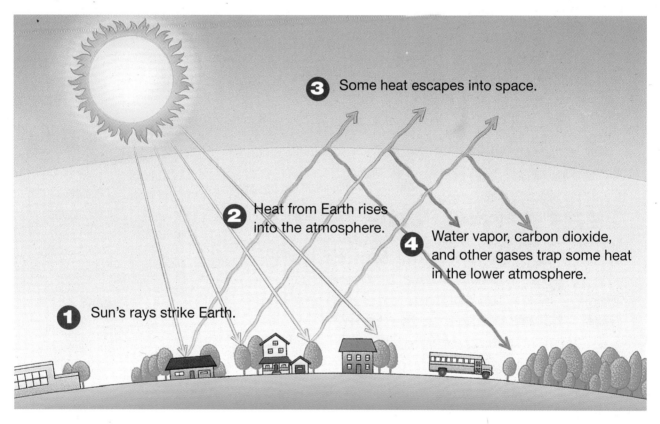

3 Some heat escapes into space.

2 Heat from Earth rises into the atmosphere.

4 Water vapor, carbon dioxide, and other gases trap some heat in the lower atmosphere.

1 Sun's rays strike Earth.

THINK IT WRITE IT

━━━━━━ **INVESTIGATION 1** ━━━━━━

1. What is air made of? How is air like other forms of matter?

2. Could there be life on Earth without the greenhouse effect? Express your ideas about what might happen if Earth lost its atmosphere.

WHY DOES AIR MOVE?

Imagine that it's summertime in a big city. The air feels hot and still. What would the air feel like by the seashore or along a big river? It's likely there would be a nice cool breeze. Why? Find out in Investigation 2 what makes the air move.

Activity

Warming the Air

What happens when the Sun's rays strike your body? Some of the light energy changes to heat and warms your body. Earth's surface is warmed by the Sun, too. Does this heating of Earth's surface change the air above it? Find out!

MATERIALS

- cardboard tube
- aluminum foil
- meterstick
- rubber band
- thermometer
- timer
- *Science Notebook*

SAFETY

Be careful when handling glass thermometers.

Procedure

1. Wrap a cardboard tube in a piece of aluminum foil. Do not cover the ends. Attach the tube to a meterstick, using a rubber band, as shown. Push the tube and rubber band along the meterstick until the bottom edge of the tube is at the 10-cm mark on the meterstick. In your *Science Notebook*, **make a chart** like the one shown.

Type of Surface	Temperature (°C)

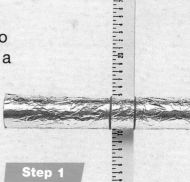

Step 1

E16

2. Go outdoors to a grassy area. Hold the meter-stick with the zero end touching the ground. Have a group member slide a thermometer into the tube. Wait at least three minutes, and then **read** the thermometer. **Record** the temperature of the air.

Step 2

UNIT PROJECT LINK

As you study weather and climate in this unit, you'll observe and record weather-related data. In the outside area that has been set aside for your class weather station, mount a thermometer on a milk carton, using a rubber band. For two weeks, record the temperature in the morning, at noon, and late in the afternoon.

3. **Talk with your group** and **predict** how the temperature of the air over other types of surfaces will vary. Repeat step 2 over two very different surfaces, such as concrete or a patch of bare soil. **Measure** the air temperature for three minutes each time. **Record** your data.

Analyze and Conclude

1. **Compare** your results in step 3 with your predictions. How did the air temperatures you recorded vary? What can you **infer** about the temperature of the surfaces from the temperature of the air above them?

2. Make a **hypothesis** to explain how the air over Earth's surface is affected by the Sun's warming of that surface.

Activity

Making an Air Scale

Does temperature affect the way air moves? In this activity you'll find out!

Procedure

1. Cut a piece of string about 20 cm long, and tie one end to the center of a meterstick.

2. Open two large paper bags fully. Turn each bag upside down. Tape one end of a 10-cm string to the center of one bag bottom. Do the same with the other bag. Tape the free end of each string to opposite ends of the meterstick. The open end of each bag should hang toward the floor.

3. On a high table, place a second meterstick in between a stack of heavy books. About one third of the meterstick should hang over the edge of the table. Tape the string from the center of the first meterstick to the end of this meterstick. The bags should hang freely and be in balance with one another.

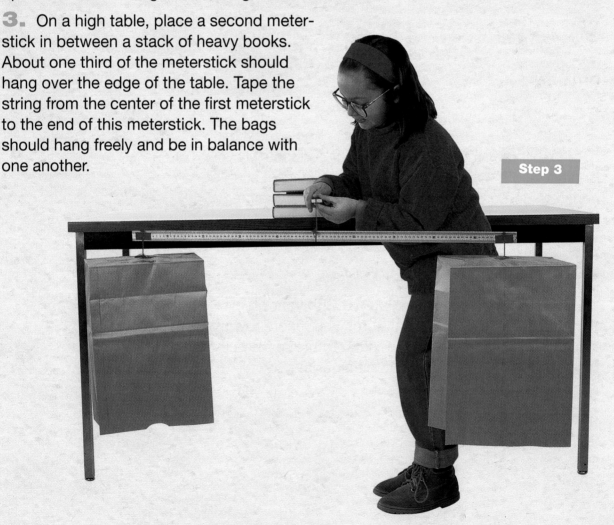

Step 3

4. Put a lamp below one of the bags, as shown. **Talk with your group** and **predict** what will happen to the bag when the lamp is turned on. **Record** your prediction in your *Science Notebook*. **Measure** and **record** the temperature inside the two bags.

5. Turn on the lamp and **observe** what happens. Again **measure** the temperature inside the two bags. **Record** your data and observations.

Analyze and Conclude

1. **Describe** what happened to the bag over the lamp. How does this result **compare** with your prediction?

2. **Compare** the temperature of the air in the two bags in steps 4 and 5. **Infer** the effect of temperature on the weight of the air in each of the bags. Give reasons for the inference you make.

Hot-Air Balloon

The hot-air balloon shown below doesn't look like a paper bag, does it? But it *does* work like the paper-bag scale you made on pages E18 and E19. Read and find out why.

4 The pilot controls how high the balloon rises. To make the balloon rise higher, the pilot burns more fuel to heat the air more. To lower the balloon the pilot lets the air cool.

3 Heat makes the particles of air inside the balloon move farther apart, so the air gets lighter. Outside the balloon the particles of air are more closely packed together, so this air is heavier. As the warm air rises and fills the balloon, the balloon goes up.

1 The pilot and passengers stand in the basket. The fuel tanks are also inside the basket. Hot-air balloons use propane gas as fuel.

2 A fuel line feeds gas to the burner. The burner hangs above the basket and below the mouth of the balloon. Flames from the burner heat the air in the lower part of the balloon.

mouth

burner

fuel line

basket

Feeling the Air

In the activity on pages E16 and E17, you saw that some surfaces on Earth are warmed more than others. This leads to greater warming of the air over some surfaces than others.

Moving Air

Look at the photos on this page. They show some of the different materials that make up Earth. In general, dark-colored materials heat up more rapidly than light-colored materials do. So the air above dark-colored surfaces heats up more rapidly than the air above light-colored surfaces.

In the activity on pages E18 and E19, you saw that by heating the air in a paper bag, that bag became lighter than an unheated bag. The bag with the heated air moved upward.

When an area of air is warmed, the particles of the warm air spread out. The warm air becomes lighter than the cooler air above it. The warm air rises and the cooler air sinks. This movement of air is called d. Some winds are very gentle. winds are so strong that they dangerous. So even if you ee the air, you can always *feel* en the wind blows!

▲ **Which of these surfaces do you think would give off the most heat?**

Cooler air over land moves out toward the water and takes the place of the rising air.

Warm air over the water rises.

LAND BREEZE

cool land

warm sea

Warm air over the land rises.

Cooler air over the water moves toward land and takes the place of the warmer air that has risen.

SEA BREEZE

warm land

cool sea

▲ **The uneven heating of land and water causes land and sea breezes.**

Land and Sea Breezes

Let's look at the movement of air between two very different areas on Earth's surface: water and land. Land loses heat faster than water. So at night, the air over land cools off more than does the air over water. Land also heats up faster than water. So during the day, the air over land is heated more than is the air over water.

You may be familiar with this uneven heating of land and water. How does it feel when you walk barefoot on the sand at a beach? Your feet may feel as if they are burning. But when you go into the water, you cool off right away. You may feel a cool breeze when you come out of the water. Look at the drawings to learn more about what causes land and sea breezes. ∎

━━━━━━━━━━━━━━━ **INVESTIGATION 2** ━━━━━━━━━━━━━━━

THINK IT WRITE IT

1. Suppose that you attach a thermometer to the wall near the ceiling of your classroom and attach another thermometer to the wall just a few centimeters above the floor. What temperature difference would you expect to find? Why?

2. What does uneven heating of Earth's surface have to do with air movement?

REFLECT & EVALUA

WORD POWER

air
atmosphere
carbon dioxide
greenhouse effect
nitrogen
oxygen
troposphere
water vapor
weather
wind

 On Your Own
Write a definition for each term in the list.

 With a Partner
Write each term in the list on one side of an index card and the definition on the other side. Use the cards to quiz your partner.

PORTFOLIO

Create a word picture of Earth and the air surrounding it for someone living on another planet. Use the terms *oxygen, nitrogen, carbon dioxide,* and *water vapor.*

Analyze Information

Study the drawing. In your own words explain how the greenhouse works and how it is similar to Earth's atmosphere.

Assess Performance

Design a way to investigate the "ocean" of air that is pressing against your body. Work with sheets of newspaper or other lightweight paper taped together. Test whether this unseen ocean presses down on your entire body at the same time.

Problem Solving

1. Why is carbon dioxide important to the survival of life on Earth? Name one other gas in Earth's atmosphere and explain its importance to living things.

2. You're in a spaceship that takes you high above the troposphere. What would the weather be like there? Explain your answer.

3. Suppose you had a scale, a pump, and a flat basketball. How could you use these items to show that air has weight?

CHAPTER 2

OBSERVING WEATHER

Have you ever noticed that the leaves on trees sometimes flip upside down in the wind? When the leaves turn like this, some people think it's a sign that rain is on the way. What signs do you observe in nature that make you think it's about to rain?

Weather Watchers

Long ago, people lived closer to nature, and their very lives depended on the weather. Here are some old-fashioned weather rhymes. Some of them describe weather patterns. Others tell about some ways to forecast weather.

Red sky at night,
Sailors' delight.
Red sky at morning,
Sailors take warning.

If bees stay at home,
The rain will soon come.
If bees fly away,
It'll be a fine day.

March winds and April showers
Bring forth May flowers.

June damp and warm
Does the farmer no harm.

In this chapter you'll become a weather watcher as you learn about air pressure, wind, and water vapor.

Coming Up

◄ What other sayings, rhymes, or songs do you know that tell about the weather?

WHAT IS AIR PRESSURE?

Air pushes down on Earth's surface. Air pushes up and sideways, too. How does the way that air pushes against things affect weather? You'll begin to find out in this investigation.

Activity

It's a Pressing Problem

Air pressure is the push of air against its surroundings. Find out if air pressure is always the same or if it changes.

MATERIALS

- plastic soda bottle with cap (2 L)
- 2 small plastic dish tubs
- hot tap water
- ice water
- timer
- *Science Notebook*

SAFETY

Be careful when using hot water. Clean up any spills immediately.

Procedure

1. Unscrew the cap of an empty plastic bottle. Wait a few seconds. Tightly screw the cap back on.

2. Fill a plastic dish tub with hot water from the tap. Fill a second plastic dish tub with ice water.

3. Talk with your group and predict what will happen
...apped bottle when it is put into hot water
...ld water.
...
...tion in
...ebook.

4. Lower the bottle into the tub of hot water. Hold as much of the bottle as you can below the water level. Keep it there for one minute. Remove the bottle and **record** your observations.

5. Repeat step 4 with the tub of ice water.

Step 5

Analyze and Conclude

1. Describe what happened to the bottle after step 4 and after step 5.

2. Compare your results with your prediction. **Talk with other groups** about their results.

3. Infer what the results have to do with **air pressure**—the push of air against its surroundings. **Explain** what led you to this inference.

INVESTIGATE FURTHER!

EXPERIMENT

Fill the plastic bottle you used in the activity with hot tap water. Let the water sit in the bottle for one minute. Hypothesize what will happen if you now empty the bottle and then quickly screw the cap back on tightly. Test your hypothesis. Compare your results with those from the activity.

Activity
Measuring Air Pressure

When you want to find out how hot or cold the air is, you use a thermometer. But how can you measure air pressure? In this activity you'll make a barometer to measure air pressure.

Procedure

1. Cut a large balloon lengthwise. Stretch it over the open top of a coffee can. Secure it with a rubber band. Tape the edge of the balloon to tightly seal the air inside the can.

2. Cut one end of a plastic straw to form a point. Tape the uncut end to the center of the stretched balloon. You have now made a **barometer** (bə räm′ət ər), a device that measures air pressure.

Step 2

3. Tape a cardboard strip on a wall so the bottom of the strip is level with the table, as shown on the next page. Place your barometer next to the strip so that the straw pointer just touches it.

4. In your *Science Notebook*, **make a chart** like the one shown.

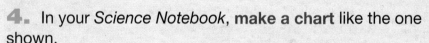

Date	Air Pressure Reading	Weather Conditions

5. Each day for one week, take a barometer reading. Draw a line on the cardboard where the straw is pointing. Label the line with the date and weather conditions, such as cloudy, windy, or rainy.

6. **Record** this data in your chart. Under the heading *Air Pressure Reading*, **record** whether the pressure is higher, or lower, than the day before.

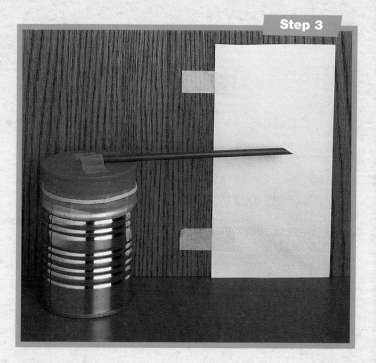

Step 3

Analyze and Conclude

1. **Describe** how the pointer moved from day to day. **Explain** how you could tell whether the air pressure was high or low.

2. **Compare** the readings on your barometer to your observations about the weather.

3. **Talk with your group** and **form a hypothesis** about how your barometer can help predict the weather.

UNIT PROJECT LINK

Compare the data your group collected from your barometer with the data collected by other groups. Choose one of the barometers to place in your class weather station. Explain why you chose this one. Then use your weather station barometer to collect data about air pressure at the same time that you make temperature readings. Add the barometer readings to your data.

Torricelli's Barometer

In the activity on pages E28 and E29, you made a device called a barometer. More than 350 years ago, the very first barometer was made—by accident.

A scientist named Evangelista Torricelli (tôr ə chel'ē) was trying to make a vacuum (vak'yōōm), a space in which there is no air or any other kind of matter. He used a large bowl and a long glass tube, open at one end and closed at the other.

Torricelli filled the tube with a heavy liquid metal, called mercury, and turned the tube upside down in the bowl. Some mercury flowed out of the tube, leaving a space at the top. The space was the vacuum Torricelli wanted to investigate.

Torricelli wondered why *all* of the mercury didn't flow out of the tube. And he questioned why the height of the mercury changed from day to day. He inferred that air was holding up the mercury in the tube.

As the diagram shows, air pushes down on the surface of the mercury in the bowl. This air pressure keeps some of the mercury inside the tube. And because air pressure keeps changing, the mercury level keeps changing. ■

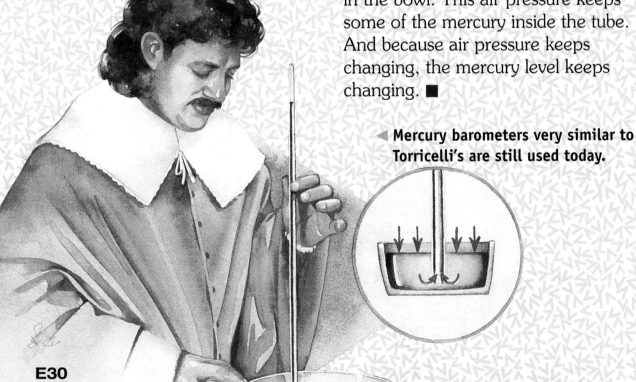

◀ **Mercury barometers very similar to Torricelli's are still used today.**

All About Pressure

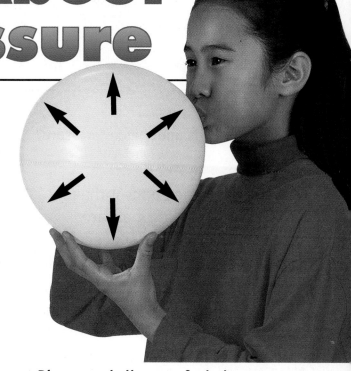

You live in an atmosphere in which the billions of particles that make up air are in constant motion. These particles move in all directions—up, down, and sideways. When air particles bump into things—a tree, a dog, a pencil, a person, or other air particles—they push. The push of air against its surroundings is called **air pressure**.

You can see the effect of air pressure when you blow up a balloon. Air pushes in all directions at once against the inside of the inflated balloon.

▲ **Blow up a balloon to feel air pressure at work.**

Gravity Rules

Look at the drawing. Where are the particles of air closest together? Near sea level or at the top of the mountain? Do you know why?

Air is matter. Like all matter, particles of air are pulled toward Earth's surface by a force called gravity. The closer you are to Earth's surface, the more particles of air there are squeezed into a given space. If you climbed to the top of the highest mountain, Mount Everest, three quarters of all the air particles in the atmosphere would be below where you were standing.

▲ **The particles of air are closest together near sea level.**

E31

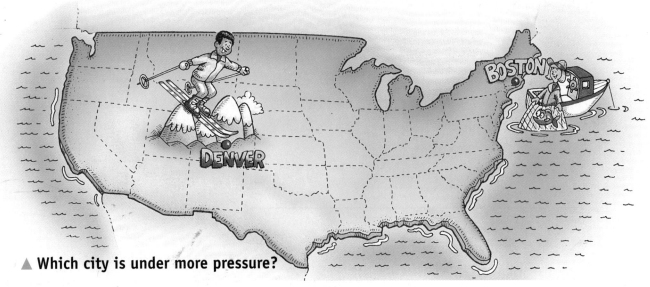

▲ **Which city is under more pressure?**

Who's Under Pressure?

What difference does it make how many particles of air are squeezed into a given space? A lot! The closer together the air particles, the more pressure the air has.

Denver is called the Mile-High City because it is about a mile above sea level. Boston is just above sea level. In which city are people under greater air pressure? If you said Boston, you're right! People living at sea level are at the "bottom" of Earth's atmosphere. All the air of the atmosphere is above them.

People in Denver are also under pressure. But the higher you go, the less air there is above you. And the farther apart the particles of air are. So the air pressure in Denver is lower than in Boston.

Measuring Air Pressure

The device used to measure air pressure is called a **barometer**. There are two main kinds of barometers—mercury barometers and aneroid barometers.

A mercury barometer works like Torricelli's barometer. A column of mercury in a tube rises and falls as air pressure changes.

An aneroid barometer is made with a sealed metal can. The can expands or contracts when air pressure changes. This barometer is similar to the one you made in the activity on pages E28 and E29.

Scientists use barometer readings to help predict the weather. Air pressure is usually measured in inches of mercury. At sea level the height of the column of mercury is 29.92 in. (75.66 cm). This is used as the standard for comparing pressure everywhere. As air pressure becomes lower, the mercury column starts falling.

◄ **An aneroid barometer**

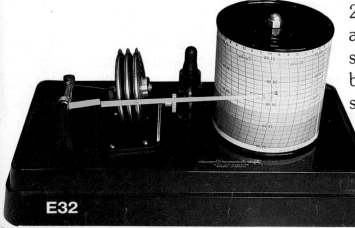

Air Pressure and Temperature

In the activity on pages E26 and E27, you saw that air pressure in the bottle increased when the air inside was heated. Air pressure in the atmosphere changes with temperature, too. But it works in the opposite way from air in a closed space, such as a bottle.

When air in the atmosphere is warmed, particles of air move farther apart. But air pressure gets lower because the particles are not enclosed and can move away from each other. When air is cooled, particles move closer together. Air pressure gets higher.

Areas where pressure is higher than the surrounding air are called **high-pressure areas**. Areas where pressure is lower than the surrounding air are called **low-pressure areas**. The difference in air pressure between such areas can cause winds. ■

Which "block" of air has greater pressure? ▼

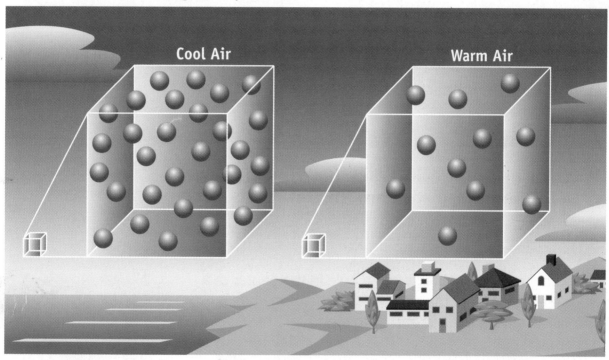

Cool Air   Warm Air

─────────── INVESTIGATION 1 ───────────

1. You're visiting one of the tall buildings of the World Trade Center in New York City. You have a barometer with you. As you ride the elevator to the 107th floor, you notice that the barometer reading goes down. Explain what happened and why.

2. What is air pressure and how is it measured?

HOW CAN YOU FIND WIND SPEED AND DIRECTION?

Look out a window to observe a flag, a tree, or some leaves on the ground. What can these observations tell you about the wind? In Investigation 2 you'll discover even better ways to measure wind speed and find wind direction.

Activity

A Windy Day

Which way is the wind blowing? In this activity you'll build a wind vane to find out!

Procedure

1. Draw a large cross through a hole in the center of a wooden board. Mark the end of each line of the cross with one of the letters *N, S, E,* and *W* to stand for *north, south, east,* and *west.*

2. Remove the rubber bulb from a dropper. Carefully push the pointed end of the dropper into the hole in the wooden board.

3. Tape the middle section from a plastic bottle to a wire hanger. Then insert the straightened end of the wire hanger into the dropper.

MATERIALS

- goggles
- wooden board with hole in center
- marker
- dropper
- middle section from plastic soda bottle (1 L)
- wire hanger (with hook straightened)
- tape
- cardboard
- scissors
- magnetic compass
- **Science Notebook**

SAFETY //////

Wear goggles during this activity.

4. Cut out an arrowhead and arrow tail from cardboard. Attach these to the hanger as shown. You have made a wind vane.

5. Place the wooden board in an open area outdoors. Use a compass to find north. Then turn the wooden board so that the *N* faces north.

6. **Observe** such things as flags and leaves to see how they move in the wind. **Discuss** your observations **with your group** members. **Infer** the direction from which the wind is blowing.

7. A **wind vane** is a device that shows the direction from which the wind is blowing. On your wind vane, the arrow will point in the direction the wind is blowing from. Use the wind vane to **find** the wind direction and **record** it in your *Science Notebook*.

8. **Make a chart** like the one shown. For one week, **observe** and **record** the wind direction. **Record** other weather conditions at the same time.

Date/Time	Wind Direction	Weather Conditions

Analyze and Conclude

1. **Compare** your findings in step 7 with the inference you made in step 6.

2. Use the data in your chart to **infer** whether the wind comes from the same direction on warm days as it does on cool days. What connections do you see between the direction of the wind and other weather conditions over a period of time? What patterns do you see? Explain.

UNIT PROJECT LINK

Choose one of the wind vanes to put in your class weather station. Use the wind vane to collect data about wind direction when you make readings for temperature and air pressure. Add your wind direction readings to your data.

Activity

How Fast the Wind Blows

Have you heard a weather reporter talk about the speed of the wind? Perhaps you've wondered how wind speed is measured. In this activity you'll build an anemometer, a device to measure wind speed.

MATERIALS

- goggles
- 4 small paper cups
- 4 plastic straws
- stapler
- tape
- crayon
- straight pin
- pencil with a new eraser
- timer
- *Science Notebook*

SAFETY ⁄⁄⁄⁄⁄

Wear goggles during this activity. Be careful when handling the straight pin.

Procedure

1. Staple one end of a plastic straw to the outside of a paper cup, near the rim. Do the same thing with three other straws and paper cups. Each straw should be sticking out to the *right* of its cup.

2. Place two cups on their sides with the straws pointed toward each other. The open ends of the cups should be facing in opposite directions. Overlap the tips of the straws about 1 cm and tape them together.

3. Repeat step 2 with the other two cups. Then crisscross the two pairs of straws, as shown. Tape the two pairs of straws together at their midpoints. Mark the bottom of one cup with an *X*.

Step 3

Step 1

4. Your teacher will insert a straight pin through the center of the cross and into the top of a pencil eraser. Don't push the pin all the way in. Your anemometer (an ə mäm′-ət ər) is complete.

5. Test your anemometer by holding the pencil and blowing into the cups. The cups should spin freely. Each time that you see the cup marked *X* on the bottom, the anemometer has made one complete spin.

6. **Talk with your group** members and **hypothesize** how your anemometer can be used to measure wind speed. **Record** and **explain** your hypothesis in your *Science Notebook*.

7. **Make a chart** like the one shown. Take your anemometer outside. **Count** how many times it spins in one minute. **Record** the number of spins at different times of the day or at the same hour each day for one week. **Record** other observations about weather conditions at the same time.

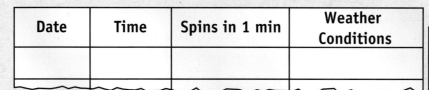

Date	Time	Spins in 1 min	Weather Conditions

Analyze and Conclude

1. Study the data in your chart. **Compare** differences in wind speed at different times and under different weather conditions. **Describe** any patterns you see.

2. **Compare** the hypothesis you made in step 6 with your results.

UNIT PROJECT LINK

Choose one of the anemometers to put in your class weather station. Explain your choice. Use the anemometer to collect data about wind speed. Add your wind speed data to the other weather findings you make on a daily basis.

Which Way Is the
Wind Blowing?

Wind is moving air. In Chapter 1 you saw that the uneven heating of Earth results in the uneven heating of air. Recall that differences in air temperature affect air pressure. Winds occur when there are differences in air pressure between two areas of air that are near each other. Winds move from areas of high pressure to areas of low pressure.

What makes some winds stronger than others? When the difference in pressure between two areas is great, winds are strong. And when high-pressure and low-pressure areas are close together, winds are also stronger.

Finding Wind Direction

The direction of the wind is the direction from which it is blowing. A wind blowing from the east to the west is called an east wind. What would a wind blowing from the northeast to the southwest be called?

A **wind vane** is a device used to find wind direction. Most wind vanes are shaped like a long arrow with a tail. When the wind blows, the arrow points into the wind. If the arrow points south, the wind is a south wind. If the arrow points between the north and the east, it's a northeast wind. How does the wind vane shown compare with the one you made on pages E34 and E35?

Another instrument used to find wind direction is a windsock. A **windsock** is a cloth bag that is

▲ **A windsock points away from the wind.**

narrow at one end and open at both ends. Air enters the wide end and causes the narrow end to point away from the direction that the wind is blowing. This is opposite to what the wind vane does.

Measuring Wind Speed

An **anemometer** is a device used to measure wind speed. It often consists of cups on spokes attached to a pole. Scientists use an anemometer like the one shown to record wind speed in kilometers per hour. What rate did you use to measure wind speed in the activity on pages E36 and E37?

If you don't have special devices to measure wind speed, you can try to figure out wind speed using the Beaufort (bō′fərt) scale. In 1805 a British naval officer named Sir Francis Beaufort made a scale that divides wind strength into 12 forces.

Part of the Beaufort scale is shown below. Beaufort made his scale by observing how wind affects sailing ships and the ocean. The scale was later changed to include observations on land.

THE BEAUFORT SCALE			
Beaufort Number	Speed in km/h (mph)	Description	Observations on Land
2	6–11 (4–7)	light breeze	leaves rustle, wind felt on face; wind vanes move
4	20–28 (13–18)	moderate breeze	dust and paper blow; small branches sway
6	39–49 (25–31)	strong breeze	umbrellas hard to open; large branches sway
8	62–74 (39–46)	gale	walking is very difficult; twigs break off trees
10	89–102 (55–63)	whole gale	much damage to buildings; trees uprooted
12	117 and up (74 and up)	hurricane	violent, widespread destruction

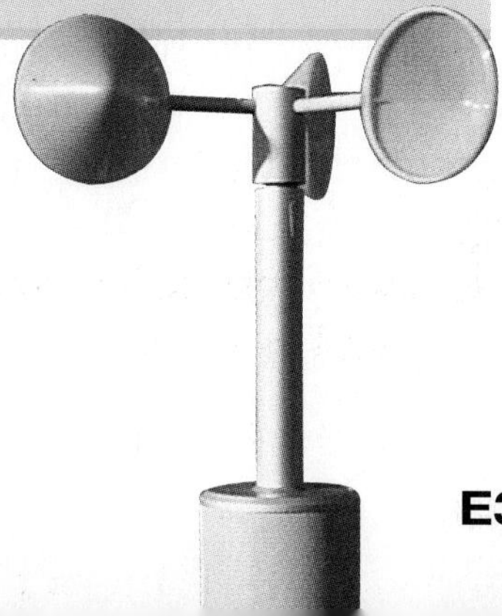

The faster the wind blows, the faster the anemometer's cups spin. ▶

◀ A wind vane points into the wind.

Wind Power

In the activity on pages E36 and E37, you saw the power of the wind. The harder the wind blew, the faster the anemometer spun. What if all that spinning energy could be put to work?

sails spun. The turning motion was used to grind grain.

In the fourteenth century, the Dutch began using windmills to pump water out of low-lying land. The traditional Dutch windmill has four arms attached to cloth sails or wooden blades. The blades spin like the propeller of a plane. The sails or blades can turn only when the wind blows directly at them.

▲ Many modern windmills work the same way as this traditional Dutch windmill.

Early Wind Machines

Windmills are machines that put the wind to work. They were first used in the Middle East, perhaps as long ago as the seventh century. In these early windmills, a wheel made of cloth sails was attached to a tall structure. As the wind blew, the

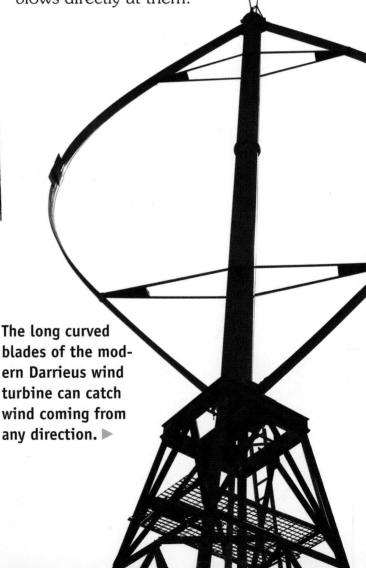

The long curved blades of the modern Darrieus wind turbine can catch wind coming from any direction. ▶

Today's Windmills

Modern windmills are designed to work at much higher wind speeds than are traditional ones. They are usually made of aluminum or other light metals. Some modern windmills, called wind turbines (tur′binz), are used to produce electricity.

The largest wind turbines are over 90 m (300 ft) tall. The tips of the blades travel as fast as 400 km/h (250 mph). The turbine is attached to a generator that produces the electricity.

Wind Energy Use Worldwide

Wind power may be one of the answers to today's energy needs. Unlike many other sources of energy, wind can't be used up and it doesn't pollute the air. Also, wind turbines can be built fairly quickly.

But wind power is not a perfect answer to energy needs. The direction and speed of the winds change

▲ **Wind farm in Altamont Pass, California**

over time and from place to place. And sometimes, of course, the wind doesn't blow at all. Wind power works best where wind speeds are high and fairly steady. Wind turbines are placed in areas where there are not too many trees, houses, or other barriers that may block the wind.

A wind farm is a system of 50 or more wind turbines working together. Each turbine turns a generator. The Altamont Pass wind farm produces enough electricity to supply several towns in California. Wind farms are being developed in other states as well as in Europe, India, China, and other parts of the world. ■

INVESTIGATION 2

1. Most people would agree that wind turbines offer benefits as an energy source for producing electricity. Identify two problems in using wind turbines as a source of energy.

2. How can you determine wind speed and wind direction?

HOW DOES WATER IN THE AIR AFFECT WEATHER?

Water vapor is a very important gas in Earth's atmosphere. In Investigation 3 you'll find out how the amount of water vapor in the air affects weather.

Activity

Make a Rain Gauge

Have you wondered how scientists measure rainfall? They use a device called a rain gauge. Make one in this activity.

MATERIALS
- flat wooden stick
- marker
- metric ruler
- aluminum soda can, top removed
- plastic soda bottle (2 L), cut in half
- *Science Notebook*

Procedure

1. Place a flat wooden stick on your desk. Use a metric ruler and a marker to draw a line 3 cm from the lower end. Label this line *1 cm*.

2. Draw another line on the stick, 3 cm above the 1-cm line. Label this second line *2 cm*. Then draw another line, 3 cm above the 2-cm line. Label this third line *3 cm*.

3. Divide the space between the lower end of the stick and the 1-cm line into ten equal parts. Repeat this for each space. Your stick should look like the one shown.

4. Place an aluminum can, with the top removed, inside the bottom half of a cut plastic soda bottle.

Step 3

E42

5. Turn the top half of the bottle upside down. Insert the neck of the bottle into the can, as shown. The top half of the bottle will serve as a funnel. You've made a rain gauge (gāj).

6. In your *Science Notebook*, **make a chart** like the one shown. Put your rain gauge outdoors where it won't be disturbed. Use your chart to **record** the amount of rainfall every day for one month. To **measure** rainfall, put the marked wooden stick along the inside wall of the can. Be sure to measure rainfall the same way each time.

Date	Amount of Rainfall

Analyze and Conclude

1. How would you measure the rainfall if the water overflowed the can?

2. How could you use your rain gauge to measure snowfall?

3. Together with your group members, **predict** how the amount of rainfall where you live will vary during different seasons in the coming year. What information will you need to make such a prediction?

UNIT PROJECT LINK

Choose one of the rain gauges to put in your class weather station. Why did you make this choice? Use the rain gauge to collect data about rainfall. Add your rainfall data to the other weather readings you make each day.

Step 5

Snow
Around the World

Over 2,000 years ago, the Chinese scholar Han Ying observed that snowflakes have six points. About 1,700 years passed before people in other places discovered this fact.

You don't have to know about the shape of a snowflake to know how much fun, or how much trouble, snow can be. Take a look at some ways that people around the world deal with "the white stuff."

▲ **UNITED STATES**   In 1880 a Vermont farm boy named Wilson A. Bentley began photographing snow crystals through a microscope. He took thousands of pictures, but not one snowflake looks exactly like another.

◀ **JAPAN**   Sapporo, a city in northern Japan, has long winters with lots of snow. Every February the city holds a week-long snow festival in which groups compete in a snow-statue contest. As you can see from the snow castle shown here, these sculptures are much bigger than an average snowman! In fact, trucks bring in 40,000 tons of extra snow for the festival.

LAPLAND Cars aren't practical in regions with heavy snowfall. The Lapps (called the Sami, in Norway) are a people who live in the northern parts of Norway, Sweden, Finland, and Russia. Instead of using cars, they train reindeer to pull sleds over the snow. ▶

◀ **THE ALPS** The northern side of the Alps mountain range receives about 305 cm (120 in.) of snow a year. People who live there must find ways to avoid avalanches (avʹə lanch əz). An avalanche is a sudden sliding of snow down a mountain. Some avalanches weigh several tons and move at speeds of 160 km/h (100 mph).

THE ARCTIC The Inuit (inʹo͞o wit) live in the Arctic, which is frozen under snow and ice for as long as nine months a year. To survive, Inuits join together to fish and to hunt. Snow is so much a part of Inuit life that their language has more than two dozen words to describe different kinds of snow. ▶

Water Vapor and Weather

Water vapor is one of the gases that make up air. The amount of water vapor in the air is called the **humidity** (hyoō mid'ə tē). Humidity changes from day to day and from place to place. Changes in humidity cause changes in the weather.

It's Relative

There is a limit to the amount of water the air can hold. But that limit isn't constant. It changes, depending on the temperature of the air. The warmer the air, the more water vapor it can hold.

The **relative humidity** is the amount of water vapor the air is holding at a given temperature compared to the total amount that it *could* hold at that temperature. If the air is holding all the water it possibly can hold at that temperature, the relative humidity is 100 percent.

When the temperature outside is high but the humidity is low, the sweat on your skin evaporates quickly. When water **evaporates,** it changes from a liquid to a gas. In the process it takes heat with it. This makes you feel cooler.

When both the temperature and the humidity are high, the water on your skin can't evaporate quickly. That's because there's already a lot

Explain how this could be true. ▼

It feels hotter today than it did yesterday.

But the temperature's the same!

of water vapor in the air, and the air can't hold much more. So the sweat remains on your skin. That's why even though the temperature is the same, you feel warmer.

Wet Weather

As the temperature drops, the air can hold less water vapor. Some of the water vapor **condenses**, or changes from a gas to a liquid.

Clouds form when water vapor in the air condenses. Although it may sometimes look like a fluffy ball of cotton, a **cloud** is billions of tiny drops of water that condensed from the air. A cloud that touches Earth's surface is called fog.

As the drops of water in clouds grow larger, they become heavier. Finally they fall to Earth. Any form of water that falls from the air to Earth's surface is called **precipitation** (prē sip ə tā'shən). Look at the photos of different kinds of precipitation shown on the next page.

Measuring Precipitation

You've probably heard weather reports in which the amount of rainfall or snowfall was given. How are these forms of precipitation measured? A **rain gauge** is used to measure the amount of precipitation. It's measured at a certain time every day for national weather reports.

SCIENCE IN LITERATURE

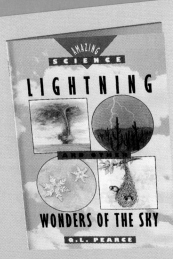

LIGHTNING AND OTHER WONDERS OF THE SKY
by Q. L. Pearce
Illustrated by Mary Ann Fraser
Julian Messner, 1989

- A parachuting pilot gets tossed around inside a thundercloud for 40 minutes!

- Another pilot falls to Earth encased in ice—turning him into a human hailstone.

- Under certain conditions you can see a halo around the Moon.

What can cause these strange things to happen? Find the explanations in *Lightning and Other Wonders of the Sky* by Q. L. Pearce. Use the Contents page at the beginning of the book to find the discussion of each natural wonder.

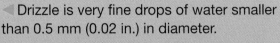

◁ Drizzle is very fine drops of water smaller than 0.5 mm (0.02 in.) in diameter.

Rain is water drops that are larger and fall faster than drizzle. ▷

◁ Snow is a solid form of precipitation made of ice crystals.

Hail is particles of ice usually ranging from the size of a pea to the size of a golf ball. Some hailstones are even larger. ▷

INVESTIGATION 3

THINK IT WRITE IT

1. Imagine that it's a cold winter day. You are outside, talking with a friend. Why can you see your breath as you talk?

2. Describe the role of water vapor in weather.

REFLECT & EVALUATE

WORD POWER

air pressure
anemometer
barometer
cloud
condense
evaporate
relative humidity
high-pressure area
low-pressure area

precipitation
rain gauge
humidity
windsock
wind vane

On Your Own
Write a definition for each term in the list.

With a Partner
Mix up the letters of each term in the list. Provide a clue for each term and challenge your partner to unscramble the terms.

BUILD YOUR PORTFOLIO

Use the complete Beaufort scale to make a record of wind speed for one week. Each day, record observations of the effect of the wind. Compare your observations with the estimated wind speeds on the Beaufort scale.

Analyze Information

Study the drawing. It shows air pressure readings, in inches of mercury, that were taken in different places at the same time on the same day. Explain the relationship between air pressure and height above sea level.

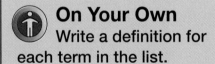

20.58

24.89

27.01

29.92

Assess Performance

Design your own windmill or wind turbine. Decide what you will use the machine to do and what materials it will be made of. Decide how big the spinning blades will be and how they will be shaped. Draw or write a description of how your wind machine will look.

Problem Solving

1. You are working in a weather station and you notice that the barometer reading is beginning to drop. What does this tell you about the air pressure of the atmosphere?

2. Explain why an aluminum can "sweats" when you take it out of the refrigerator on a hot day.

3. You are trying to fly a kite. How can you use a wind vane and an anemometer to help?

CHAPTER 3

WEATHER PATTERNS

Blame it on the weather reporter. When you listened to the radio, the weather reporter said it was going to be sunny for your outdoor field trip. But then it rained all day. In this chapter you'll find out what goes into predicting the next day's weather.

Storm Pilot

You might think that studying weather is not very exciting. But seeing how Anton Seimon learns about rainstorms, blizzards, hurricanes, and tornadoes will change your mind. He flies a plane above, around, and even *into* these storms.

Anton Seimon studies storms to better understand how they form and to help other people predict storms. He uses simple instruments, such as thermometers, and not-so-simple devices, such as radar. He sometimes drops packages of instruments from the plane into a storm that is too strong to fly into. These instruments gather important data, such as wind speed and air pressure.

"My work is very exciting," he says. "Studying the information we collect is almost as exciting as flying into a storm." What would you ask Anton Seimon about his work?

Coming Up

▲ Anton Seimon flies a plane like this one into the storms he studies.

INVESTIGATION 1

WHAT CAN CLOUDS TELL YOU ABOUT THE WEATHER?

You're about to head out the door. You notice thin, wispy white clouds high in the sky. Should you take an umbrella or your sunglasses? Find out how clouds can help you predict the weather.

Activity

Kinds of Clouds

Are there different types of clouds in the sky? Discover the answer in this activity.

MATERIALS
• *Science Notebook*

SAFETY
Never look directly at the Sun.

Procedure

Choose three different times of day to carefully **observe** clouds. **Write a description** in your *Science Notebook* of how the clouds look and where they appear in the sky. Then **draw** pictures of the clouds. With your group, **classify** the clouds you saw. Share your results with other groups.

Analyze and Conclude

1. How many different cloud shapes did you see? Did any of the clouds change shape?

2. What colors were the clouds? How high were they in the sky?

3. Explain how your group classified the clouds.

Activity

Cloudy Weather

Can the types of clouds in the sky help you predict what the weather will be? In this activity you'll find out.

MATERIALS
- thermometer
- *Science Notebook*

SAFETY

Be careful when handling glass thermometers. Never look directly at the Sun.

Procedure

1. Think about the types of clouds you've seen in the sky. **Predict** which types of clouds may occur in certain types of weather. **Record** your predictions in your *Science Notebook*.

2. **Make a chart** like the one shown.

Date	Time	Cloud Description	Weather Conditions

3. Twice a day for one week, **observe** the types of clouds you see. **Record** a description of the clouds in your chart.

4. **Record** the weather conditions at the same time you make your cloud observations. Note whether it is sunny, cloudy, rainy, or snowy. Use a thermometer to **measure** the temperature of the air.

Analyze and Conclude

1. **Compare** your findings with the predictions you made.

2. **Compare** differences in cloud types at different times and for different weather conditions. **Hypothesize** how clouds might be used to predict the weather.

Step 4

E53

The Weather From Space

STS
SCIENCE
TECHNOLOGY
& SOCIETY

Clouds are one factor scientists use to forecast the weather. **Weather satellites** are devices in space that are used to take pictures of clouds and to collect other weather information. One important type of weather satellite is called GOES, short for Geostationary Operational Environmental Satellite. This type of satellite travels at the same speed that Earth spins. So a GOES can keep track of weather over the same area day and night.

Weather satellites send images of the clouds over Earth to weather stations on the ground. The satellites also measure moisture in the atmosphere as well as the temperature of land and of water. Such data can help farmers know when cold, icy weather is coming so that they can protect their crops.

GOES can also be used to warn people when big storms are on the way. Weather satellites can track storms over long distances. In 1992, Hurricane Andrew was tracked from space for thousands of kilometers over many days. ∎

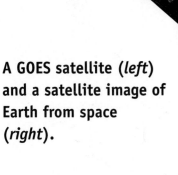

A GOES satellite (*left*) and a satellite image of Earth from space (*right*).

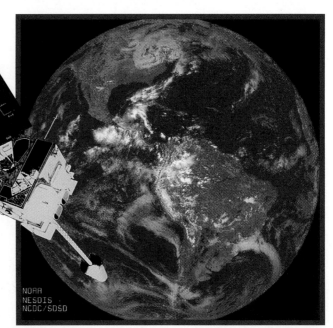

NORA
NESDIS
NCDC/SDSD

Watching the Clouds Go By

Imagine that you are in a place with no newspapers, radio, or TV. How can you tell what the weather is going to be? Believe it or not, the answer is right outside your window. Just take a look at the sky. The types of clouds that you see can help you predict the coming weather.

But where do clouds come from? Like a magic trick, clouds appear out of the air. That's because they form in air. Look at the diagram to see how a cloud forms.

Cloud Families

Recall the way you classified clouds in the activity on page E52. You probably noticed that there were clouds of many different shapes and sizes. In 1803 a scientist named Luke Howard found a way to group clouds by the way they looked. He grouped the clouds into three main families—cumulus (kyoo'myoo ləs) clouds, stratus (stra'təs) clouds, and cirrus (sir'əs) clouds.

▲ Cumulus clouds

Cumulus clouds are puffy clouds that look like cauliflower. They form when large areas of warm, moist air float upward from Earth's surface.

A cloud forms when warm, moist air rises and cools. ▼

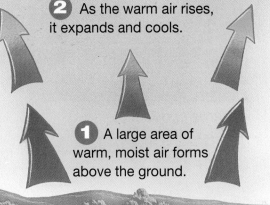

3 Water vapor condenses into tiny drops of water that come together to form a **cloud.**

2 As the warm air rises, it expands and cools.

1 A large area of warm, moist air forms above the ground.

E55

Types of Clouds

CIRRUS CLOUDS Often a sign that rainy or snowy weather is on its way

CIRROCUMULUS CLOUDS Thin, high clouds that mean changing weather

ALTOCUMULUS CLOUDS Fluffy gray clouds that can grow into rain clouds

CIRROSTRATUS CLOUDS Thin milk-colored sheets that often mean rain is on the way

ALTOSTRATUS CLOUDS Mean that stormy weather is coming soon

CUMULONIMBUS CLOUDS Thunderheads that bring thunderstorms with rain, snow, or hail

CUMULUS CLOUDS Appear in sunny summer skies

STRATOCUMULUS CLOUDS Mean that drier weather is on the way

STRATUS CLOUDS Low clouds that often bring drizzle

NIMBOSTRATUS CLOUDS Thick dark blankets that may bring snow or rain

▲ Stratus clouds

▲ Cirrus clouds

Stratus clouds are like flat gray blankets that seem to cover the sky. Stratus clouds form when a flat layer of warm, moist air rises very slowly.

Cirrus clouds look like commas or wisps of hair high in the sky. Cirrus clouds form when the air rises high enough for ice crystals to form.

Sometimes scientists talk about nimbostratus or cumulonimbus clouds. *Nimbus* is a Latin word that means "rain." When you see *nimbus* or *nimbo-* in a cloud name, you know the cloud is a rain cloud.

Clouds are also grouped by height above the ground. Some clouds are close to the ground, some are high in the sky, and some are in between. Clouds that form high in the sky have the prefix *cirro-* in front of their

family name. Clouds that form at a medium height have the prefix *alto-* in front of their family name.

Weather Clues From Clouds

When you did the activity on page E53, you may have noticed that certain types of clouds appeared in the sky before a rainstorm. Or you may have seen that other types of clouds showed up before fair weather.

Different types of clouds give clues about the weather to come. Examine the different cloud types shown on page E56. Which cloud types might tell that rain is coming? Which might tell that the weather will be changing soon? Which types did you see when you did the activities on pages E52 and E53? ■

── **INVESTIGATION 1** ──

1. You are going to a picnic and see that the sky is filled with a layer of gray clouds. Should you go to the picnic, or should you stay inside? Explain.

2. How can clouds seen from the ground help people predict the weather? What kinds of information do weather satellites provide?

How Can Maps Help You Predict Weather?

You've probably used maps to find cities and streets. But you can also use a map to find out about weather. Investigation 2 will show you how.

Activity

MATERIALS
- weather maps
- *Science Notebook*

Weather Maps

How can a weather map be used to predict the weather? Find out in this activity.

Procedure

1. Look on weather map 1 for a high-pressure area, marked with the letter *H*. Find the same high-pressure area on map 2. Note whether the *H* is in the same place or if it has moved. If it has moved, note in what direction it moved. Now repeat this with map 3. In your *Science Notebook*, **describe** what happened to the high-pressure area over the three-day period.

2. Look on the weather maps for a low-pressure area, marked with the letter *L*. Note whether the *L* is in the same place on all three maps or if it moved. If it moved, note in what direction it moved. **Record** what happened to the low-pressure area over the three-day period.

WEATHER MAP SYMBOLS

	Rain
	Snow
	High Pressure
	Low Pressure
	Wind Direction
49/32	High and Low Daily Temperatures (°F)
	Clear Skies
	Partly Cloudy
	Cloudy
	Warm Front
	Cold Front

3. Look on map 1 for the lines with the little triangles and half circles. These lines show fronts. A **front** is a place where two masses, or areas, of air meet. Cold fronts are shown by the lines with triangles. Warm fronts are shown by the lines with half circles. Find the fronts on maps 2 and 3. Note whether the fronts are always in the same place or if they move. **Record** your observations.

4. **Predict** what weather map 4 will look like. **Draw** a picture of your prediction. Your teacher will give you a copy of weather map 4 so that you can check your prediction.

Analyze and Conclude

1. How do the locations of high-pressure areas, low-pressure areas, and fronts on weather map 4 compare with your prediction?

2. **Hypothesize** how weather maps can help you predict the weather.

UNIT PROJECT LINK

Make a wall chart of daily weather maps for your weather station. Each day, cut out the weather map from your local newspaper. Mount it on your wall chart. Compare that map with the map for the day before. Describe any changes.

Activity

Predicting the Weather

Earlier you made devices that measure weather conditions. Data from devices like these are used to make weather maps. You can use your devices to predict the weather.

MATERIALS

- thermometer
- barometer
- wind vane
- compass
- anemometer
- rain gauge
- crayons or colored pencils
- *Science Notebook*

Procedure

1. In your *Science Notebook*, **make a chart** like this one.

Date/Time	Weather Conditions	Measurement or Observations
	Temperature	
	Air pressure	
	Wind direction	
	Wind speed	
	Rain/sleet/snow	
	Cloud type	
	Cloud cover	
	Prediction for tomorrow	

2. Use your weather devices to **collect information** about temperature, air pressure, wind direction, wind speed, and amount of rain, sleet, or snow. **Record** your measurements and observations in your chart. Include the date and time.

Step 2

E60

3. **Observe** the types of clouds in the sky. **Record** your observations.

4. **Estimate** how much of the sky is covered by clouds. To **record** your estimate, **draw** a small circle on your weather chart. Then color in part of the circle to show how much of the sky is covered by clouds.

5. Use the information you collected and information from other sources, like newspaper weather maps, to **predict** tomorrow's weather. **Compare** your forecast, or prediction, with those of other students.

Analyze and Conclude

1. Listen to the radio, watch TV, or read a newspaper weather report to find out the weather forecast for tomorrow. How do your predictions compare with the forecast? If the forecasts do not agree, **hypothesize** about the reason for the difference.

2. Do you think it's possible to always tell exactly what the weather will be? Explain.

UNIT PROJECT LINK

For five days, use the weather devices in your class weather station to measure weather conditions. Use your observations and a weather map to predict the weather each day. Keep track of how often you make the correct prediction. Do your predictions improve over time?

Weather Wisdom

People have been predicting the weather since long before forecasts appeared on TV or in newspapers. But not everyone looks at devices such as barometers and thermometers. Instead, some people observe how plants and animals behave. Look at the map to see some of the signs people have used in different parts of the world to predict the weather.

UNITED STATES Some say if a groundhog sees its shadow on February 2, winter will continue for six more weeks.

ENGLAND The flowers of the scarlet pimpernel open in sunny weather and close up tightly before it rains.

JAPAN Some people hang strands of kelp, or seaweed. If rain is coming, the kelp swells and feels damp.

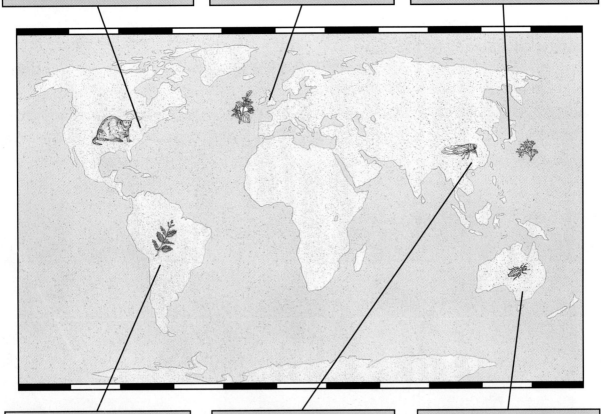

PERU If the leaves of this plant fold up an hour before sunset, the next day will be overcast and stormy.

CHINA In China there is a saying, "Hearing the cicadas in the rain foretells the coming of fine weather."

AUSTRALIA Some believe that if mound-building termites are very active, then wet weather is on the way.

Weather in the News

A **weather forecaster** is someone who makes predictions about the weather. Maybe you've heard a weather forecaster predict bright, sunny skies when, in fact, it rained all day. How do people predict the weather? Why is it such a tough job?

The Weather Detectives

Being a forecaster is a bit like being a detective trying to solve a mystery. First, the forecaster must gather clues, or information, about the current weather. The forecaster gets information from all over the world about such things as current wind speed and direction, cloud type, air pressure, moisture in the air, and temperature.

Once forecasters have gathered the information, they have to decide what the information means. They are like detectives who must sort through the many clues they have uncovered. Luckily, the forecaster gets to use computers to help solve the "mystery." All the different pieces of information are put into a computer. The computer then puts all the pieces together and produces different types of weather maps, like the ones shown below.

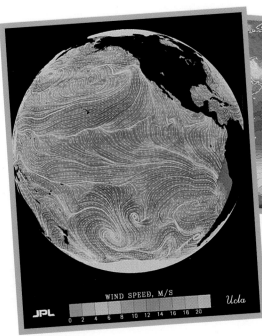

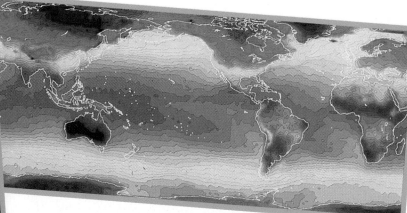

Weather forecasters use computer-generated maps like this wind map (*left*) and this temperature map (*above*).

Weather Clues

Think back to the weather map activity on pages E58 and E59. You found the symbols for cold fronts and warm fronts and high- and low-pressure areas. These areas and fronts are clues a weather forecaster uses to make a prediction. But what do these clues mean?

You know that air surrounds Earth. Now imagine that the air is divided into large bodies, or areas. Some of these areas are warm and others are cold. Each different body of air is called an air mass. An **air mass** is a body of air that has the same general temperature and air pressure throughout.

Often different air masses move so that they contact each other. A **front** is a place where two different types of air masses meet. A **cold**

COLD FRONT When the edge of a cold air mass comes in contact with the edge of a warm air mass, the cooler air pushes under the warm air, forcing the warm air mass to rise. Clouds form in the warm air as it is forced upward. ▶

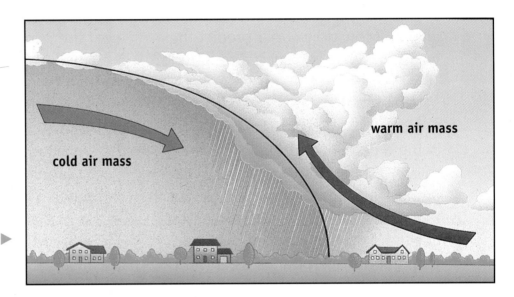

cold air mass

warm air mass

WARM FRONT When a warm air mass moves forward into a cold air mass, the warmer air rides up over the cooler air. Clouds form as the air rises and cools. ▶

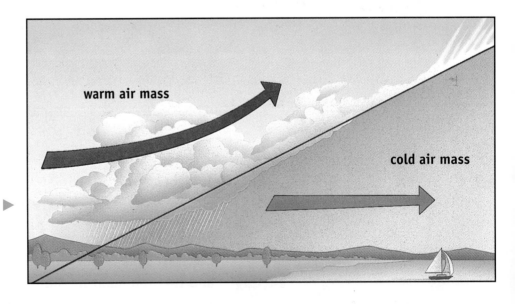

warm air mass

cold air mass

An approaching front darkens the sky and brings stormy weather. ▶

front forms when a cold air mass moves into a warm air mass. Cold fronts often produce thunderstorms. A **warm front** forms when a warm air mass moves into a cold air mass. Warm fronts often bring light rain.

Weather forecasters also look at air pressure to help them predict how the weather will change. In a high-pressure area, or high, the air pressure is higher than in the air surrounding it. High-pressure areas usually bring dry, clear weather.

In a low-pressure area, or low, the air pressure is lower than in the surrounding air. Low-pressure areas usually bring wind, clouds, and rain.

Now the forecaster has enough clues to help solve the mystery. So the forecaster can make a weather prediction. Weather predictions are not always correct. Sometimes the weather conditions change so quickly that the information the forecasters have isn't up-to-date. And sometimes the weather doesn't follow "normal" patterns.

Scientists are developing new ways to gather and study weather information. These new methods will help forecasters improve their weather predictions. ■

INVESTIGATION 2

1. Suppose you are a weather forecaster for your town. What data would you gather to make a prediction about the next day's weather?

2. What are four types of information that appear on weather maps?

HOW CAN YOU STAY SAFE DURING DANGEROUS WEATHER?

The weather may range from calm and quiet to stormy and even dangerous. In Investigation 3 you'll find out about different kinds of dangerous weather and how you can stay safe.

Activity

Storm Safety

In this activity find out how you can plan ahead and be prepared for severe weather.

Procedure

With your group, make a Weather Safety booklet. In your *Science Notebook* list the types of severe weather that may occur in your area. These may include thunderstorms, lightning, snowstorms, hurricanes, or tornadoes. Find out which radio and TV stations to listen to in case of severe weather and what safety measures you should take. **Record** what you learn in your Weather Safety booklet.

Analyze and Conclude

1. Where should you go if you are warned that severe weather is about to strike your area?

2. What things should you do or not do during severe weather?

ity

Tube

tornado? These dan-
can cause a lot of
ver seen a tornado,
you'll be mak-

MATERIALS

- 2 plastic soda
  bottles (2 L)
- water
- tornado tube
- *Science Notebook*

Step 3

E67

Light and
Sound Sh

KABOOM! You hear a sharp crack of thunder. A **thunderstorm** is a storm that produces heavy rain, strong winds, lightning, and thu Every year there are about lion thunderstorms arou These storms occur a and in places where ther is very hot an

kilo t

Stormy Weather

Thunderstorms h

Activ

Tornado

Have you ever seen a
gerous twisting storms
damage. If you have ne
don't worry. In this activit
ing a model of one.

- - - - - - - - - - - - - - - - - - -

Procedure

1. Fill a plastic soda bottle about two-thirds full of water.

2. Screw one end of a tornado tube onto the bottle. Make sure the end fits tightly. Then screw an empty bottle into the other end of the tube. Make sure it also is screwed in tightly.

3. Turn the bottle with the water in it upside down. Hold on to the tornado tube. Quickly move the bottles in five or six circles so the water inside swirls. **Observe** as the water drains from one bottle into the other. **Record** your observations in your *Science Notebook*.

Analyze and Conclude

1. **Describe** the motion of the water as it moved from one bottle to the other.

2. **Hypothesize** how the movement of air in a tornado is similar to the movement of air and water in your model.

meters above the surface make the air rise faster and higher than usual, forming cumulonimbus clouds, or thunderheads. A single thunderhead may be several kilometers wide and up to 10 km (6 mi) high.

Swirling winds within the clouds carry water droplets and ice crystals up and down several times. This action causes the droplets and crystals to grow in size. When the raindrops and ice crystals become large enough and heavy enough, rain or hail begins to fall.

ws a series of lightning flashes. ▼

Lightning and Thunder

Water and ice particles inside a thunderhead are thrown together by strong winds. This action produces static electricity. The energy from the static electricity is released as a flash of light and heat, called lightning. As a lightning bolt moves through the air, the air around it can become as hot as 30,000°C (54,000°F). This is more than five times as hot as the surface of the Sun!

When a lightning bolt flashes, it heats the air in its path. The air expands very rapidly causing the rumbling we call thunder.

Although you might not think so, lightning and thunder happen at the same time. But we see lightning before we hear thunder, because light travels faster than sound.

Thunderstorm Problems

Although thunderstorms cool the air and ground, they can also cause problems. Sometimes there is so much rain from a sudden thunderstorm that floods occur. Sudden and violent floods are called **flash floods**. Heavy rain or hail from thunderstorms can damage crops.

Lightning can injure and even kill people. It can cause fires. It can damage power lines and stop the flow of electricity. It can also interfere with radio and TV signals. ■

SCIENCE IN LITERATURE

PROFESSOR FERGUS FAHRENHEIT AND HIS WONDERFUL WEATHER MACHINE
by Candace Groth-Fleming
Illustrated by Don Weller
Simon & Schuster, 1994

The townsfolk of Dry Gulch are suffering from drought. There hasn't been a cloud in the sky for weeks. The mayor calls them together to discuss the matter. But what can they do about the weather? In walks a stranger who offers the impossible. He claims he can deliver rain to order—a drizzle or a downpour.

Find out what happens next when you read *Professor Fergus Fahrenheit and His Wonderful Weather Machine* by Candace Groth-Fleming. Be sure to read the "Author's Note" on the last page, where she explains who the rainmakers were.

Staying Safe in a Storm

In the past, people weren't able to predict when storms, hurricanes, or tornadoes would occur. But today, with the help of tools like weather satellites, scientists can better predict the weather.

Think back to the activity you did on page E66. What kinds of safety precautions did you include for thunderstorms, hurricanes, and tornadoes? Here are some more precautions you should follow.

STAYING SAFE DURING A FLASH FLOOD

Flash floods are sometimes the result of heavy thunderstorms or hurricanes. There are a couple of things you can do to keep yourself safe during a flood.

- Stay away from rivers, streams, and creeks. Water in these bodies can move very quickly.

- Don't try to walk or drive through water if you can't see the ground beneath the water.

- If a flood occurs, move to higher ground as quickly as possible.

STAYING SAFE FROM LIGHTNING

When lightning is occurring in your area, follow these rules.

- If you are outside, stay away from tall trees and buildings. Lightning usually strikes the tallest objects in an area.

- Avoid metal objects, such as metal baseball bats and umbrellas. These objects can attract lightning.

- Don't take a bath or shower or touch electrical appliances. Water, metal pipes, and metal wires can carry the electricity from lightning.

In the Tucson mountains in Arizona, a flash flood turns a dry arroyo, or gully (*left*), into a dangerous rush of muddy water (*below*).

STAYING SAFE DURING A HURRICANE

If you are caught in a hurricane, here are some things you can do.

- Get as far away from ocean beaches as possible. The huge waves produced by hurricanes are very dangerous.
- Stay inside in a basement, under a stairwell, or in another sheltered area.
- Stay away from windows. Glass can break in hurricane winds and injure people.
- Listen to local TV and radio stations for additional information.

STAYING SAFE DURING A TORNADO

If a tornado is sighted in your area, follow these precautions.

- If you are outside, try to stay in a ditch or other low area. This will help protect you from flying objects.
- If you are inside, try to stay in a basement or a storm cellar. If there is no basement or storm cellar, stay in a closet or bathroom.
- Stay away from windows and doors that lead outside. These can be blown apart by the winds of a tornado.

The Fiercest Storms on Earth

What are hurricanes and tornadoes? What causes these storms? Why are they known as the fiercest storms on Earth?

Hurricanes—The Largest Storms

Hurricanes have different names in different parts of the world. In the Pacific Ocean they are typhoons, in the Indian Ocean they are cyclones, and in Australia they are willy-willies. **Hurricanes** are large, violent storms that form over warm ocean water.

To be called a hurricane, the storm must have winds of at least 117 km/h (74 mph). Some hurricanes have winds of more than 240 km/h (150 mph)! Look back at the Beaufort scale on page E39. How does the Beaufort scale describe hurricanes?

Hurricanes start out as small thunderstorms over an ocean. Several of these storms may join to form a larger storm. This storm grows bigger as it takes in heat and moisture from the warm ocean water. As the storm grows, the wind increases. This causes

These satellite photos of Hurricane Andrew show the storm's location as it moved from Florida to Louisiana. The photos were taken over a three-day period in August 1992. ▼

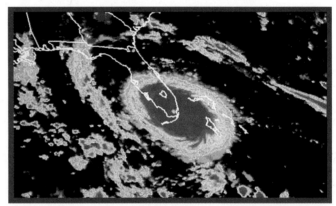

the clouds to spin. The diagram below explains how a hurricane forms.

In the middle of a hurricane is a hole, called the eye of the hurricane. Within the eye the weather is calm. There is little wind and no rain. Sometimes people are fooled into thinking that a hurricane is over when the eye is overhead. But it isn't over. The other half of the storm is on its way.

Hurricanes are the largest storms on Earth. The storm can cover an area as wide as 600 km (360 mi). This area is five times bigger than Washington, D.C.

Hurricanes on the Move

Once a hurricane forms, it begins to travel. As it moves, the winds blow harder. The winds can rip trees out of the ground and blow the roofs off houses. The winds can also produce giant ocean waves as tall as a house. These waves can wash away beaches and sink boats. The rain from a hurricane can also cause flooding.

Luckily, hurricanes don't last very long once they reach land. When the storm moves over land or over cold ocean water, it loses its source of energy and dies down.

4 A circular wall of clouds with heavy rains and strong winds develops around the eye. As the warm air moves up, it spreads out.

5 In the eye the air sinks slowly, the winds are light, and there are no clouds.

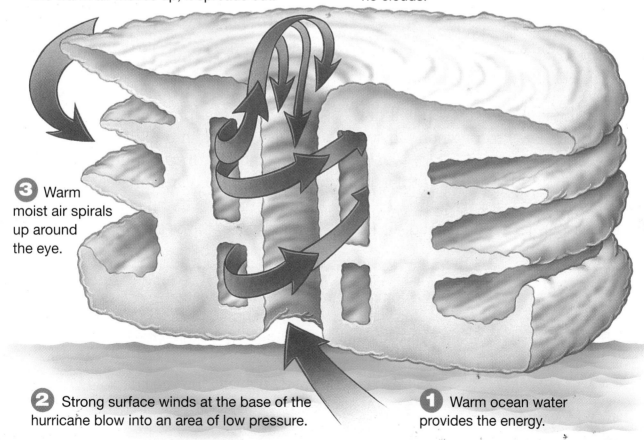

3 Warm moist air spirals up around the eye.

2 Strong surface winds at the base of the hurricane blow into an area of low pressure.

1 Warm ocean water provides the energy.

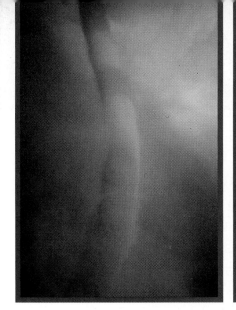

▲ **A tornado may skip across the ground like someone playing leapfrog. Whatever it touches is likely to be destroyed.**

Twister!

Sometimes a thunderstorm gives birth to a tornado. A **tornado**, sometimes called a twister, is a funnel-shaped storm of spinning wind. Think back to the activity on page E67. The shape of the spinning water is the same shape as a tornado. But unlike the water in the bottle, the air in a tornado spins upward.

Tornadoes can develop without warning. They form when a column of warm air begins to spin. As air flows up into this swirling column, it spins very fast, forming the well-known funnel-shaped cloud.

Even though tornadoes don't cover as much area as hurricanes, they can be just as dangerous. The speed of the winds in the center of a tornado can be as high as 500 km/h (300 mph). This is twice the speed of the winds in the worst hurricane!

In tornadoes the air pressure is very low. The strong winds blowing into these low-pressure areas can sweep objects into the tornado, including dirt, trees, and roofs of buildings. The winds may be strong enough to move and destroy large trees, cars, trains, and houses. ■

INVESTIGATION 3

1. Compare hurricanes and tornadoes. What are some ways in which the two types of storms are similar? What are some ways in which they are different?

2. Describe the safety precautions you should take if you are caught outside during a thunderstorm.

REFLECT & EVALUATE

WORD POWER

air mass
cirrus clouds
cold front
cumulus clouds
flash flood
front
hurricane
stratus clouds
thunderstorm
tornado
warm front
weather forecaster
weather satellite

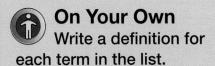 **On Your Own**
Write a definition for each term in the list.

With a Partner
Use the terms in the list to make a word-search puzzle. See if your partner can find the hidden terms and tell you what each one means.

Make a poster of safety guidelines for one type of dangerous weather.

Analyze Information

Study the drawing. Then explain how hurricanes form.

Assess Performance

Work with a group to create a radio or TV weather forecast. Gather the information you need to make your forecast. When you present your forecast to the class, explain how you made your prediction.

Problem Solving

1. Suppose you want to predict the next day's weather, but you don't have any weather devices. How can clouds help you make the prediction?

2. What are some of the uses of weather forecasts? What are some of the problems with them? Describe five types of information that a forecaster uses to make a forecast.

3. Describe two safety precautions people can take for each of the following types of dangerous weather: thunderstorms, hurricanes, and tornadoes.

SEASONS AND CLIMATE

Do you live in the northern part of the United States? If so, you may go sledding in winter and swimming in summer. If you live in southern California or Florida, you may not have as great a change between seasons. But every place on Earth has seasons.

To Name the Moon

The Algonquins, a Native American people, gave a name to each full moon to keep track of the seasons. According to the Algonquins, spring begins when the crows first return, in the month we call March. That is the time of the Crow Moon. April is the month of the Sprouting Grass Moon. At the peak of spring is the Flower Moon.

In June comes the Strawberry Moon. The heat of summer begins the Thunder Moon, and August is time for the Sturgeon Moon. Summer ends with the Harvest Moon. October's moon is the Hunter, and chilly November is the month of Frost Moon. The winter brings Long Nights Moon, then the howling winds of Wolf Moon. By February, food is scarce. That month's moon is named Hunger.

In this chapter you'll investigate seasons and climate. How would you name the moon for the seasons where you live?

Coming Up

◀ This Algonquin uses a shaving horse to prepare wood for making harvest baskets.

WHAT CAUSES THE SEASONS?

Which activities do you like to do in summer? in winter? How do the differences in weather during summer and winter affect what you do? In Investigation 1 you'll find out what causes summer and winter!

Activity

Sunshine Hours

Find out if the number of hours of sunlight changes from season to season.

- - - - - - - - - - - - - - - -

Procedure

1. The table shows the times the Sun rises and sets in the middle of each month. **Interpret the data** in the table to **predict** whether the number of hours of sunlight is greater in winter or in summer. **Discuss** your prediction with your group, then **record** it in your *Science Notebook*.

2. Using graph paper, set up a graph like the one shown. Note that *Time of Day* should be on the left side and *Month of Year* should be along the bottom. Then **make a graph** using the data in the table.

Sunrises and Sunsets (Standard Time) for the Middle of Each Month		
Month	**Sunrise (A.M.)**	**Sunset (P.M.)**
Jan.	7:20	5:00
Feb.	6:55	5:34
Mar.	6:11	6:07
Apr.	5:23	6:38
May	4:44	7:09
June	4:31	7:30
July	4:44	7:27
Aug.	5:12	6:56
Sept.	5:41	6:09
Oct.	6:11	5:20
Nov.	6:45	4:44
Dec.	7:15	4:36

SUNSHINE HOURS

3. On your graph, mark a dot to show the time the Sun rises for each month. Connect the dots.

4. Mark another dot to show the time the Sun sets for each month. Connect these dots.

5. Use a yellow crayon to color the space between the two lines on your graph paper. Keep the graph in your *Science Notebook*.

Analyze and Conclude

1. What does the yellow space on your graph represent?

2. Interpret your graph. Are the number of hours of sunlight greater in summer, or in winter? **Compare** your results with your prediction.

3. Use the data on your graph to **infer** why the temperature of the air in the summer tends to be higher than the temperature of the air in the winter.

Changing Seasons

▲ **How do the changing seasons affect what you do?**

It's the first day of summer! You and your friends are planning a trip to the nearest swimming pool. At the same time, students your age in Australia are spending the first day of winter in school. How can it be summer in one part of the world and winter in another? And why are there different seasons at all?

The Tilting Earth

As Earth moves, or revolves, around the Sun, different places on Earth's surface are heated differently by the Sun. To understand why this happens, imagine Earth has a line running through it, like the one shown in the picture on page E81. This imaginary line is called Earth's **axis** (ak'sis).

The Earth spins, or rotates, around its axis. It takes Earth about 24 hours, or one day and night, to complete this turn.

There is a second imaginary line that circles the middle of Earth. This line is called the **equator** (ē kwāt'-ər). Find the equator on the picture on page E81. The half of Earth that is above the equator is called the

Northern Hemisphere. The half below the equator is called the **Southern Hemisphere**.

When Earth revolves around the Sun, its axis is not straight up and down. Instead, Earth's axis is tilted slightly. The tilt of Earth's axis stays almost the same throughout a year. So as Earth revolves around the Sun, sometimes the Northern Hemisphere is tilted toward the Sun, and sometimes it is tilted away from the Sun.

AXIS Earth's axis is an imaginary line that runs from the North Pole through Earth's center to the South Pole.

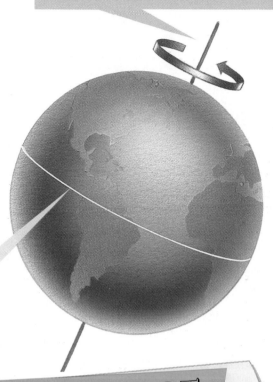

EQUATOR The equator divides Earth into the Northern Hemisphere and the Southern Hemisphere.

SCIENCE IN LITERATURE

THE THIRD PLANET
EXPLORING THE EARTH FROM SPACE
by Sally Ride and
Tam O'Shaughnessy
Crown Publishers, 1994

Imagining how Earth moves in space is hard to do. So is imagining how Earth looks from space. In *The Third Planet: Exploring the Earth From Space* by astronaut Sally Ride and author Tam O'Shaughnessy, you'll find out how the rotation of Earth allows a satellite to take pictures of many views of our planet.

You'll see how Earth's atmosphere gets thinner as it reaches into space. You'll learn that the best way to predict a hurricane is from above. And you'll see how drought affects the living things of North Africa. Share an astronaut's sense of wonder at how our planet works.

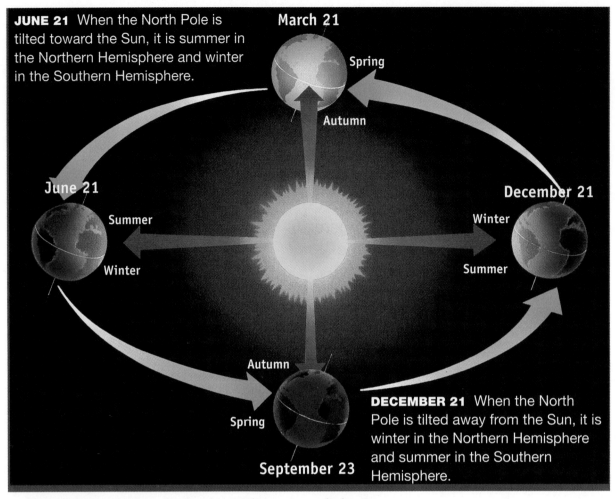

JUNE 21 When the North Pole is tilted toward the Sun, it is summer in the Northern Hemisphere and winter in the Southern Hemisphere.

March 21

Spring

Autumn

June 21

Summer

Winter

December 21

Winter

Summer

Autumn

Spring

DECEMBER 21 When the North Pole is tilted away from the Sun, it is winter in the Northern Hemisphere and summer in the Southern Hemisphere.

September 23

▲ The seasons change as Earth revolves around the Sun.

UNIT PROJECT LINK

Use your weather station to collect data for a two-week period during different seasons of the year. Compare weather data such as high and low temperatures, amounts of precipitation, and air pressure for each of the seasons. Discuss the patterns in seasonal weather you observe for your location.

Seasons in the Sun

Study the picture above. As Earth revolves around the Sun, there are changes in the way the Sun's rays strike Earth's surface. These changes cause the temperature of Earth's surface and atmosphere to change. This leads to the change in seasons.

Remember that the tilt of Earth's axis does not change much. What *does* change is the position of the axis in relation to the Sun's position.

The picture on page E83 shows that during the winter, sunlight

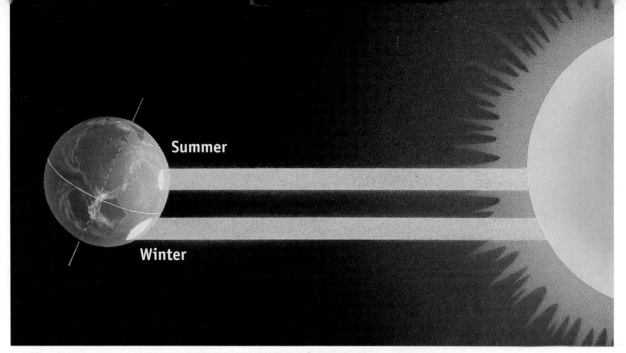

▲ **The Sun's rays strike Earth at a greater slant during winter.**

strikes Earth at a slant. When light strikes at a slant, it spreads out and covers more area. The greater the slant, the less the ground in this area is heated. This is the main reason why temperatures are colder in winter than in summer.

In summer, sunlight strikes Earth more directly. The light does not spread out as much and covers less area than it does in winter. So the ground is heated more. This is the main reason why temperatures are warmer in summer.

The number of hours of daylight also affects the temperature. When the North Pole is tilted toward the Sun, the Sun is high in the sky, and there are more hours of daylight. The longer the Sun shines on an area, the more energy can be absorbed and the warmer the temperatures can become.

When the North Pole is tilted away from the Sun, the Sun is low in the sky, and there are fewer hours of daylight. Because the Sun has less time to heat Earth's surface, temperatures are cooler. In the activity on pages E78 and E79, which season, according to the graph, has the most hours of daylight? ■

INVESTIGATION 1

1. Give two reasons why the Sun heats Earth more in summer than it does in winter.

2. Make a drawing to show the positions of the Northern Hemisphere in summer and in winter. Be sure to include the Sun in your picture.

WHAT FACTORS AFFECT CLIMATE?

Climate is the average weather conditions of a place over a long period of time. In Investigation 2 you'll find out what factors cause Earth to have different climates.

Activity

Microclimates Everywhere!

Temperature and wind are important factors in determining climate. Find out if two places close to each other can have different climates.

MATERIALS
- cardboard tube
- aluminum foil
- rubber band
- meterstick
- thermometer
- wind vane
- magnetic compass
- *Science Notebook*

SAFETY
Be careful when handling thermometers.

Procedure

1. In your *Science Notebook*, **make a chart** like the one shown.

Building Side	Temperature (°C)	Wind Direction

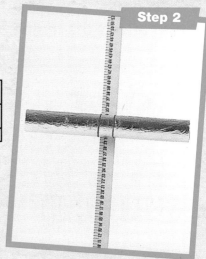

Step 2

2. Cover the outside of a cardboard tube with aluminum foil. Fasten the tube to a meterstick with a rubber band as shown. Move the tube so that the lower edge of the tube is at the 30-cm mark.

3. **Predict** whether temperature and wind direction will be the same, or different, on each of the sides of your school building.

4. Take a thermometer and a wind vane outside your school. Stay close to one side of the building and **measure** the temperature 30 cm from the ground. **Determine** the wind direction, too. **Record** this data in your chart.

5. Repeat step 4 for the other sides of the building. **Record** all data in your chart.

Step 4

Analyze and Conclude

1. **Compare** your prediction in step 3 with your results. What differences, if any, did you find on different sides of your school?

2. Different sides of a building have different microclimates. *Micro-* means "very small." From your study, how would you **define** *microclimate*?

3. Which microclimate was the warmest? Which was the coolest? **Infer** why temperature would vary on different sides of the building.

4. Was the wind direction different on different sides of the building? What factors would affect the way the wind blows on one side of your school building?

INVESTIGATE FURTHER!

EXPERIMENT

Hypothesize what would happen if you repeated this experiment over a longer period of time. Would the same sides of the building always be windier or warmer than others? Discuss your predictions with your group. Repeat the experiment once a month for the next three months. How did your predictions compare with your results?

Florida Is Not North Dakota

What is the weather in your area normally like in the summer? What is it like in the winter? People in different parts of the world will have different answers to these questions. That's because different places have different climates. The **climate** of an area is the average weather conditions over a long period of time.

POLAR CLIMATE In the Arctic and Antarctic, the temperature is usually below freezing. These areas do not receive as much energy from the Sun as other parts of Earth.

TEMPERATE CLIMATE Between the equator and the poles are areas that generally have warm, dry summers and cold, wet winters.

TROPICAL CLIMATE The places closest to the equator are usually hot and rainy for most of the year. Temperatures are high because these areas receive the most energy from the Sun.

E86

Hot or Cold, Wet or Dry

Two important parts of an area's climate are its average temperature and its average yearly rainfall. The average temperature of an area depends a great deal on how far the area is from the equator. In general, areas close to the equator are warmer than areas farther from the equator. For example, North Dakota is farther from the equator than Florida is, so North Dakota is usually colder than Florida.

The map below shows the location of three main types of climates. They are polar, tropical, and temperate.

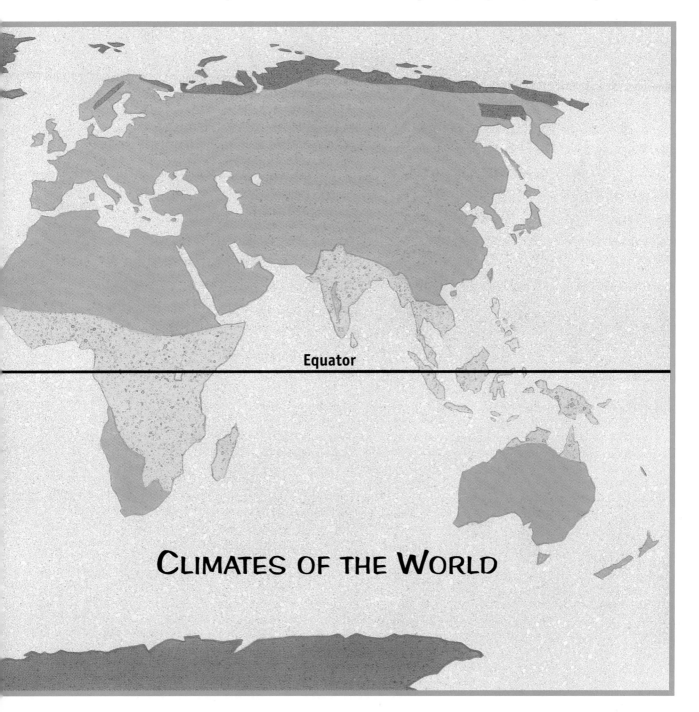

Equator

CLIMATES OF THE WORLD

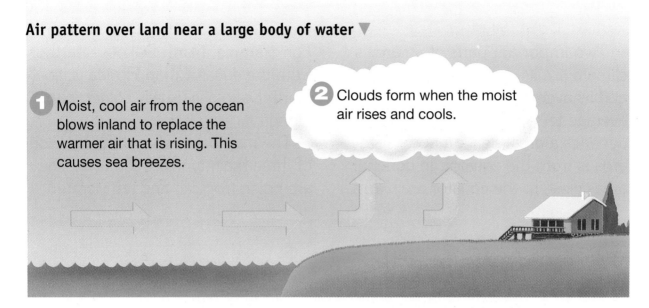

1 Moist, cool air from the ocean blows inland to replace the warmer air that is rising. This causes sea breezes.

2 Clouds form when the moist air rises and cools.

Areas with a **tropical climate** are usually hot and rainy year-round. Areas with a **temperate climate** generally have summers that are warm and dry and winters that are cold and wet. Areas with a **polar climate** are usually very cold. Which climate do you think you live in?

Climate Controls

Think back to the activity on pages E84 and E85, in which you investigated microclimates around your school building. What factors affected the temperature of an area? What factors affected the way the wind was blowing in an area?

Just as certain things affect micro-climates, certain features, such as oceans and mountains, can affect the climate in an area. In the diagrams on this page and the next, you can see why features such as oceans and mountains affect climate.

Air pattern over plains ▼

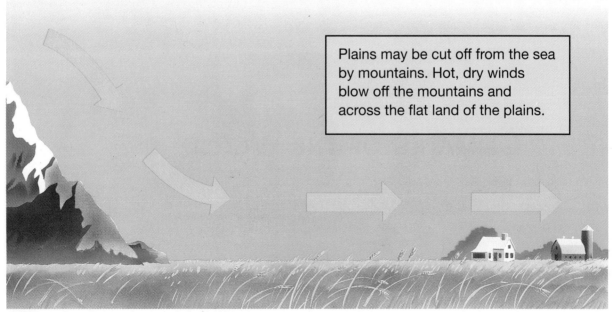

Plains may be cut off from the sea by mountains. Hot, dry winds blow off the mountains and across the flat land of the plains.

If you live near an ocean or large lake, your climate may be cloudier and wetter than the climate of places farther from the water. The summers in your area may be cooler, and the winters may be warmer.

An area in the middle of the plains or far from any large body of water will likely have a different climate. These areas probably will have little rain, hot summers, and cold winters.

If you live near a mountain on the side least protected from the wind, your area may often have strong winds and lots of rain. But if you live near a mountain on the side most protected from the wind, your climate will probably be dry. ■

INVESTIGATE FURTHER!

RESEARCH

Locate San Francisco, California, and Wichita, Kansas, on a map of the United States. Both cities are about the same distance from the equator. Record whether each city is near a large body of water. Predict which city will have a greater change in the average daily temperature from January to June. Compare your prediction with the data that appears in an almanac. What can you infer about the effect that being near water has on weather conditions?

Air pattern over a mountain ▼

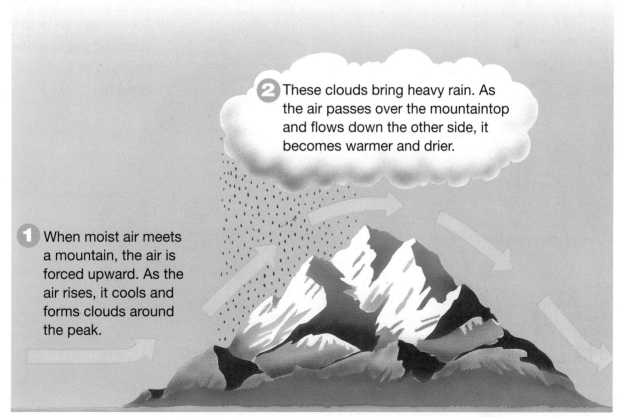

2 These clouds bring heavy rain. As the air passes over the mountaintop and flows down the other side, it becomes warmer and drier.

1 When moist air meets a mountain, the air is forced upward. As the air rises, it cools and forms clouds around the peak.

Clues to Earth's Climate

The world's climate has gone through many changes. These changes have lasted from just a few years to thousands of years. Scientists who study Earth's climate look for clues to find out why these changes in climate have taken place.

Tree Rings

One way that scientists learn about climate changes is by studying trees. Most trees grow a new ring every year. You can see the tree rings in the picture. If a ring is wide, the weather affecting that tree was probably moister and warmer than normal that year. If a ring is narrow, the weather was probably drier and colder than normal that year. By studying tree rings, scientists can track warm and cold periods several thousand years into Earth's past.

◀ Tree rings can help scientists determine changes in Earth's climate.

▲ Finding fossils in unexpected places may indicate changes in Earth's climate.

Fossil Clues

A second place in which scientists can find clues about climate is in fossils. Fossils are imprints or remains of animals and plants that lived in the past. Sometimes, scientists find fossils in unusual places. This kind of finding can be a clue that the climate in an area has changed. For example, some fossilized camel bones were found in the Arctic. But camels usually live in hot desert areas. Scientists hypothesize that these fossils show that the Arctic was once much warmer than it is now. Fossils can give clues to what Earth's climate was like millions of years ago.

Ice Cores

A third method that scientists use to find out about past climates is to drill holes in glaciers and pull out long columns of ice, or ice cores. Scientists then analyze these ice cores. Finding traces of certain chemicals can give clues about past climate changes. The scientist in the photo is wearing surgical clothing to keep the ice core from getting dirty.

Covered in Ice

Great changes in Earth's climate usually occur very slowly. At times, Earth has been much warmer than it is now. At other times, Earth has been much colder than it is now, and ice sheets covered large areas of the world. These cold periods are called **ice ages**. The last ice age ended about 10,000 years ago. During that time, ice sheets covered much of Earth's land, including large parts of the United States! ■

▲ A scientist saws off a piece of an ice core for testing.

Weather Records

Have you ever thought that a certain rainstorm was the worst one you'd ever seen? Or, on a hot day, have you ever thought that it couldn't get any hotter? Imagine what it would be like to live some- place that had no rain for 400 years. Think about how you would feel to live someplace that only gets sunlight for half of the year. Find out where these places are as you read about some of the windiest, wettest, driest, hottest, and coldest places on Earth!

The Windiest Place
- Winds coming off Commonwealth Bay, Antarctica, can reach 320 km/h (200 mph).

The Fastest Wind Gust
- A wind speed of 415 km/h (231 mph) was recorded on April 12, 1934, on Mount Washington in New Hampshire. This area is known for unpredictable and dangerous weather.

Mount Washington, New Hampshire ▶

STOP
THE AREA AHEAD HAS THE WORST WEATHER IN AMERICA. MANY HAVE DIED THERE FROM EXPOSURE, EVEN IN THE SUMMER. TURN BACK NOW IF THE WEATHER IS BAD.
WHITE MOUNTAIN NATIONAL FOREST

The Coldest Place
- Polus Nedostuphosti (Pole of Cold), Antarctica, has an average temperature of −58°C (−72°F). This area near the South Pole gets sunlight for only about half the year.

The Lowest Temperatures
- The lowest recorded temperature on Earth was −88°C (−127°F) in Vostok, Antarctica, on July 22, 1983.
- In the United States a low temperature of −62°C (−80°F) was recorded on January 23, 1971, in Prospect Creek, Alaska.

South Pole, Antarctica ▶

The Hottest Place
- Dallol, Ethiopia, has an average temperature of 34°C (94°F). Dallol is very close to the equator and is shielded from the Indian Ocean by mountains.

The Highest Temperatures
- The highest temperature recorded on Earth was in Al'Aziziyah, Libya, where the temperature reached 58°C (136°F) on September 13, 1922.
- The highest temperature recorded in the United States was 57°C (134°F) on July 10, 1913, in Death Valley, California.

◀ Death Valley, California

The Wettest Places

- Mawsynram, in India, has about 1,186 cm (467 in.) of rainfall per year.
- The state of Louisiana averages 142 cm (56 in.) of rainfall per year.

   In these areas the warm, wet winds blow in off the water. As the winds blow over the land, the air rises and cools. This creates thick clouds and heavy rains.

The Greatest Rainfall

- In one day, from March 15 through March 16, 1952, nearly 187 cm (74 in.) of rain fell in Cilaos, on the island of Réunion, in the Indian Ocean.

▼ **Mawsynram, India**

The Atacama Desert, Chile ▲

The Driest Places

- Arica, Chile, averages less than 0.01 cm (0.004 in.) of rainfall per year. Chile is near very cold water, so the winds blowing toward land are usually dry and don't form many clouds.
- In the state of Nevada, about 23 cm (9 in.) of rain falls per year. Much of Nevada is sheltered from ocean winds by the Sierra Nevada, a mountain range. The winds that come down from the mountains contain little water vapor.

The Longest Dry Spell

- Desierto de Atacama (the Atacama Desert) in Chile had almost no rain for 400 years! This dry spell ended in 1971.

INVESTIGATION 2

THINK IT WRITE IT

1. What are the two main factors that affect the climate of an area? Discuss the three different types of climates.

2. Suppose you live near mountains and your friend lives near a large body of water. Describe what type of climate each of you would be likely to have.

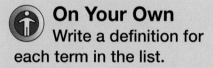
WORD POWER

axis
climate
equator
ice ages
Northern Hemisphere
polar climate
Southern Hemisphere
temperate climate
tropical climate

On Your Own
Write a definition for each term in the list.

With a Partner
Mix up the letters of each term in the list. Provide a clue for each term, and challenge your partner to unscramble the terms.

BUILD YOUR PORTFOLIO

Make a poster that uses words and pictures to describe the three main types of climates. Show what it would be like to live in each climate.

Analyze Information

Study the drawing. In your own words, explain how the tilt of Earth's axis and the slant of the Sun's rays cause the seasons.

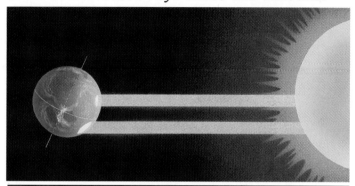

Assess Performance

Design a model to show Earth's revolution around the Sun. Show how your model can be used to demonstrate change in seasons.

Problem Solving

1. Imagine that you and a friend live in different cities. The cities are the same distance from the equator, but they have very different climates. What are some of the factors that might explain this difference?

2. Explain why it is usually warmer in the United States in June than it is in January.

3. Antarctica is the coldest continent on Earth. In the summer the temperature inland usually ranges from −15°C to −35°C (5°F to −31°F). Explain why Antarctica is so cold year-round.

Throughout this unit you've investigated questions related to weather and climate. How will you use what you've learned and share that information with others? Here are some ideas.

Hold a Big Event
to Share your Unit Project

Invite other classes and your parents to visit your classroom. With your group, give weather forecasts like the ones seen on TV. If possible, ask someone to videotape the forecasts. Take your visitors on a tour of your weather station. Demonstrate how each instrument works and explain how your instruments are similar to the ones used by professional weather forecasters.

Research

Find out more about one of the topics in this unit. If you're interested in "state-of-the-art" weather forecasting, do research about the National Weather Service. This government service uses computers, weather balloons, satellites, and other new technology.

Take Action

Share what you've discovered about weather safety with other classes in your school. Display your storm safety posters and explain why these precautions are necessary.

Experiment

Plan a long-term project based on an activity in this unit. You may want to use your weather station to practice predicting the weather. Have a contest to see who is the most accurate weather forecaster in your class.

UNIT F

THE BODY'S DELIVERY SYSTEMS

Theme: Systems

GET READY TO

OBSERVE & QUESTION

How do diseases spread?

How is it that you can feel great one day but become sick the next? Tiny living things all around you can make you sick. Luckily, things you do keep you from getting sick and help fight disease if you do get sick. For example, to stay healthy, you should get regular exercise. What else should you do to keep your body systems healthy?

EXPERIMENT & HYPOTHESIZE

How does the respiratory system work?

Take a deep breath. Now let it out. How much air can you hold in your lungs? Do a hands-on activity to find the answer to this question. Then learn how you can make a model that shows how the lungs work.

INVESTIGATE!

RESEARCH & ANALYZE

As you investigate, find out more from these books.

- ***SURE HANDS, STRONG HEART: The Life of Daniel Hale Williams*** by Lillie Patterson (Silver Burdett Ginn, 1995). In 1893 the phrase "Sewed Up His Heart!" became closely associated with the name of Dr. Daniel Hale Williams. Read about this amazing African American doctor in this book.

- ***Body Science*** by Anita Ganeri (Dillon Press, 1992). Have you ever wanted to know why running makes you pant or gives you a "stitch" in your side? Well, now you can find out in this fascinating book on the human body.

WORK TOGETHER & SHARE IDEAS

How can you plan a Body Maze Quiz Show?

Working together, you'll have a chance to plan and produce a question-and-answer quiz show, complete with commercials. Throughout this unit, look for the Unit Project Links to help you write quiz-show questions about the body's delivery systems.

CHAPTER 1

THE INS AND OUTS OF BREATHING

Your breathing occurs so automatically that you probably don't even think about it. But that's not the case if you have a bad cold. Then you're very aware of your breathing, because it's so difficult. How do you breathe? What happens to the air you breathe in?

Lifeguards Wanted

Have you ever envied those lifeguards at the pool or beach? It may seem that they earn money by simply sitting around. But that's not so.

Every summer, junior lifeguard training programs take place along the beaches of the United States. The programs are open to boys and girls from ages 9 to 17. The training includes push-ups and sit-ups as well as long beach runs and long-distance swims. Lifeguards must be in good condition to rescue a swimmer struggling in the ocean.

Young lifeguards must learn some basic first aid for treating cuts and cramps. They also learn how to give CPR—a procedure that can help a person start breathing again. In this chapter you'll find out more about the ins and outs of breathing.

Coming Up

◀ A volunteer from the American Red Cross gives CPR training to a junior lifeguard.

F5

INVESTIGATION **1**

WHAT HAPPENS WHEN YOU BREATHE?

Take a deep breath. Hold it. Now let it out. Where does the air go that you breathe in? In Investigation 1 you'll learn how you breathe and what happens when you do.

Activity

MATERIALS
- tape measure
- *Science Notebook*

Breathe In and Out

Do this activity and observe what happens to your body when you breathe in and out.

- - - - - - - - - - - - - - - - - -

Procedure

Predict how the size of your chest changes as you breathe in and out. Record your prediction in your *Science Notebook*. Then put a tape measure around your chest. Measure the size of your chest after you breathe in and again after you breathe out. Record your measurements. Find the difference between the two numbers. Compare your results with those of others.

Analyze and Conclude

How did your chest size change when you breathed in? How did it change when you breathed out? What causes these differences? What other changes occur as you breathe?

Activity

Breathing Rates

MATERIALS
- chair
- timer
- *Science Notebook*

How often do you breathe in during one minute? This number is your breathing rate. What things can affect your breathing rate? Find out by doing this activity.

Procedure

1. Find your breathing rate at rest. Sit in a chair in a relaxed position. Have a group member set a timer for one minute. Breathe normally. **Count** how many times you breathe in during one minute. **Record** this number in your *Science Notebook*.

2. **Predict** how your breathing rate will change if you sit bent over with your chest to your knees. **Record** your prediction.

3. **Count** and **record** how many times you breathe in during one minute while you are bent over with your chest to your knees.

4. **Predict** how exercise will affect your breathing rate. **Record** your prediction.

5. Run in place for one minute. Then **count** and **record** how many times you breathe in during one minute.

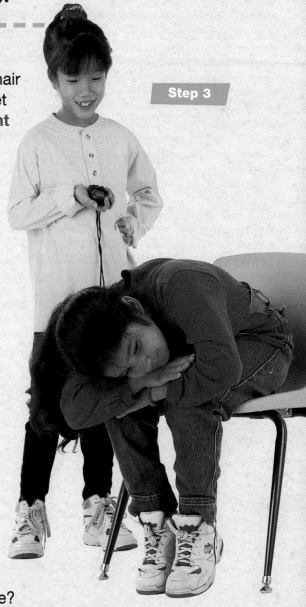

Step 3

Analyze and Conclude

1. How did sitting in a bent-over position affect your breathing rate? **Infer** why this position affected your breathing.

2. How did exercise affect your breathing rate? **Infer** why exercise had this effect.

3. **Hypothesize** about other things that could affect your breathing rate. Explain your ideas.

Activity

A Breathing Machine

Without special devices you can't look inside your chest to observe how your lungs work. But you can make a working model of a lung in this activity.

Procedure

1. Work with a group to **build a model** of a lung. Pull the opening of a small balloon over one end of a drinking straw. Use tape to attach the balloon to the straw.

2. Cut the neck off a large balloon. Stretch the balloon over the cut end of a bottle. Secure the balloon with tape.

3. Push the end of the straw with the small balloon into the mouth of the bottle. Then use modeling clay to seal the mouth of the bottle and to hold the straw in place.

4. **Predict** what will happen to the small balloon when you pull down and push up on the large balloon. **Record** your prediction in your *Science Notebook*.

5. **Observe** what happens when you pull down and then push up on the large balloon. **Make drawings** of your observations.

Step 3

Analyze and Conclude

1. What happened to the small balloon when you pulled down on the large balloon? What happened when you pushed up?

2. Based on observations of your model, **hypothesize** what happens in your body when you breathe.

Breathing Basics

How long can you stay underwater? You have to come up for air after only a short time. That's because your body needs oxygen (äks'i jən), one of the gases in the air. But your body can't store oxygen the way it stores fat. You have to take in fresh air all the time. And you must let out the "used air" before taking in another breath. **Breathing** is what your body does when it takes in fresh air, containing oxygen, and lets out the used air.

The body parts that work together to bring air into and push it out of your body make up the **respiratory** (res'pər ə tôr ē) **system**. Look at the drawing below of the respiratory system as you read about how this body system works.

Air Enters

What happens after you take a breath through your nose? First, your nose both warms and moistens the air. Small hairs inside the nose trap dust and other particles in the air. Then the clean air moves from your nose to the back of your throat. There the air enters the windpipe.

THE RESPIRATORY SYSTEM

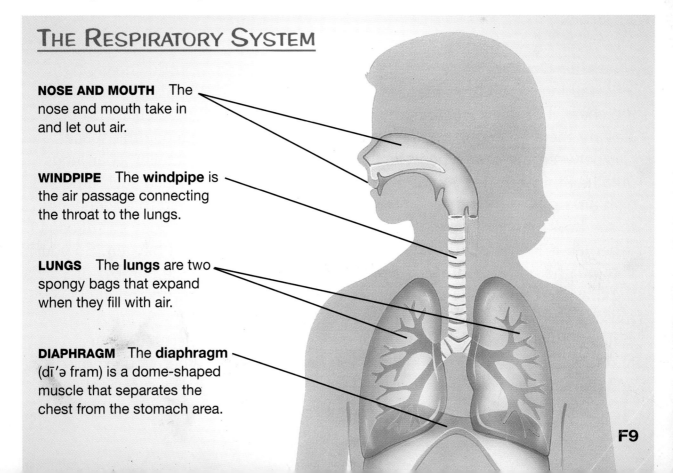

NOSE AND MOUTH   The nose and mouth take in and let out air.

WINDPIPE   The **windpipe** is the air passage connecting the throat to the lungs.

LUNGS   The **lungs** are two spongy bags that expand when they fill with air.

DIAPHRAGM   The **diaphragm** (dī'ə fram) is a dome-shaped muscle that separates the chest from the stomach area.

F9

INHALING

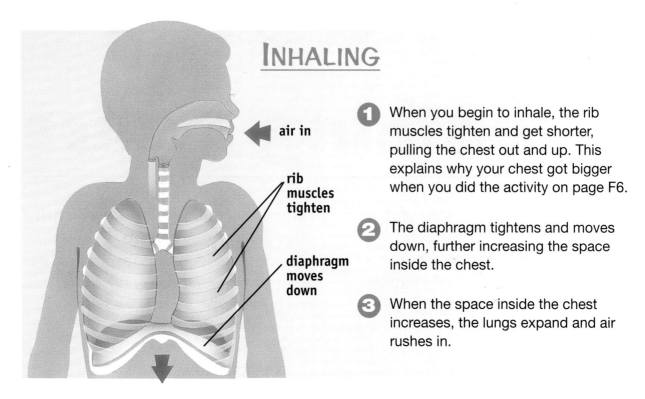

air in

rib muscles tighten

diaphragm moves down

① When you begin to inhale, the rib muscles tighten and get shorter, pulling the chest out and up. This explains why your chest got bigger when you did the activity on page F6.

② The diaphragm tightens and moves down, further increasing the space inside the chest.

③ When the space inside the chest increases, the lungs expand and air rushes in.

Feel your windpipe by gently moving your hand up and down the front of your neck. The bumps are rings of **cartilage** (kärt′′l ij), a tough but bendable body material. Because cartilage makes the windpipe stiff, your windpipe doesn't collapse when you breathe in.

Muscles Do the Work

Breathing depends on muscles in the chest. The main breathing muscles are the diaphragm and the muscles between the ribs. When you breathe in, or **inhale,** your lungs fill with air. Look at the drawing above to see how muscles help you inhale. When air is forced out of the lungs, you breathe out, or **exhale.** Look at the drawing on page F11 to see how muscles help you exhale.

The model you made in the activity on page F8 shows how the lungs and diaphragm work. When you pull

down on the large balloon, the small balloon inflates, or fills with air. This happens because you make more space in the bottle for air. Compare how your model works to how your diaphragm and lungs work.

Breathless!

Sometimes you change the space inside your chest just by changing your position. What happened when you bent over in the activity on page F7? Because you made the space inside your chest smaller, your lungs couldn't fill up as much each time you inhaled. You had to breathe faster because your body still needed the same amount of oxygen. So your **breathing rate**, the number of times you inhale in one minute, increased.

Exercise also increases your breathing rate. When you exercise, your body uses up its supply of

EXHALING

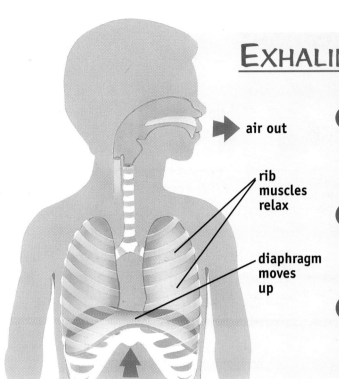

air out

rib muscles relax

diaphragm moves up

1 When you begin to exhale, the rib muscles relax and get longer and the chest gets smaller.

2 The diaphragm relaxes and moves up, making less space inside the chest.

3 Air is forced out of the lungs as the space in the chest gets smaller.

oxygen more quickly. The only way to get more oxygen into your body is to breathe faster and more deeply.

Exercise is good for you because it makes your breathing muscles work harder and become stronger. ■

SCIENCE IN LITERATURE

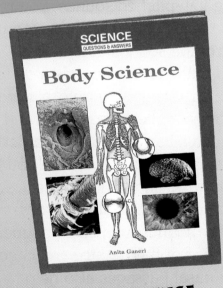

BODY SCIENCE
by Anita Ganeri
Dillon Press, 1992

Did you know that . . .

- Someone had a sneezing fit that lasted over 2 years?

- One man had an attack of hiccups that lasted 70 years?

- A cough moves at about 96 km/h (60 mph)?

These are some of the amazing facts found in *Body Science* by Anita Ganeri. And if you're wondering what sneezing, hiccuping, and coughing have to do with breathing, you'll find that out, too!

Give a Yell!

Your lungs aren't just for breathing. Whenever you talk, laugh, sing, or yell, you also use your lungs. And you use other body parts.

Can you feel a lump in your throat that goes up when you swallow? This is your larynx (lar'iŋks), or voice box. Sometimes it's called the Adam's apple. Because the larynx is at the top of the windpipe, all the air you breathe passes through it.

Vocal Point

If you touch your fingers to your throat while you are speaking or singing, you can feel the movement of your vocal cords. The vocal cords are two elastic bands inside the larynx. Look at the close-up drawing on page F13 to see the larynx and the vocal cords inside it.

Sing High, Sing Low

How do you control the sounds you make? Look again at the drawing of the larynx. Two vocal cords stretch across the inside of the larynx. When you breathe normally, the vocal cords are relaxed and V-shaped, letting air pass through. To make sounds, you tighten the vocal cords. They move closer together, so the opening between them is smaller. Then air is pushed out of the lungs and through the larynx. Air passes between the vocal cords and makes them vibrate. These vibrations produce sound.

Catch the Pitch

Have you ever pulled the neck of an inflated balloon so that it squeaks as the air goes out? If you pull the neck of the balloon tighter, the sound gets higher in pitch. The same sort of thing happens in your larynx.

To make high-pitched sounds, you tighten your vocal cords. Then they vibrate faster as air goes past. To make low-pitched sounds, you relax your vocal cords. How else can you control the sounds you make?

To make louder sounds, you force more air through your vocal cords. In normal speech, you relax and tighten your vocal cords in order to make different sounds. Can you talk without moving your tongue? Probably not. You shape words and change sounds with your tongue, lips, roof of the mouth, and cheeks. Your nasal passages also help to change sounds. What happens when you pinch your nose while you are talking?

How You Make Sounds

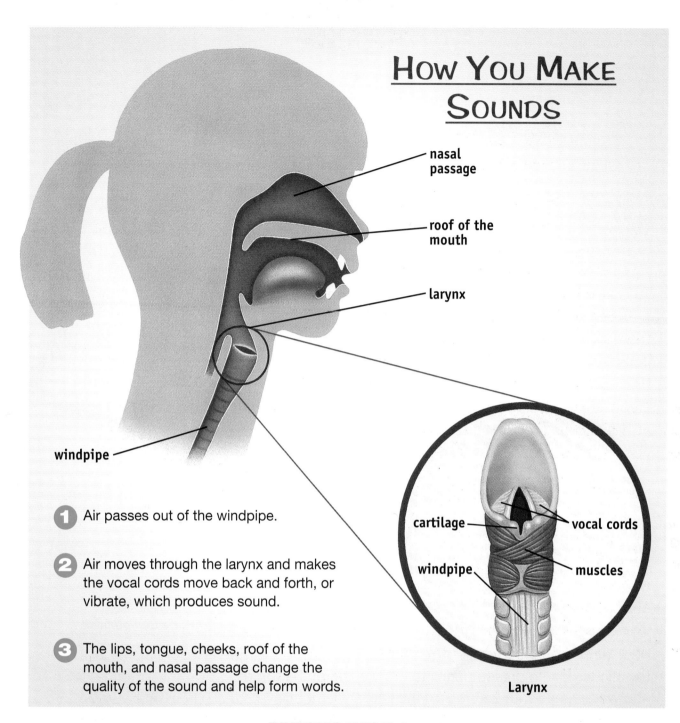

- nasal passage
- roof of the mouth
- larynx
- windpipe

1 Air passes out of the windpipe.

2 Air moves through the larynx and makes the vocal cords move back and forth, or vibrate, which produces sound.

3 The lips, tongue, cheeks, roof of the mouth, and nasal passage change the quality of the sound and help form words.

- cartilage
- vocal cords
- windpipe
- muscles

Larynx

INVESTIGATION 1

1. Describe how air is forced into and out of your lungs as you inhale and exhale. Explain the role of the diaphragm in this process.

2. In women, the larynx is usually smaller and the vocal cords are shorter than in men. Explain how this affects the sounds of women's voices and of men's voices.

HOW DOES THE RESPIRATORY SYSTEM WORK?

INVESTIGATION 2

Air is made up of several gases, but oxygen is the only one your body needs. Your lungs make it possible for your body to take oxygen out of the air and get rid of waste gases. In Investigation 2 you'll learn how the lungs do their work.

Activity

Take a Deep Breath

When you breathe in, you can feel your lungs fill up. How much air can your lungs hold? Try this activity and you'll find out!

Procedure

1. Work with your group. Add 250 mL of water to a large plastic jar. Use a grease pencil to draw a line at the top of the water line. Write *250 mL* on the line.

2. Repeat step 1, but write *500 mL* on the second line. Continue adding water and marking the jar until you have 3,500 mL of water in the jar.

3. Add enough water to fill the jar to the very top. Then fill a dishpan half full with water.

4. Put the lid on the jar. With the help of group members, turn the jar upside down in the pan of water. Remove the lid as a group member steadies the jar.

Step 2

F14

Step 4

5. Put one end of a length of rubber tubing into the jar. Place a drinking straw in the other end of the tubing. Tape the straw to the tubing. Each group member should use his or her own straw.

6. **Predict** how much air you exhale in a normal breath. **Record** your prediction in your *Science Notebook*.

7. Take a normal breath and then exhale through the straw. **Record** about how much air you exhaled.

8. Refill the jar. Repeat steps 2 through 6, but this time take a deep breath. Again **record** how much air you exhaled.

Analyze and Conclude

1. What forces the water out of the jar? Explain how forcing the water out allows you to measure the volume of air you exhale. Volume is the amount of space something takes up.

2. How does the volume of your normal breath of air compare with the volume of your deep breath?

3. **Hypothesize** whether the volume of your deep breath is equal to the total amount of air your lungs can hold.

INVESTIGATE FURTHER!
....
EXPERIMENT
How does exercise affect the amount of air you exhale? Run in place for one minute. Then measure how much air you exhale. Record this volume and compare it with your normal volume. Share your results with your classmates.

Gas Exchange

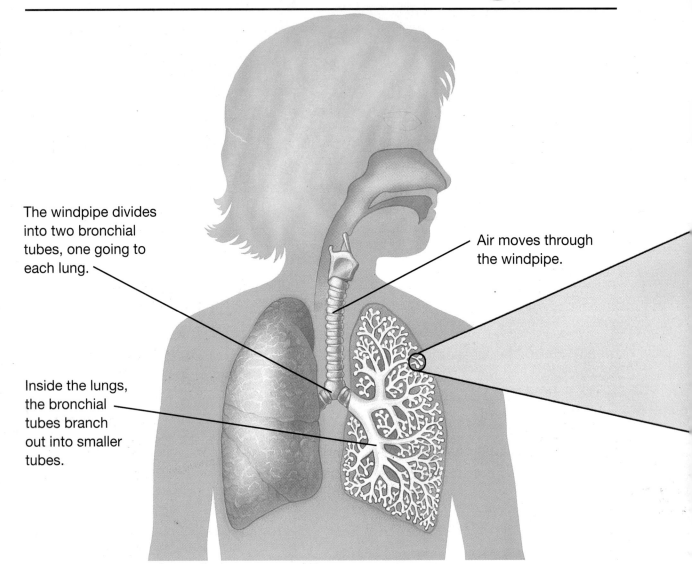

The windpipe divides into two bronchial tubes, one going to each lung.

Inside the lungs, the bronchial tubes branch out into smaller tubes.

Air moves through the windpipe.

You've learned how your lungs fill with air. The next step is getting oxygen out of the air and into your bloodstream. This part of breathing happens inside the lungs. The lungs are really no more than bags that fill with air when you inhale. They also absorb, or take in, oxygen from the air and get rid of waste gases.

When You Inhale

Look at the drawings on this page and on the next. Follow the path air takes once you've inhaled.

When you inhale, air moves from the windpipe to the two **bronchial tubes**. It ends up in the air sacs. The **air sacs** are chambers that have very thin walls. They are surrounded by tiny thin-walled blood vessels called capillaries (kap'ə ler-ēz). The oxygen in the inhaled air passes through the thin walls of the air sacs and into the capillaries, where it enters the bloodstream. The millions of tiny air sacs in each lung provide lots of surface area for absorbing oxygen.

cells use oxygen and give off carbon dioxide is called **respiration**.

Gas In, Gas Out

How does your body get rid of carbon dioxide? Carbon dioxide moves out of the cells and into the bloodstream. Blood carries carbon dioxide to the capillaries that surround the air sacs of the lungs. Look at the drawing to see how carbon dioxide and oxygen are exchanged in the air sacs.

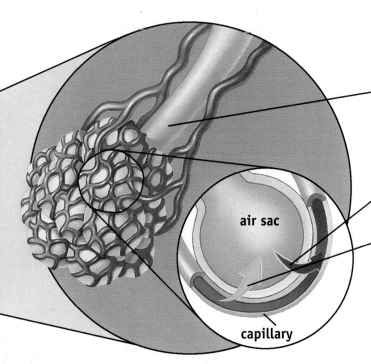

The smallest tubes are thinner than hairs and open into air sacs.

Oxygen moves from the air sac into the capillary.

Carbon dioxide moves from the capillary into the air sac.

air sac

capillary

◀ **Carbon dioxide and oxygen are exchanged in the air sacs.**

Releasing Energy

Oxygen is carried by the bloodstream to every cell of the body. The **cell** is the basic unit that makes up all living things. In the body cells, oxygen joins with materials from digested food, releasing energy. The cells need energy to do their jobs.

When energy is released, carbon dioxide and water vapor are given off as waste gases. Carbon dioxide is a colorless gas found in the air and in living things. The process by which

INVESTIGATE FURTHER!

· ·

RESEARCH

Find out why your nose runs and what causes a sneeze. Read the book *Why Does My Nose Run? (And Other Questions Kids Ask About Their Bodies)* by Joanne Settel and Nancy Baggett.

When You Exhale

After oxygen and carbon dioxide have been exchanged in the air sacs, your breathing muscles force the waste gases out of your lungs. When you exhale, carbon dioxide and water vapor from your lungs go up the bronchial tubes. These waste gases pass through the windpipe and leave the body through your nose or mouth. After you've exhaled, some air always remains in your windpipe, bronchial tubes, and air sacs.

Recall from the activity on pages F14 and F15 that the amount of gases you exhaled depended on how deeply you inhaled. Recall also that different people's lungs are different sizes. The amount of air people can inhale varies from person to person.

▲ **Yawning is one way to get more oxygen to the blood.**

Controlling Your Breathing

Too much carbon dioxide in your blood can be harmful. Sensors in some blood vessels act like watchdogs. If sensors show a high level of carbon dioxide in your blood, they send a signal to the part of your brain that controls respiration. As a result, you breathe more quickly or more deeply. Yawning is another way your body responds to a high level of carbon dioxide in the blood.

Of course, *you* can control your breathing, too. You can make yourself take big or small breaths. And you can breathe faster or slower. But you don't need to remember to breathe. You breathe all the time, whether or not you think about it. ■

UNIT PROJECT LINK

As you move through this chapter, think of some challenging quiz questions about the parts of the respiratory system and how the respiratory system works. Record the questions and their answers. Then use other resources to find out some new things about the respiratory system. Write some true-false or multiple-choice questions about this new information.

Why You Hiccup

Sometimes your breathing muscles seem to have a mind of their own! One unhappy surprise you can get from them is a case of hiccups.

How You Hiccup

When you breathe normally, your diaphragm tightens in one smooth movement. But when you have hiccups, the diaphragm goes on the blink and contracts, or tightens, suddenly. And it usually happens over and over again.

The sudden contraction of a muscle is called a spasm (spaz'əm). Each time the diaphragm contracts in this way, air is sucked into your lungs quickly. Look at the drawing below to see how you hiccup.

HOW YOU HICCUP

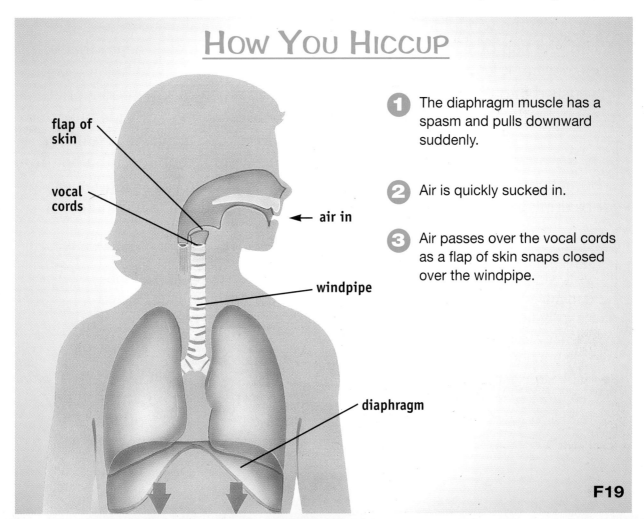

flap of skin

vocal cords

← air in

windpipe

diaphragm

1 The diaphragm muscle has a spasm and pulls downward suddenly.

2 Air is quickly sucked in.

3 Air passes over the vocal cords as a flap of skin snaps closed over the windpipe.

Breathing into a bag

Eating a spoonful of sugar

Which methods have you used to stop hiccups?

The *hic* noise of a hiccup comes partly from a flap of skin as it closes suddenly over your vocal cords. It's the same flap of skin that automatically covers the windpipe when you swallow. This flap keeps food from going down the windpipe. When you hiccup, the flap of skin acts like a safety device. It keeps food from getting sucked into your lungs if you hiccup when you're eating.

Is It Something You Ate?

Sometimes hiccups start when you eat or drink too much too fast, causing a sudden stretching of the stomach. Hiccups can also start if you swallow air when you laugh or cry.

Hiccups are a normal part of life. Luckily, most attacks of hiccups last only a few minutes. You've probably heard of several ways to cure hiccups. Have you ever heard that you can get rid of them by holding your breath? When this method works, it's because carbon dioxide builds up in the blood. This buildup can stop hiccups. But if that doesn't work, try to relax. Hiccups usually go away by themselves after a few minutes. ■

INVESTIGATION 2

1. When people get sick with pneumonia (noō-mōn′yə), liquids build up in their air sacs. Based on what you've learned, how can pneumonia affect respiration?

2. What happens during respiration? How do body cells get oxygen? How do wastes from body cells get to the lungs?

REFLECT & EVALUATE

WORD POWER

air sac   diaphragm
breathing   exhale
breathing rate   inhale
bronchial tube   lungs
cartilage   respiration
cell   windpipe
respiratory system

On Your Own
Write a definition for each term in the list.

With a Partner
Use the terms in the list to make a word search puzzle. Trade puzzles with your partner.

BUILD YOUR PORTFOLIO

Make a labeled diagram to show the pathway of air when you inhale and when you exhale. Include air sacs and capillaries in your diagram.

Analyze Information

Study the drawing. Then describe how sounds are produced when you talk or sing.

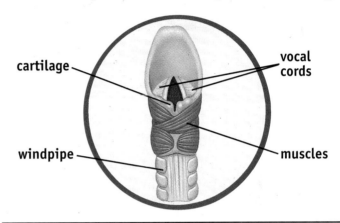

Assess Performance

Plan an activity to measure and compare the breathing rates of people of different ages. After your teacher has reviewed your plan, carry it out. Make inferences about any differences you find. Compare your results and inferences with those of your classmates.

Problem Solving

1. Your nose is lined with hairs. How do these hairs help protect your lungs?

2. Why do people get the air knocked out of their lungs when they fall down hard?

3. When people have an asthma attack, the tiny tubes in their lungs that lead to the air sacs tighten and swell. How do you think this condition affects breathing?

2

MOVING AND REMOVING MATERIALS

Your body is like a busy machine. New materials are constantly coming into your body. Waste materials that are produced in all parts of your body need to be removed. What body system moves materials throughout your body? What body system works to get rid of wastes? Find out in Chapter 2.

Saving at the Blood Bank

Materials that keep a person alive are carried through the body by blood. When someone is ill or injured, the person may need to receive extra blood. The blood often comes from a blood bank.

Every day about 40,000 units of blood are needed by people in the United States. The blood centers of the American Red Cross supply about half of this blood. Before blood is given to anyone, it's tested. The Red Cross wants to make sure the blood is free of disease.

Florence Paau is the supervisor of blood testing at the Red Cross laboratory in Columbus, Ohio. She has a daughter, Alexis, who is five years old. Every few weeks Alexis needs to receive a unit of blood to keep her healthy. Florence Paau and workers like her who test blood want to make sure that Alexis and others receive healthy blood.

◄ Florence Paau, supervisor of blood testing, and daughter Alexis

F23

HOW DOES BLOOD FLOW THROUGH YOUR BODY?

Your body contains an amazing network of tubes called blood vessels. How does blood move through this huge network? You'll learn the answer in Investigation 1.

Activity

MATERIALS
• rubber ball
• timer
• *Science Notebook*

Pump On!

How hard does a human heart work to pump blood? Try this activity and find out!

Procedure

Squeeze a rubber ball hard, and then release it. **Predict** how many times you can squeeze the ball in one minute. **Record** your prediction in your *Science Notebook*. While a group member times you, count how many times you can squeeze the ball in one minute. **Record** the number. Next, try to squeeze the ball 70 times in one minute. See how long you can continue at that rate. **Record** your results.

Analyze and Conclude

1. On average, the heart beats about 70 times per minute. How long could you squeeze the ball at the rate of 70 squeezes per minute without stopping?

2. What does this activity tell you about the heart?

Activity
Pulse Point

MATERIALS
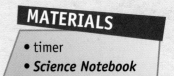
- timer
- *Science Notebook*

You've learned that the average person's heart beats about 70 times each minute. Find out how hard your own heart is working and what factors affect it.

- -

Procedure

1. Find your pulse (puls) in your wrist, as shown. The **pulse** is the throbbing you can feel in a blood vessel caused by the beating of the heart.

2. **Count** how many times your heart beats in 15 seconds. **Multiply** that number by 4 to get your heartbeat rate for one minute. **Record** your heartbeat rate in your *Science Notebook*.

3. **Predict** whether your heartbeat rate will change if you exercise. **Record** what you think the rate for one minute will be after exercising.

4. Run in place for one minute. Immediately afterward, **calculate** your heartbeat rate as you did in step 1. **Record** this rate.

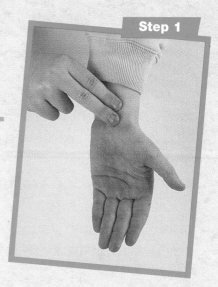
Step 1

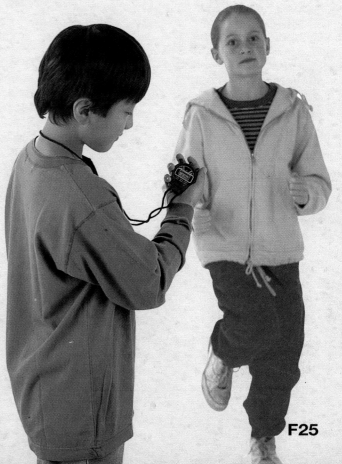
Step 4

Analyze and Conclude

1. **Compare** your heartbeat rate before and after exercise. How does it compare with your prediction?

2. **Infer** why exercise would cause changes in your heartbeat rate.

3. **Hypothesize** about other things that could affect your heartbeat rate. Tell why you think these things would affect heartbeat rate.

The Circulatory Story

Your body has a transport system made up of a network of tubes called blood vessels. Blood vessels are like one-way highways that transport materials in a loop around your body. Look at the picture. The movement of blood through your body is called **circulation** (sɤr kyoo lā'shən).

Blood is pushed through the blood vessels by the **heart**, a muscular body part about the size of your fist. The **circulatory** (sɤr'kyoo lə tôr ē) **system** includes the heart, blood vessels, and the blood. They work together to carry food and oxygen to cells and to carry wastes from cells.

BODY CIRCULATION

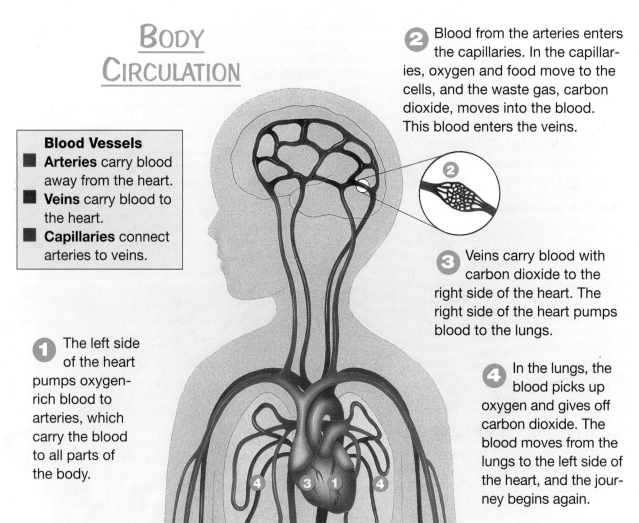

Blood Vessels
- **Arteries** carry blood away from the heart.
- **Veins** carry blood to the heart.
- **Capillaries** connect arteries to veins.

2 Blood from the arteries enters the capillaries. In the capillaries, oxygen and food move to the cells, and the waste gas, carbon dioxide, moves into the blood. This blood enters the veins.

3 Veins carry blood with carbon dioxide to the right side of the heart. The right side of the heart pumps blood to the lungs.

1 The left side of the heart pumps oxygen-rich blood to arteries, which carry the blood to all parts of the body.

4 In the lungs, the blood picks up oxygen and gives off carbon dioxide. The blood moves from the lungs to the left side of the heart, and the journey begins again.

CIRCULATION THROUGH THE HEART

1 Between heartbeats, the heart relaxes and both atriums fill up with blood.

2 When the atriums contract, blood is forced from the atriums through one-way openings. The right atrium pumps blood into the right ventricle. The left atrium pumps blood into the left ventricle.

3 When the ventricles contract, blood is pumped out of the heart. The right ventricle pumps blood to the lungs. The left ventricle pumps blood to the rest of the body.

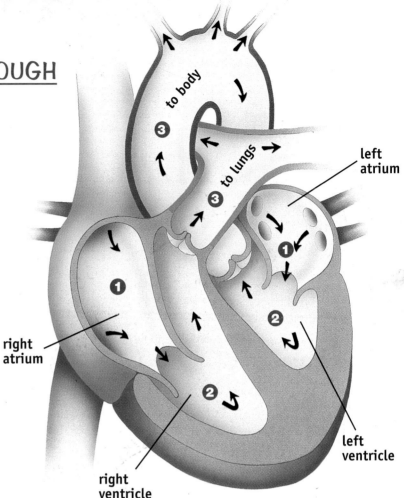

to body

to lungs

left atrium

right atrium

right ventricle

left ventricle

Heart—The Power Organ

The heart provides the force that makes the circulatory system work. Look at the picture above. Notice that the heart is divided into two halves. Each half has an upper chamber, called an **atrium** (āˈtrē-əm), that receives blood. Each atrium is connected to a lower chamber, called a **ventricle** (venˈtri kəl), that pumps blood out.

Each half of the heart works as a separate pump to send blood along two different paths. The heart chambers contract, or squeeze, which keeps the blood moving. Follow the path of blood through the heart.

Your heart beats about 100,000 times in just one day. Why doesn't your heart get tired like you do after exercising? Think back to the activity on page F24. The muscles in your hand probably got tired squeezing the ball. Your heart doesn't get tired because it's made of a different kind of muscle from the kind that moves your hand.

Muscles need oxygen to work. When you overwork your hand muscles, for example, the oxygen supply can't keep up with the demand. When that happens, your hand gets tired. However, your heart gets oxygen with every breath you take.

F27

The Blood-Vessel Highway

The blood vessels form a closed loop through which the heart pumps blood. There are three kinds of blood vessels—arteries, veins, and capillaries. Arteries have thick, muscular walls. They have to be able to stretch when the heart pumps blood into them with great force. The arteries branch many times into smaller and smaller arteries.

The smallest arteries lead into capillaries. The capillaries have such thin walls that gases and nutrients can pass through them into the cells. The capillaries lead to the smallest veins. Veins become larger and larger as they go back to the heart.

You can feel your heart beating when you feel your pulse. The **pulse** is the throbbing caused by blood rushing into the arteries each time the ventricles contract. The arteries expand and contract as blood rushes through them. You can feel a pulse wherever arteries are close to the skin, such as at the wrist.

Was your pulse rate higher after you exercised during the activity on page F25? When your muscles work harder, they need more energy to keep contracting. Your muscle cells use oxygen as they work. When your muscles work harder, your heart pumps blood faster. Then your muscles can get more oxygen.

SCIENCE IN LITERATURE

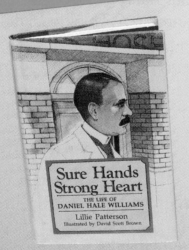

SURE HANDS, STRONG HEART
THE LIFE OF DANIEL HALE WILLIAMS
by Lillie Patterson
Illustrated by David Scott Brown
Silver Burdett Ginn, 1995

The newspaper headline read, "Sewed Up His Heart." The year was 1893, and the hero of the day was Daniel Hale Williams. Dr. Williams did what most other doctors dared not to do. He cut open a man's chest to repair a tear in the covering of the patient's heart.

Read about this remarkable doctor and his accomplishments, including being the first African American to start a new hospital. The life story of "Doctor Dan" is well told in *Sure Hands, Strong Heart* by Lillie Patterson.

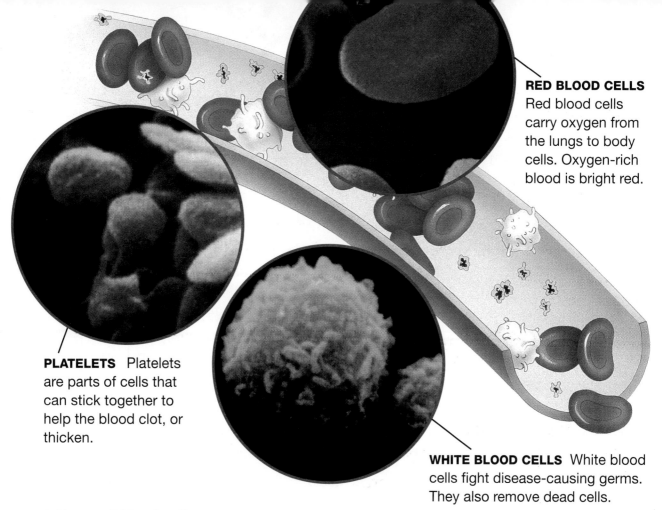

RED BLOOD CELLS
Red blood cells carry oxygen from the lungs to body cells. Oxygen-rich blood is bright red.

PLATELETS Platelets are parts of cells that can stick together to help the blood clot, or thicken.

WHITE BLOOD CELLS White blood cells fight disease-causing germs. They also remove dead cells.

▲ Types of blood cells

Liquids and Solids in Blood

Blood is a tissue made up of several types of cells and a liquid called plasma. The solid part of blood includes three different kinds of cells—red blood cells, white blood cells, and platelets. The blood cells float in the liquid part of blood called plasma. Plasma is mostly water, but it also contains nutrients, wastes, and chemicals the body needs. The pictures above describe the job done by each type of blood cell.

Your blood has many different jobs. It delivers nutrients and oxygen to your cells and carries away wastes. Your blood also fights infections and helps with clotting. It helps keep your body temperature steady by taking heat from more active parts of your body and bringing it to cooler parts. The blood can do all these jobs because the heart circulates blood through the body. ■

INVESTIGATE FURTHER!

RESEARCH

Find out how exercise improves the respiratory and circulatory systems. Read the book *Arnold's Fitness for Kids Ages 11–14* by Arnold Schwarzenegger with Charles Gaines.

Heart of the Matter

Early doctors performed limited surgery. They had little knowledge about the inside of the body. Today, with modern tools, doctors have learned more about the circulatory system than early scientists could ever have dreamed of. Study the time line to find out how this knowledge has grown.

William Harvey, an English doctor, shows that blood flows away from the heart in arteries. He also demonstrates that the heart pumps blood in a circle around the body.
A.D. 1628

The Chinese write that blood flows in a circle and is controlled by the heart. They think some blood vessels carry air.
ABOUT 2600 B.C.

1816
Rene Laennec, a French doctor, listens to the heart with a wooden tube, the first stethoscope.

ABOUT 150 B.C.
Galen, a doctor in ancient Rome, learns that the heart is made of muscle and that arteries carry blood, not air. He thinks that blood moves from one side of the heart to the other through holes.

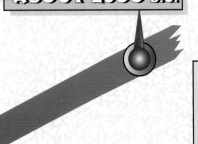

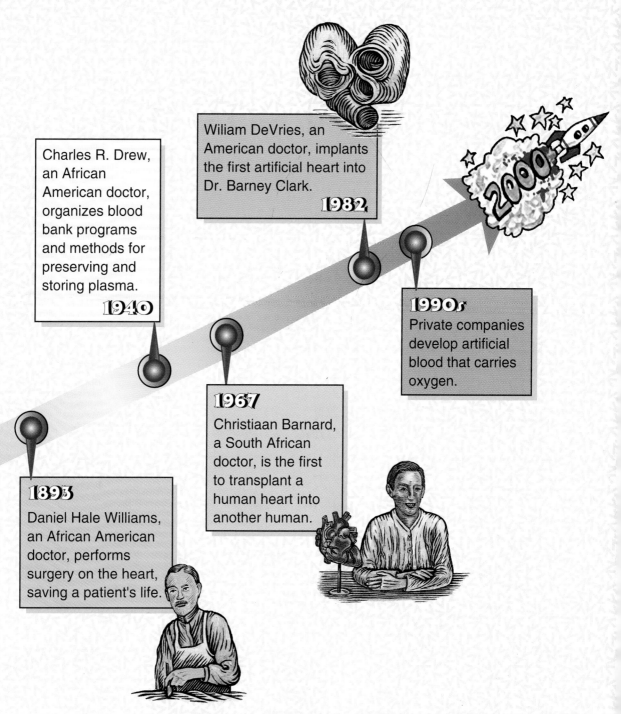

Charles R. Drew, an African American doctor, organizes blood bank programs and methods for preserving and storing plasma.

1940

Wiliam DeVries, an American doctor, implants the first artificial heart into Dr. Barney Clark.

1982

1990s
Private companies develop artificial blood that carries oxygen.

1967
Christiaan Barnard, a South African doctor, is the first to transplant a human heart into another human.

1893
Daniel Hale Williams, an African American doctor, performs surgery on the heart, saving a patient's life.

2000

UNIT PROJECT LINK

As you move through this chapter, think of quiz questions about the parts and workings of the circulatory and excretory systems. Write some true-false or multiple-choice questions. Record the questions and the answers to them. Save your questions for the Big Event.

G-Force

 Imagine you're an astronaut returning to Earth from space. It could be a thrilling experience, as long as the G's don't get you! G's can cause problems for your circulatory system.

What's a G?

A G is a unit of force equal to the force put on your body by Earth's gravity. You may already know that gravity is the force of attraction between two bodies because of their mass. When you sit in a chair, you push into the chair with a force that is the same as Earth's gravity. This amount of force is equal to your weight. It is referred to as 1 G.

If you're in a car or plane when it goes faster or turns, you can feel a force pushing you. Then you're beginning to feel more than 1 G, but only slightly more.

Pilots feel G-forces, too. A pilot feels twice as much force at 2 G's than at 1 G. And the pilot feels twice as heavy. These effects increase as the G's build. From 4 G's to 6 G's, the pilot can start to black out, or faint.

Astronauts feel very strong G-forces as they return to Earth. In

▲ **Astronauts wear anti-G suits to lessen the effect of G-forces when returning to Earth.**

fact, the G-forces are so strong that there is a very great danger of the astronauts fainting.

Anti-G Suit

How do G's cause pilots and astronauts to black out? An increase in G's causes blood to collect in the pilot's lower body. It's difficult for this blood to get back to the heart. That's because so much force is pulling the blood downward. When this happens, the brain doesn't receive enough blood. Too little blood to the brain causes the pilot to black out.

Astronauts and pilots have a way to delay blackouts. They do this by tightening the muscles around their stomach and by leaning backwards. This action prevents the blood from collecting in the large blood vessels around the stomach. But for very high G-forces, they wear anti-G suits. These suits increase pressure on the stomach and legs.

How does an anti-G suit work? As the G-forces increase, the anti-G suit is inflated. This can happen automatically, or the suit can be inflated by the pilot. The squeezing force of the suit pushes the blood out of the legs and back toward the heart. Then the heart can pump enough blood to the brain so that the pilot won't black out. The suit can get so tight that it's hard for the wearer to talk in a normal voice. ■

This test pilot is wearing an anti-G suit. ▼

A Medical Mystery

Why would a medical treatment work well in one part of the world and have mixed results in another? This medical mystery stumped scientists until they learned more about blood.

The mystery begins more than 500 years ago with the Incas. The Incas were people who lived along the western coast of South America. Inca doctors learned how to give blood transfusions to injured people who lost a lot of blood. A blood transfusion is when blood from one person is given to another person. Inca doctors let the blood pass from a blood vessel of a healthy person, through a tube, to a blood vessel of an injured person. This was often a lifesaving measure.

When blood transfusions were tried in Europe in the 1600s, many patients died. In 1818 an English doctor, James Blundell, saved 11 of 15 patients by giving them blood. He noticed that when transfusions failed, the blood cells in the patient were stuck together.

In 1901 the mystery began to unfold. Karl Landsteiner, an Austrian-born doctor working in the United States, found that people have different blood types. He named these blood types A, B, AB, and O. He learned that blood from a donor, the person who gives blood, must be matched to the person who receives it. If not, the blood cells

▲ Scientists now know that most native South Americans have type O blood.

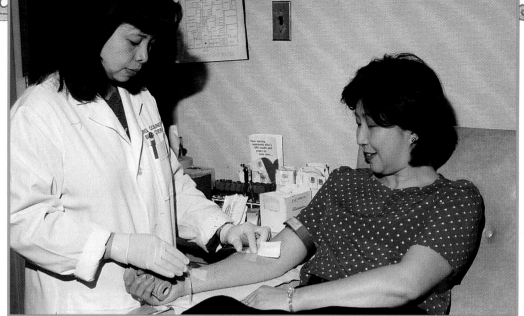

◀ After you donate blood, it's tested to find out what type it is.

clump or stick together. This clumping of cells causes illness or death.

Look at the table to see which blood types can receive blood from which donors. What clues does the table give for solving the mystery?

Scientists now think the reason the Incas were successful in blood transfusions was because most of them had type O blood. In western Europe the most common blood types were A and O. It's likely that many early blood transfusions in western Europe failed because of mismatched blood, which caused the blood cells to stick together.

Your Blood Type	Donor Blood You Can Receive
A	A or O
B	B or O
AB	A, B, AB, or O
O	O

Today, blood is typed when it's drawn. That means it's tested to find out what type it is. Then each unit of blood is labeled by type. As a safety measure, some donor red blood cells are mixed in a tube with some of the patient's plasma. If they clump, the blood isn't used. ■

INVESTIGATION 1

1. How does the heart rate change during and after exercise? Why is this change helpful?

2. What are the parts of the circulatory system? Describe how they work together to cause blood to circulate throughout the body.

HOW DOES YOUR BODY GET RID OF WASTES?

Your body gets energy when it "burns" nutrients. Just as burning wood produces ash, "burning" nutrients produces wastes in your body. In this investigation you'll find out what these wastes are and how your body gets rid of them.

Activity

Skin Scan

MATERIALS
- hand lens
- *Science Notebook*

What's the largest body part? How does it help you get rid of wastes? Find out.

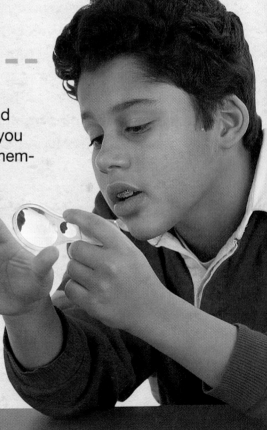

Procedure

Observe the skin on your arms and hands with a hand lens. In your *Science Notebook*, record all the features you observe. Then compare observations with your group members. As a group, list the things the skin does for the body. Record your group's list. Give reasons for each item you put on the list.

Analyze and Conclude

1. What are some of the features you saw on your skin? What do you think these features do for the body?

2. How do you think the skin helps the body get rid of wastes?

Activity

Drink Up!

MATERIALS
- metric measuring cup
- plastic cup
- marker
- *Science Notebook*

Your body needs a lot of water to help it get rid of wastes. You take in much of this water in liquids that you drink. In this activity you'll measure how much liquid you drink.

Procedure

1. **Predict** how much liquid you'll drink in one day. Include all liquids, even frozen ones such as ice pops. **Record** your prediction in your *Science Notebook*.

2. **Make a chart** like the one shown.

DRINKS IN A DAY		
Time	Type of Liquid	mL of Liquid

3. Make a plastic cup into a liquids measurer. Use a measuring cup to add 50 mL of water to the plastic cup. Use a marker to mark the water line. Label this mark *50 mL*. Add another 50 mL and mark the new water line. Label this mark *100 mL*. Continue marking the cup in this way to its top. Use your liquids measurer as your drinking glass for one day.

Step 3

50 ml

4. In your chart, **record** all the liquids you take in during one day. **Record** the time you take in the liquid, the type of liquid, and the amount. Rinse out the measurer each time you use it.

Analyze and Conclude

1. How much liquid did you take in during the day?

2. Why is it important to drink plenty of liquids?

The Waste Works

Your body is a lot like a factory. You take in fuel when you eat. This fuel is changed to make it useful to cells. The changed food is carried to your cells by the circulatory system. In your cells the fuel provides energy for the work of the body—building, repairing, and moving.

Like a factory, your body produces wastes. The wastes of the body can harm you if they're allowed to build up. Luckily, your body has a way to get rid of all the wastes it produces. The body system that rids the body of harmful wastes produced by the cells is called the **excretory** (eks′krə tôr ē) **system**. Look at the picture of the excretory system below.

Some people think that the intestines are also part of the excretory

THE EXCRETORY SYSTEM

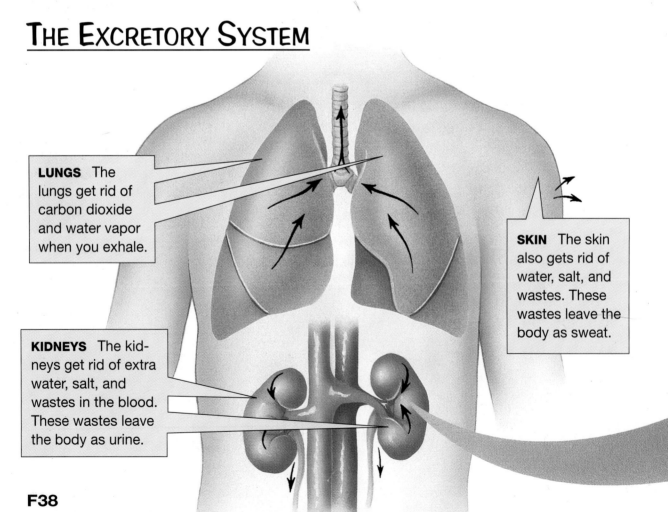

LUNGS The lungs get rid of carbon dioxide and water vapor when you exhale.

SKIN The skin also gets rid of water, salt, and wastes. These wastes leave the body as sweat.

KIDNEYS The kidneys get rid of extra water, salt, and wastes in the blood. These wastes leave the body as urine.

system. But they're not. They're part of the digestive system because they get rid of undigested food.

The Kidneys

The **kidneys** are excretory body parts that clean and filter the blood. They are on either side of your spine at about waist level. Each day about 190 L (50 gal) of blood flow through blood vessels to your kidneys.

Each kidney contains about a million tiny tubes packed close together. These tubes are filtering units. Each filtering tube is closed at one end and pushed inside itself to make a cup-shaped part. A ball of capillaries fits inside the cup-shaped end of the tube. The picture below shows how one of these tiny filtering units works. Follow the path of blood and the path of waste materials.

The combined work of all the filtering units in the kidneys produces a lot of wastes and water. Look at the picture on the next page to see where the wastes and water go. After wastes are removed, the blood returns to the heart and circulates through the body.

A filtering unit in a kidney ▼

■ Artery
■ Vein
■ Filtering tube

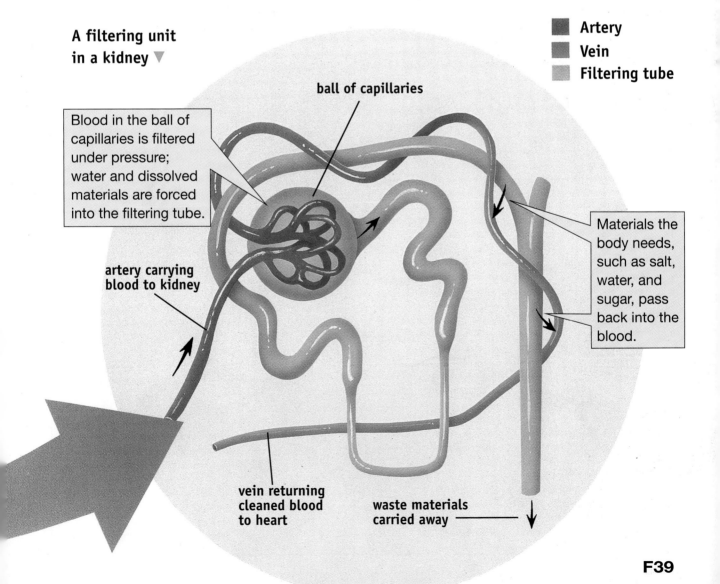

ball of capillaries

Blood in the ball of capillaries is filtered under pressure; water and dissolved materials are forced into the filtering tube.

artery carrying blood to kidney

Materials the body needs, such as salt, water, and sugar, pass back into the blood.

vein returning cleaned blood to heart

waste materials carried away ⟶ ↓

F39

How the Kidneys Work

By changing the amount of wastes and water that pass into the urine, the kidneys help keep a healthy balance of salt and water in your body.

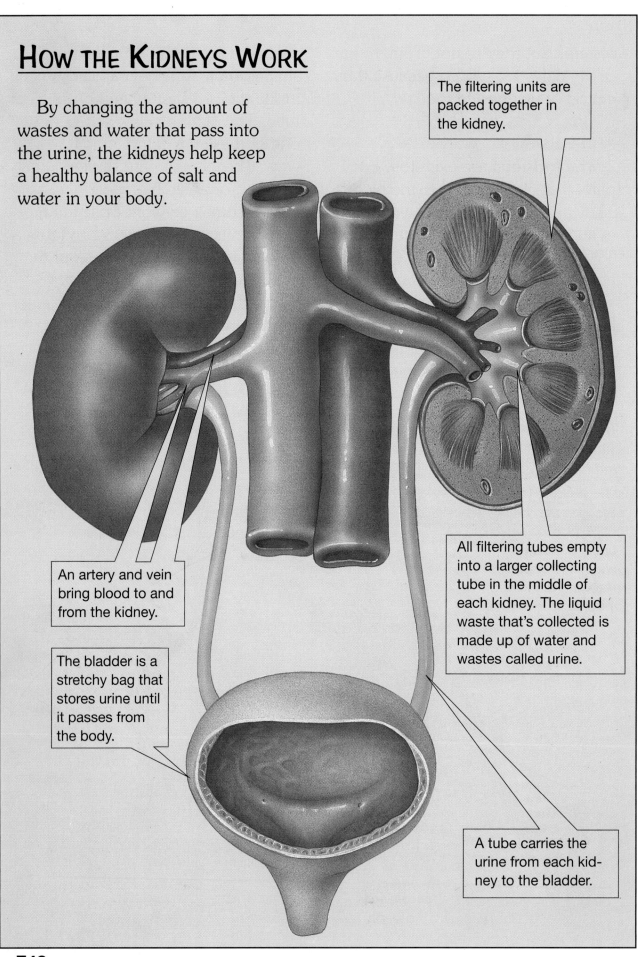

The filtering units are packed together in the kidney.

An artery and vein bring blood to and from the kidney.

The bladder is a stretchy bag that stores urine until it passes from the body.

All filtering tubes empty into a larger collecting tube in the middle of each kidney. The liquid waste that's collected is made up of water and wastes called urine.

A tube carries the urine from each kidney to the bladder.

The Skin

In addition to the lungs and kidneys, the skin is also part of the excretory system. The skin is a very large part of the body. It weighs about 4 kg to 7 kg (9 lb to 15 lb). Notice in the picture below that small coiled tubes connect the sweat glands to pores on the skin's surface. Sweat comes out of the pores. You probably saw pores in your skin in the activity on page F36.

Why Sweat?

Sweating might seem annoying at times, but it's important to health. Sweating serves two purposes. One is to get rid of salt wastes. If you've ever tasted sweat, you know it tastes salty. The other is to cool down your body. Heat is lost from your body when the drops of water on your skin change to a gas, or evaporate. As the water on your skin evaporates, it cools you down. ■

THE SKIN

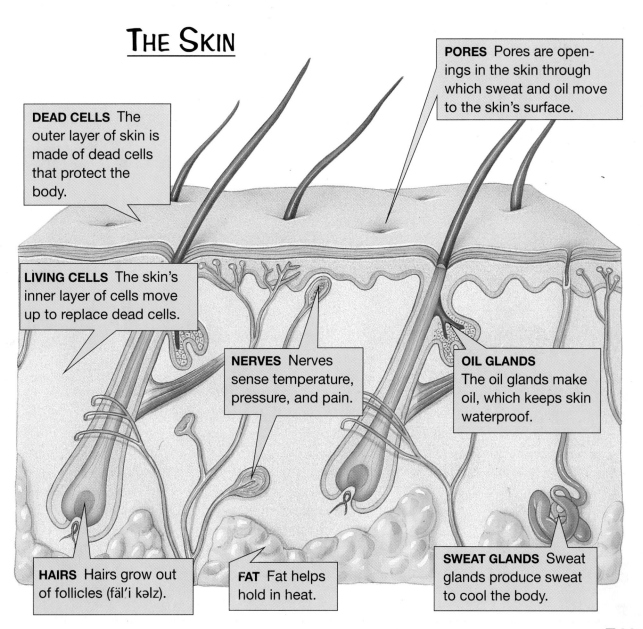

PORES Pores are openings in the skin through which sweat and oil move to the skin's surface.

DEAD CELLS The outer layer of skin is made of dead cells that protect the body.

LIVING CELLS The skin's inner layer of cells move up to replace dead cells.

NERVES Nerves sense temperature, pressure, and pain.

OIL GLANDS The oil glands make oil, which keeps skin waterproof.

HAIRS Hairs grow out of follicles (fäl′i kəlz).

FAT Fat helps hold in heat.

SWEAT GLANDS Sweat glands produce sweat to cool the body.

Goose Bumps

Does your skin get covered all over with little bumps when you are cold or frightened? You probably call these bumps goose bumps. Goose bumps form where the hairs come out of your skin. Did you ever wonder why you get them? Look at the picture below to see what causes goose bumps.

Animals with fur or hair also get cold. When they do, the muscles on their hairs contract, causing the hairs to stand straight out. The hairs trap air. This layer of air next to their skin helps them keep warm.

Why do you get goose bumps when you're frightened? Perhaps furry animals can give us a clue. When furry animals are frightened, they fluff out their fur. Then they look bigger, and scarier, to enemies.

Since humans don't have a thick coat of hair, goose bumps can't help you stay warm or frighten enemies. But they can let you know it's time to put on a sweater or to stop watching a scary movie! ■

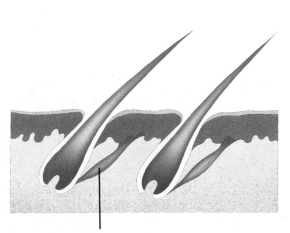

1 Muscles in skin are relaxed and hairs lie down flat.

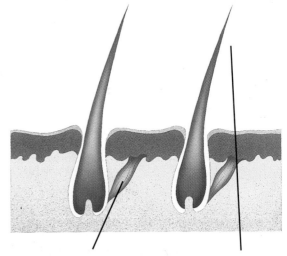

2 When nerves in your skin signal your brain that it's cold, small muscles at the bottom of each hair contract and pull each hair up.

3 This pulling causes the hair to stand out straight from your skin. As the hair stands out, it pulls on the skin around it, forming a bump.

Keeping Things Even

If you play hard, especially on a hot day, you probably get pretty sweaty. What's the first thing you do when you come inside? More than likely, you get a drink of water. Why do you want water after you've been sweating hard?

Water Balance

It might surprise you to learn that your body is more than two-thirds water. Water is in your blood, inside your cells, and between your cells. But your body doesn't store water very well. Every day, you lose about 2 L (2 qt) of water when you breathe, sweat, and pass urine.

When you lose water, your brain signals your body to take in more water by making you feel thirsty. So when you drink water after you've been sweating a lot, you're replacing water your body has lost.

To remain healthy, you have to replace all the water you lose. The amount of water you take in compared to the amount of water that goes out is called water balance. You take in a lot of water by drinking and eating. How much water did you take in during one day when you did the activity on page F37?

Why is it so important to keep a good balance of water in your body? You've learned how water in sweat helps control body temperature. Water is needed to digest food. The body also needs water to dissolve most of the nutrients, gases, and other materials that are carried to and from the cells by the blood.

The waste materials in urine also have to be dissolved in water.

The more you exercise, the thirstier you'll get. ▶

F43

If the water lost from the body is not replaced, the work of the body slows down. In a short time, serious health problems will develop.

The kidneys play a big role in keeping the body's water balance. If there's too much water in the body, the kidneys remove more water from the blood. If there's too little water in the body, the kidneys remove less water from the blood. But over time, having too little water in the body can harm the kidneys. Therefore it's very important to always drink lots of water. This is especially true when you're sick or when it's hot and you've been very active.

Every day you should take in about 2 L (2 qt) of water. But this doesn't mean you have to drink that much water. Remember, you also get water from juices, other drinks, and food. Just make sure there's enough water in your diet to replace all the water you lose. That way you'll always keep a balance of water. ■

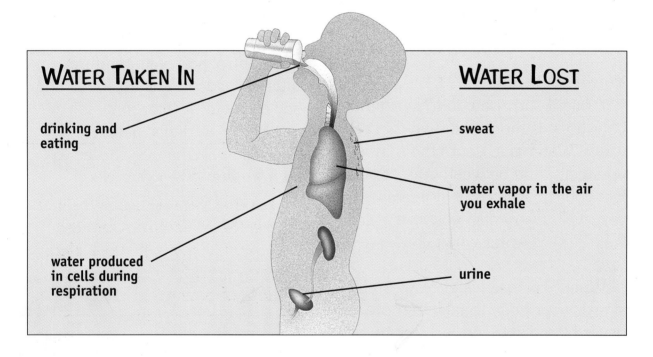

WATER TAKEN IN

drinking and eating

water produced in cells during respiration

WATER LOST

sweat

water vapor in the air you exhale

urine

INVESTIGATION 2

1. When people have a fever, doctors urge them to drink lots of liquids. Based on what you know about water balance, infer why doctors give this advice.

2. What are the major body parts of the excretory system? Describe how they work to get rid of wastes.

REFLECT & EVALUATE

WORD POWER

arteries   heart
atrium   kidneys
blood   pulse
capillaries   veins
circulation ventricle
circulatory system
excretory system

On Your Own
Review the terms in the list. Then make a diagram to represent the circulatory system, using as many terms from the list as possible.

With a Partner
Write each term in the list on one side of an index card—one term per card. Write its definition on the other side. Use the cards to quiz your partner.

BUILD YOUR PORTFOLIO

Make a labeled diagram to show the differences between arteries, veins, and capillaries.

Analyze Information

Study the drawing. Then explain how the lungs, kidneys, and skin each work as part of the excretory system.

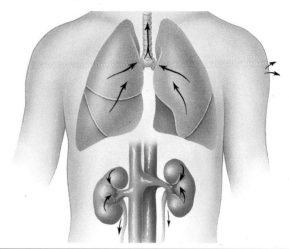

Assess Performance

Design an experiment to find out how different kinds of exercise affect heartbeat rate. After your teacher has reviewed your plan, carry out the experiment. Compare your results with those of others.

Problem Solving

1. Many of the veins in your body have one-way valves in them. Why do you think these valves are necessary?

2. Imagine that you didn't sweat. Why would this be harmful to your body?

3. Explain whether you think this statement is true or false: A person can live much longer without food than without water.

CHAPTER 3

KEEPING YOUR SYSTEMS HEALTHY

Many things that you do each day are possible because all your body systems work together. But sometimes, things get into your body that affect how well your systems work. What are some things that can affect your body's systems? What can you do to keep your body working at its best?

Disease Police at Work

Tracking down a disease is like hunting for a criminal. A few years ago, people living near Lyme, Connecticut, began reporting rashes, headaches, and pain in different parts of their bodies. Dr. Allen Steere began to hunt for clues as to why people were having these symptoms. Dr. Steere is a scientist who studies the spread and control of diseases.

Dr. Steere observed that all the people who were sick lived near woods that had many deer. He found that tiny living things that caused the disease were carried by ticks that fed on deer. The disease studied by Dr. Steere is called Lyme disease. Thanks to a hard-working disease detective, people now know how to avoid Lyme disease. In this chapter you'll learn about ways to keep your body systems free of disease. And you'll find out about substances that can harm your body systems.

Coming Up

◀ Dr. Allen Steere practices medicine
at New England Medical Center.

HOW DO DISEASES SPREAD?

All around you are tiny living things that can make you sick. Luckily your body has ways to protect you from these germs. In Investigation 1 you'll learn what causes diseases and what your body does to fight them off.

Activity
Pass It On

Have you ever noticed that when one member of your household gets sick, often everyone ends up getting the same illness? In this activity you'll learn how an illness can spread.

Step 2

Procedure

1. Have one student in the class start with a full sheet of construction paper. The paper represents a cold that the student has.

2. The student with the cold should cut the construction paper into three equal-sized pieces. The student should then pass on the cold to two classmates by giving them each a piece of paper.

3. Each of the new students with the cold should cut their papers into three pieces. They each should pass on the cold by giving away two of their pieces of paper to other classmates. Continue in this way until every student in the class has the cold.

4. As the cold passes through the class, **make a diagram** of names in your *Science Notebook*, using the diagram below as a model. **Record** each student's name as that person gets the cold.

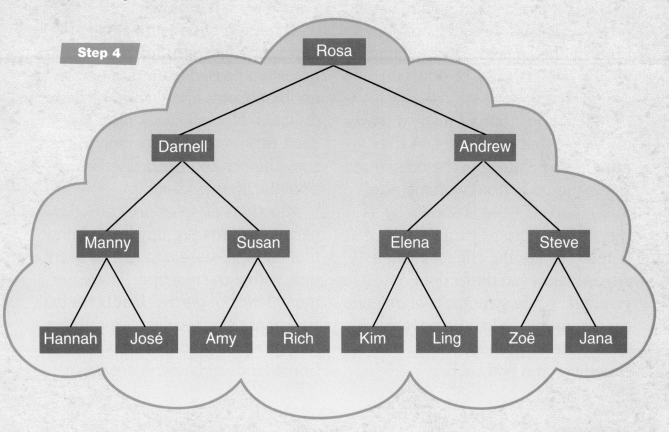

Step 4

Rosa — Darnell, Andrew
Darnell — Manny, Susan
Andrew — Elena, Steve
Manny — Hannah, José
Susan — Amy, Rich
Elena — Kim, Ling
Steve — Zoë, Jana

Analyze and Conclude

1. What is the total number of students who have the cold after the second pass? What is the total after the fourth pass? If your class had enough students for six passes, how many students would have the cold?

2. **Infer** some ways that a real cold spreads from one person to others. How is the passing of the "cold" in this activity similar to the way a cold really spreads? How is it different?

3. **Infer** some ways to prevent the spread of a cold.

The Disease Handbook

Did you ever wake up with a stuffy nose and a sore throat? If so, you've probably had a cold. Do you know what a cold really is, or how you "catch" a cold?

A cold is just one of many diseases (di zēz'əz) that people get. A **disease** is any change in the body that keeps the body from working normally. Each disease is known by its signs, or symptoms (simp'təmz). Symptoms are the changes that a disease causes in the body. For example, some symptoms of influenza, commonly called the flu, are fever, vomiting, chills, feeling tired, coughing, and body aches.

Causes of Disease

There are two main kinds of diseases. Infectious (in fek'shəs) diseases are passed from one person to another. Colds and flu are infectious diseases. Noninfectious diseases can't be spread from person to person. Cancer and heart disease are noninfectious diseases.

Infectious diseases are caused by germs. **Germs** are tiny living things that cause disease and can be seen only with a microscope. There are many kinds of germs. **Bacteria** (bak-tir'ē ə) are single-celled living things that grow just about everywhere. Some kinds of bacteria are germs.

These bacteria that live in your small intestine (*left*) and in your lungs (*right*) don't cause disease.

Viruses are the smallest germs. They are about 100 times smaller than most bacteria. Scientists aren't even sure viruses are living. But viruses do cause disease.

Germs cause disease when they get inside a person's body. Some germs make poisons that damage or kill the body's cells. Other germs enter the cells and kill them directly. Each infectious disease is caused by a different kind of germ. Look at the table to find out about some infectious diseases.

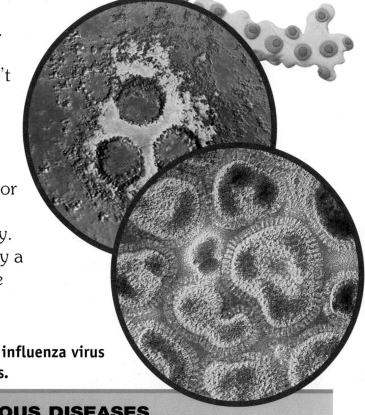

The chickenpox virus (*top*) and an influenza virus (*bottom*) cause infectious diseases.

INFECTIOUS DISEASES

Disease	Cause	How It's Spread	Symptoms
Chickenpox	virus	droplets in air; direct contact	slight fever; small, itchy red bumps on skin
Common Cold	virus	droplets in air; direct contact	sneezing, sore throat, runny nose, headache, coughing
Diphtheria	bacteria	direct contact; infected milk	sore throat, fever, swollen neck glands
Influenza (Flu)	virus	droplets in air; direct contact	chills, fever, muscle pain, sore throat, nausea, vomiting
Measles	virus	droplets in air; direct contact	fever, cough, spots on gums, rash
Pertussis (Whooping Cough)	bacteria	droplets in air	cough with "whooping" sound, vomiting
Polio	virus	direct contact	headache, stiff neck and back, fever, rarely
Tetanus	bacteria	dirt in cut or deep puncture	stiff, painful jaw and neck

If you sneeze (*top*), you should cover your mouth (*right*) to help stop the spread of germs.

How People Catch Colds and Other Diseases

In the activity on pages F48 and F49 you saw that infectious diseases can quickly spread from one person who has the disease—an infected person—to another person. But exactly how are these diseases spread?

Some diseases, such as colds and flu, are spread through the air. Every time an infected person coughs or sneezes, tiny droplets filled with germs escape into the air. Then whoever breathes in this air can catch the disease. Other diseases are spread through direct contact with an infected person or with objects on which germs have settled. Colds and flu can spread in these ways, too.

F52

Insects and other animals can also spread disease to people. Do you remember Dr. Allen Steere, the doctor who discovered the cause of Lyme disease? It was the bite of a deer tick that passed the bacteria to people. The tiny deer tick is shown in the photo on the right.

Mosquitoes can also spread diseases such as malaria and yellow fever. Tsetse flies, found in Africa, spread a harmful disease called sleeping sickness. When animals bite, they can pass on germs that cause disease to their victims.

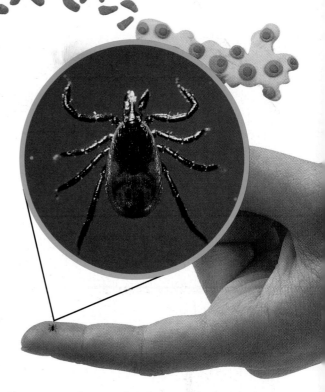

Close-up photo of a deer tick (*top*) and life-sized photo of a deer tick (*bottom*)

Knowing how diseases are spread can help you stay healthy. Some suggestions for avoiding illness are listed in the table to the left. These measures won't keep you from *ever* getting sick, but they will reduce the chances. ■

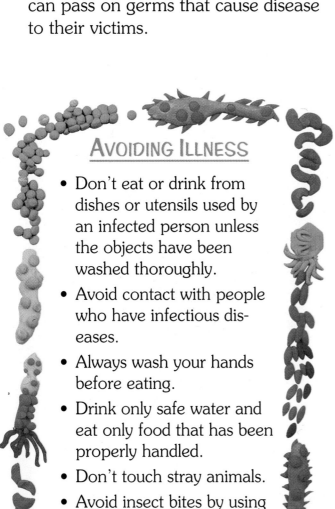

AVOIDING ILLNESS

- Don't eat or drink from dishes or utensils used by an infected person unless the objects have been washed thoroughly.
- Avoid contact with people who have infectious diseases.
- Always wash your hands before eating.
- Drink only safe water and eat only food that has been properly handled.
- Don't touch stray animals.
- Avoid insect bites by using insect repellent.

INVESTIGATE FURTHER!

TAKE ACTION

Work with your group to make a list of things an infected person can do to keep from spreading his or her illness to others. Then make a poster to teach others about one or more of the ideas on your list. Display the poster in your school.

Fighting Back

Don't forget to wash your hands! Eat all your vegetables! You'd better clean that cut! It's late; go to sleep! Have you ever heard these reminders? They're all good things for you to do because each can help your body fight disease.

The best way to help your body fight disease is to keep your body healthy. You can do this by eating well, getting regular exercise, and getting enough sleep. These things will help your body stay strong so that it can fight germs. Keeping your body clean will also help keep germs from entering your body.

Your Body's Defenses

You know that germs are all around you. What keeps you from being sick all the time? You might not think so, but your skin plays an important part in keeping you well. Your skin is your body's first line of defense against germs. The skin acts like a wall to keep germs out. The only way germs can get through the

To help your body fight disease, you should get regular exercise.

skin is by entering through an opening such as a cut or scrape. That's why it's important to clean cuts and scrapes carefully.

Germs can also enter the body through the mouth, eyes, and nose. In the mouth, germs mix with saliva (sə lī'və), a watery liquid. Chemicals in saliva kill many germs.

▲ Sneezing and tearing help get rid of germs. Eyelashes help keep germs from entering the eyes.

A thick, sticky liquid, called mucus (myoo'kəs), lines the nose, mouth, eyes, and other body openings. Germs get caught in mucus and are prevented from entering the body. Tears help wash out germs, too.

If you've ever had a fever, you know about another way your body fights germs. A fever may make you feel awful, but it serves a useful purpose. The high temperature of a fever can stop germs from growing or it can kill them.

INVESTIGATE FURTHER!

RESEARCH

Read the book *Kids to the Rescue—First Aid Techniques for Kids* by Maribeth and Darwin Boelts. Then make a poster that tells the importance of first aid in helping to prevent disease.

The Immune System

Your body also has a system, called the **immune** (im myo͞on') **system**, that destroys germs. When a germ enters the body, certain body cells make a chemical. The chemical, called an **antibody**, helps destroy germs in the body. Cells of the body produce different antibodies for different kinds of germs.

Antibodies attach to the outsides of germs and kill them. If the same kind of germ ever enters the body again, the cells "remember" it. They quickly produce antibodies to destroy the germs before disease can be caused. The body is now immune to the disease caused by that germ.

Medicine to the Rescue!

Sometimes your immune system needs a little help fighting germs. If the disease is caused by bacteria, a doctor might prescribe an antibiotic (an tī bī ät'ik). An antibiotic is a drug that kills bacteria. However, antibiotics have no effect on viruses.

Antibiotics are one kind of prescription (prē skrip'shən) medicine. A prescription medicine is a drug you can obtain only if you have a written order from a doctor.

Cold medicines and pain relievers are other kinds of medicines you might be given when you're sick. Many of these medicines are called over-the-counter medicines because

SCIENCE IN LITERATURE

SURE HANDS, STRONG HEART
THE LIFE OF DANIEL HALE WILLIAMS

by Lillie Patterson
Illustrated by David Scott Brown
Silver Burdett Ginn, 1995

Daniel Hale Williams learned to be a doctor in exciting times. Scientists had recently discovered that many diseases and infections were caused by bacteria, germs too small to be seen with the unaided eye. Yet antibiotics, which would save many lives in the future, had not yet been discovered.

"Doctor Dan" fought bacteria by making sure they didn't enter his patients' bodies. Read Chapter 7 of *Sure Hands, Strong Heart* by Lillie Patterson to find out how Dr. Williams performed surgery, without infection, right in his patient's dining room!

they can be bought without a doctor's prescription. Over-the-counter medicines help relieve some symptoms of disease, including fever, headache, and stuffy nose.

Both prescription and over-the-counter medicines can help the body fight disease. But if these medicines aren't taken according to the directions, they can harm the body. Remember that only a parent or guardian should give you medicine. They know when and how the medicine should be used.

Get Your Shots!

Do you remember getting shots at the doctor's office before you started attending school? These shots, or **vaccinations**, were given to you to make you immune to certain diseases. There are vaccinations available for diphtheria, flu, measles, polio, pertussis (whooping cough), and tetanus. One of the most recent vaccines available in the United States is for chickenpox.

Vaccinations help stop the spread of diseases. Smallpox is an example of a disease that was completely wiped out because of vaccinations. It is hoped that, in the future, vaccinations will help stop the spread of other serious diseases. ■

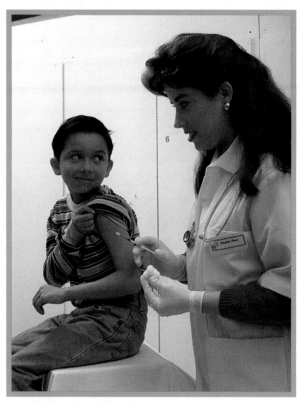

▲ **Vaccinations protect you from getting certain diseases.**

INVESTIGATION 1

1. Suppose a family member has a cold. What are some things you can do to keep from getting the cold?

2. What causes disease? What are some ways diseases are spread?

F57

INVESTIGATION 2

WHAT ARE HARMFUL AND HELPFUL DRUGS?

You've probably taken medicine that a doctor prescribed. It's likely that the medicine helped make you well. But some drugs can be harmful if they are misused. In Investigation 2 you'll find out how some drugs can be harmful.

Activity

Ad Advice

Alcohol, cigarettes, medicines, coffee, tea, and colas all contain drugs. Find out which of these products that contain drugs are advertised in magazines.

Procedure

1. Look through magazines. List each ad you find that shows products that contain drugs. **Record** your list in your *Science Notebook*.

2. **Decide** whether the ads try to get people to do things that are healthful or things that are unhealthful. Explain your decisions.

Step 3

F58

3. Choose and cut out two ads that try to get people to do unhealthful things. With your group, **analyze** how these ads try to get people to use the products advertised. Consider the choices of pictures, colors, and words in the ads. **Compare** how the ads are alike and how they are different.

4. With your group, **create** an ad for a healthful product. **Study** the other ads to get ideas on the best ways to advertise your product. **Compare** your ad with those of your classmates.

Analyze and Conclude

1. How many magazine ads try to get people to do healthful things? How many try to get people to do unhealthful things?

2. How do the ads try to get people to do things considered unhealthful? **Infer** which group, or groups, of people the ads are aiming to reach. Give reasons for your inference.

3. How do ads that try to get people to do unhealthful things affect you? How can you be less affected by these ads?

INVESTIGATE FURTHER!

RESEARCH

Go to a library and find magazines aimed at different age groups. Compare the kinds of ads shown in the magazines. How do the numbers of ads trying to get people to do unhealthful things compare in magazines for children, teens, and adults? Compare your findings with those of your classmates.

Secondhand Smoke No Joke

STS
SCIENCE
TECHNOLOGY
& SOCIETY

Have you ever noticed the smell of smoke on your clothes after you've been around people who smoke cigarettes? Many people don't like the way cigarette smoke smells. But as some medical studies show, the smell isn't the worst problem with cigarette smoke. Breathing **secondhand smoke**, or the smoke from another person's tobacco, can be dangerous to your health.

When cigarettes and other tobacco products are burned, they produce many harmful chemicals. Over time, these chemicals can cause cancer, heart disease, and lung problems. When nonsmokers breathe in someone else's smoke, they take in the same harmful chemicals that the smoker takes in. These chemicals can harm nonsmokers just as they harm smokers.

To protect the health of nonsmokers, many states have passed laws that ban smoking in public places. In some states, smoking has been banned inside schools, airports, and shopping malls. Many workplaces have also become smoke-free areas. Some people also ask visitors in their homes not to smoke. ■

People breathing secondhand smoke may have the same health problems that smokers themselves have. ▼

Straight Talk on Drugs

What do you think of when you hear the word *drug*? Do you think of something that's sold in a drugstore or something that's sold on the street? A **drug** is any chemical that changes the way the mind and body work. In the activity on pages F58 and F59 you studied magazine ads for products that contain drugs.

Kinds of Drugs

Many drugs help the body by easing pain or treating disease. These drugs are usually called medicines. Medicines should be taken only on a doctor's or parent's advice.

Some drugs are found in products that people use. Alcohol is a drug found in beer, wine, and liquor. Nicotine (nik′ə tēn) is a drug found in tobacco products. By law, alcohol and nicotine can be used only by adults. Caffeine (ka fēn′) is a drug found in small amounts in coffee, tea, chocolate, and colas.

Some drugs are so dangerous that it's against the law for anyone to use them. These drugs are **illegal drugs**. Marijuana, heroin, LSD, and cocaine are illegal drugs.

▲ Remember that only an adult should give you medicine. Never take a prescription medicine that belongs to someone else.

UNIT PROJECT LINK

As you move through this chapter, think of quiz questions about the body's immune system and how drugs affect the body's systems. Write some true-false or multiple-choice questions. Record the questions and their answers. Save your questions for the Big Event.

The Dangers of Drugs

All drugs may cause harm. Illegal drugs are always dangerous because they're very strong, can cause very serious health problems, can cause addiction, and can kill you if you take too much. Someone who is addicted to a drug feels he or she cannot live without that drug.

Drug addiction ruins people's lives. People can't do their jobs properly. Students who use drugs often do poorly in school or drop out of school. Family problems develop because drug addicts often think only of their own needs.

Why Start?

Why do people ever start taking drugs? Often people try drugs to escape from problems. For example, people may use drugs when they are under pressure at work, home, or school. Some people try drugs to feel grown-up or to fit in with a group. But there's never a good reason to take illegal drugs. Illegal drugs cause nothing but problems.

▲ **These foods contain a drug called caffeine. Too much caffeine can increase the heart rate and cause other health problems.**

If you're ever encouraged to try drugs, including tobacco or alcohol, don't be afraid to say no. You'll be saying yes to a healthier life. One of the best decisions you'll ever make is the decision to be drug-free. ∎

INVESTIGATION 2

1. What are some kinds of helpful drugs? How do they affect the body? What are some kinds of harmful drugs?

2. Imagine that some older students are trying to get you to use an illegal drug. How can you make it clear to them that it's something you don't want to do?

REFLECT & EVALUATE

WORD POWER

antibody
bacteria
disease
drug
germs
illegal drugs
immune system
secondhand smoke
vaccinations
viruses

On Your Own
Write a definition for each term in the list.

With a Partner
Have your partner match each definition to the correct term.

PORTFOLIO
Make a labeled drawing to show how your body protects itself from disease. Include symbols for the immune system in your drawing.

Analyze Information

Study the photograph. Then explain how the behavior of this person can help to stop the spread of disease.

Assess Performance

Imagine everyone you come in contact with during the day has a cold. Record each time you're exposed to cold germs and how you were exposed. At the end of the day, evaluate your notes. Then make a list of things you could do to protect yourself from catching a cold.

Problem Solving

1. Some hand soaps are advertised as being antibacterial. What does this mean? When would it be good to use antibacterial soaps?

2. Suppose you're sick and you have symptoms very similar to those your friend had when she was ill. Should you take some of her prescription medicine? Explain your answer.

3. Imagine that a person in your household smokes. How can you protect yourself from this person's secondhand smoke?

Throughout this unit you've investigated questions about the body's delivery systems. How will you use what you've learned and share that information with others? Here are some ideas.

Hold a Big Event
to Share Your Unit Project

With your classmates, plan and produce your Body Maze Quiz Show. Your show can be modeled after a television quiz show or it can be an original idea. Use the questions from the Unit Project Links on the respiratory, circulatory, excretory, and immune systems and on how drugs affect the body's delivery systems. Prepare a short commercial with your group on how to take care of one of the body systems you studied in this unit. If you want, you can videotape your show. Then invite other classes, friends, and family members to be the audience as you put on your show or show the videotape.

Research

Look back through this unit for a topic that interests you, and then find out more about that topic. For example, you might find out how exercise helps your respiratory and circulatory systems. Or you could choose to learn more about how drugs harm the body. Go to the library to learn more about it.

Take Action

In this unit you've learned about many practices that help keep your body and its systems healthy. Select one of these and make a poster that illustrates it. Your poster should persuade others to follow that practice. Display your poster in your school.

SCIENCE Handbook

THINK LIKE A SCIENTIST

You don't have to be a professional scientist to act and think like one. Thinking like a scientist mostly means using common sense. It also means learning how to test your ideas in a careful way.

In other words, *you* can think like a scientist.

Make a Hypothesis

Plan and Do a Test

Make Observations

To think like a scientist, you should learn as much as you can by observing things around you. Everything you hear and see is a clue about how the world works.

Ask a Question

Look for patterns. You'll get ideas. Ask questions like these.

- Do all birds eat the same kind of seeds?

- How does the time that the Sun sets change from day to day?

Make a Guess Called a Hypothesis

If you have an idea about why something happens, make an educated guess, or hypothesis, that you can test. For example, let's suppose that your hypothesis about sunset time is that it changes by one minute each day.

Plan and Do a Test

Plan how to test your hypothesis. Your plan would need to consider some of these problems.

- How will you measure the time that the Sun sets?

- Will you measure the time every day?

- For how many days or weeks do you need to measure?

Record and Analyze What Happens

When you test your idea, you need to observe carefully and write down, or record, everything that

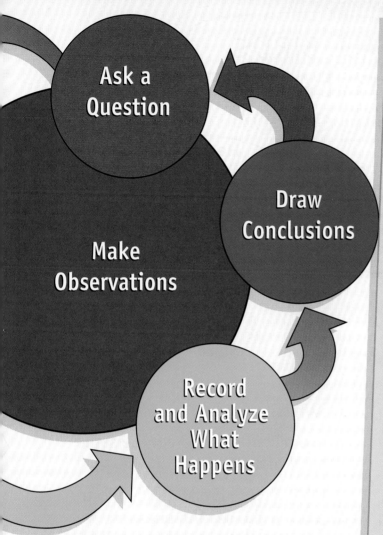

Ask a Question

Draw Conclusions

Make Observations

Record and Analyze What Happens

To think like a scientist, you need to practice certain ways of thinking.

Always check for yourself.
Ask, "How do I know it's true?" Be willing to find out for yourself.

Be honest and careful about what you observe.
It's easy to only look for the results you expect. It's harder to see the unexpected. But unexpected results lead scientists to ask more questions. They also provide information on how things work.

Don't be afraid to be wrong.
Based on their observations, scientists make many hypotheses. Not all of these hypotheses turn out to be correct. But scientists can learn from wrong "guesses," because even wrong guesses result in information that leads to knowledge.

Keep an open mind about possible explanations.
Make sure to think about all the reasons why something might have happened. Consider all the explanations that you can think of.

happens. When you finish collecting data, you may need to do some calculations with it. For example, you might calculate how much the sunset time changes in a week.

Draw Conclusions

Whatever happens in a test, think about all the reasons for your results. Sometimes this thinking leads to a new hypothesis.

If the time of the sunset changes by one minute each day, think about what else the data shows you. Can you predict the time that the Sun will set one month from now?

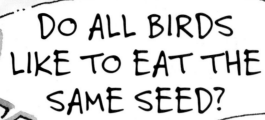

DO ALL BIRDS LIKE TO EAT THE SAME SEED?

Here's an example of an everyday problem and how thinking like a scientist can help you explore it.

Emily and Michael had filled up their bird feeder with a mixture of different seeds. They noticed at the end of the day that not all the seeds had been eaten. Some types of seed were completely gone. But others were left in the feeder or scattered on the ground.

Emily thought she knew why. She thought that the peanuts were probably too big for some of the birds to eat. A lot of the tiny millet seed mix was left. So Michael figured that the birds didn't like the way millet seed tasted.

Make Observations

Ask a Question

They thought about the birds that they'd seen at the feeder and came up with questions they wanted to answer.

Which seed do birds prefer?

Do all birds like to eat the same kind of seed?

Michael and Emily decided to try to answer the second question because it seemed more interesting. Also, they both felt very unsure about what the answer might be.

Scientific investigations usually begin with something that you've seen or read about. As you think about what you already know, you'll discover some ideas that you're not sure about. This can help you ask a question that you really want to answer.

Make a Hypothesis

Make Observations

To find out if all birds like the same kind of seed, Emily and Michael watched the birds visit the feeder. But they couldn't see which seeds the birds were eating. Emily thought about what made sense to her. She hypothesized that different birds ate different kinds of seeds, and that bigger birds probably ate bigger seeds.

Michael wasn't sure. It seemed that none of the birds ate the tiny millet. He thought that the birds would probably eat whatever tasted best. But both students thought that different birds would eat different kinds of seeds. So, they chose that idea as their hypothesis. A hypothesis is a possible answer to a question.

When you use what you've observed to suggest a possible answer to your question, you are making a hypothesis. Make sure that your hypothesis is an idea that you can test.
If you can't think of an experiment or a model to test your hypothesis, try changing it. Sometimes it's better to make a simpler hypothesis that answers only part of your question.

blue jay

cardinal

finch

sparrow

Make Observations

Plan and Do a Test

Emily and Michael worked together to plan an experiment that would test their hypothesis. They got some flat, plastic dishes and put a different kind of bird seed in each one. Then they put out the dishes. They planned to watch each dish and to keep a record of which birds came to each one.

On the first day, a squirrel knocked over some dishes and took many seeds. As a result, it was hard for Emily and Michael to tell the amount of seeds in each dish that had been eaten by the birds. Also, it was hard to describe and keep track of the birds that they saw.

Michael and Emily changed their experiment. They measured equal amounts of each type of seed into each dish for the next day. Then they put the dishes out of reach of the squirrels. To help identify the kinds of birds, they used a field guide. They also planned to describe birds by their size.

One way to try out your hypothesis is to use a test called an experiment. When you plan an experiment, make sure that it helps you to answer your question. Try to imagine what might happen when you do your experiment. Sometimes things happen that make the experiment confusing or make it not work properly. If this happens, you can change the plan for the experiment, and try again.

Make Observations

Record and Analyze What Happened

Emily kept track of the birds at some of the dishes. Michael kept track of the birds at the others. At the end of the day, Emily and Michael put the data they collected in a chart similar to the one shown below.

Bird(size)	peanut	millet	thistle	safflower	striped sunflowers (with hulls)
sparrows (small)	0	58	1	42	0
finches (small)	0	2	35	0	0
jays (big)	6	0	0	3	29
cardinals (medium)	2	0	0	21	17

Number of visits to dish

Emily and Michael analyzed the data. They noted that most of the birds liked one kind of seed, but that some birds liked two kinds. It didn't seem as if many peanuts had been eaten. They decided that maybe the squirrels had eaten the peanuts from the mixed-seed feeder. They both had noticed that different types of birds ate different types of seeds. Michael and Emily considered what they had found.

Make Observations

Draw Conclusions

When you do an experiment, you need to write down, or record, your observations. Some of your observations might be numbers of things that you count or measure, called data. When you record your data, you need to organize it in a way that helps you to understand it. Graphs and tables are helpful ways to organize data. Then think about the information you have collected. Analyze what it tells you. Look for patterns. Look for surprises.

They decided that their hypothesis was supported by the data. But, it seemed as if some types of birds liked some of the same foods as other birds. For example, both the cardinals and the jays liked sunflower seeds.

They still didn't know why certain birds like certain seeds. Michael remembered that his gerbil likes to eat sunflower seeds and that it uses its sharp teeth to crack open the seeds. Emily remembered that the cardinals and jays were bigger birds than the other birds. They both wondered whether they could predict what kinds of seeds a bird would eat if they knew how big the bird was. They had a whole new set of questions to explore.

After you have analyzed your data, you should use what you have learned to draw a conclusion. A conclusion is a statement that sums up what you learned. The conclusion should be about the question you asked. It should not be about other ideas that turned up during the experiment.

SAFETY

The best way to be safe in the classroom is to use common sense. Prepare yourself for each activity before you start it. Get help from your teacher when there is a problem. Most important of all, pay attention. Here are some other ways that you can stay safe.

Stay Safe From Stains

- Wear protective clothing or an old shirt when you work with messy materials.
- If anything spills, wipe it up or ask your teacher to help you clean it up.

Stay Safe From Flames

- Keep your clothes away from open flames. If you have long or baggy sleeves, roll them up.
- Don't let your hair get close to a flame. If you have long hair, tie it back.

Stay Safe From Injuries

- Protect your eyes by wearing safety goggles when you are told that you need them.
- Keep your hands dry around electricity. Water is a good conductor of electricity, so you can get a shock more easily if your hands are wet.
- Be careful with sharp objects. If you have to press on them, keep the sharp side away from you.
- Cover any cuts you have that are exposed. If you spill something on a cut, be sure to wash it off immediately.
- Don't eat or drink anything unless your teacher tells you that it's okay.

Stay Safe During Cleanup

- Wash up after you finish working.
- Dispose of things in the way that your teacher tells you to.

MOST IMPORTANTLY

If you ever hurt yourself or one of your group members gets hurt, tell your teacher right away.

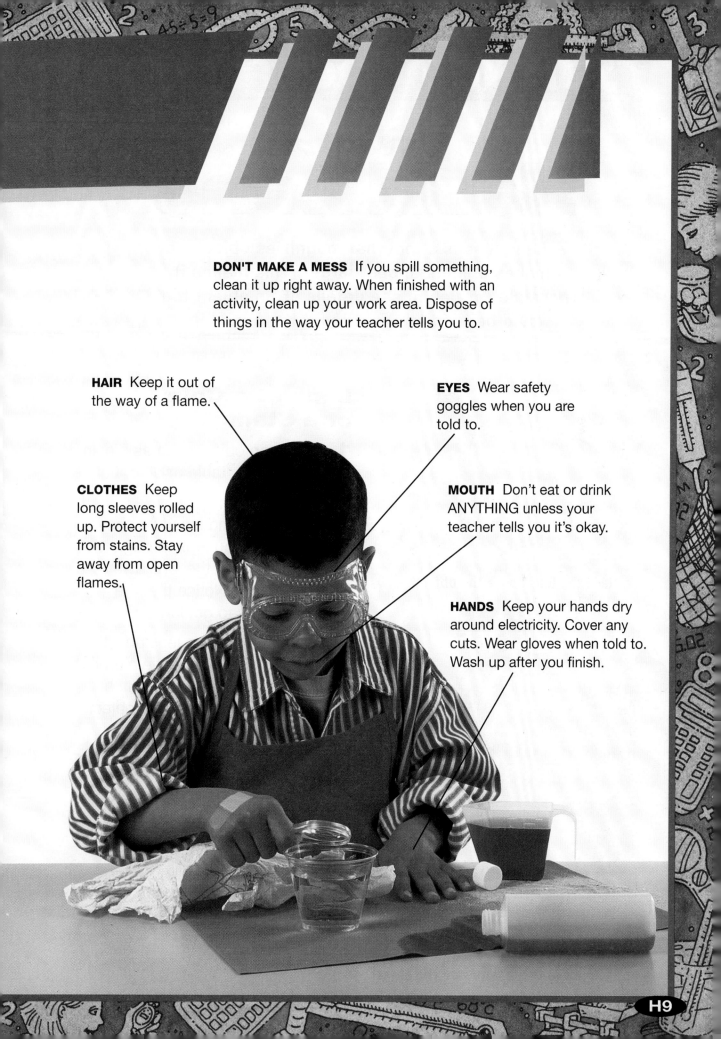

DON'T MAKE A MESS If you spill something, clean it up right away. When finished with an activity, clean up your work area. Dispose of things in the way your teacher tells you to.

HAIR Keep it out of the way of a flame.

EYES Wear safety goggles when you are told to.

CLOTHES Keep long sleeves rolled up. Protect yourself from stains. Stay away from open flames.

MOUTH Don't eat or drink ANYTHING unless your teacher tells you it's okay.

HANDS Keep your hands dry around electricity. Cover any cuts. Wear gloves when told to. Wash up after you finish.

Using a
Hand Lens

A hand lens is a tool that magnifies objects, or makes objects appear larger. This makes it possible for you to see details of an object that would be hard to see without the hand lens.

▲ Place the lens above the object.

Look at a Coin or a Stamp

1. Place an object such as a coin or a stamp on a table or other flat surface.

2. Hold the hand lens just above the object. As you look through the lens, slowly move the lens away from the object. Notice that the object appears to get larger.

3. Keep moving the lens until the object begins to look a little blurry. Then move the hand lens a little closer to the object until the object is once again in sharp focus.

▲ Move the lens slowly toward you.

If the object becomes blurry, you need to move the lens toward the object. ▶

Using a Calculator

After you've made measurements, a calculator can help you analyze your data. Some calculators have a memory key that allows you to save the result of one calculation while you do another.

Find an Average

The table shows the amount of rain that fell each month of one year. Use a calculator to find the average monthly rainfall.

1. To add the numbers, enter a number and then press the plus sign (+). Repeat until you enter the last number. Then press the equal sign (=).

2. If you make a mistake, push the clear entry key (CE). Enter the number again, and then continue adding.

3. Your total should be 1,131. You can use the total to find the average. Just press divide (÷) and enter 12, the number of months in a year.

4. Your answer should be 94.25.

Rainfall	
Month	**Rain (mm)**
Jan.	214
Feb.	138
Mar.	98
Apr.	157
May	84
June	41
July	5
Aug.	23
Sept.	48
Oct.	75
Nov.	140
Dec.	108

clear entry

divide

equal

plus

Using a Balance

A balance is used to measure mass. Mass is the amount of matter in an object. Place the object to be massed in the left pan of the balance. Place standard masses in the right pan.

Measure the Mass of an Orange

1. Check that the empty pans are balanced, or level with each other. When balanced, the pointer on the base should be at the middle mark. If it needs to be adjusted, move the slider on the back of the balance a little to the left or right.

2. Place an orange on the left pan. Then add standard masses, one at a time, to the right pan. When the pointer is at the middle mark again, each pan holds the same amount of matter and has the same mass.

3. Add the numbers marked on the masses in the pan. The total is the mass in grams of the orange.

Using a
Tape Measure or Ruler

Tape measures and rulers are tools for measuring the length of objects and distances. Scientists most often use units such as meters, centimeters, and millimeters when making length measurements.

Use a Tape Measure

1. Wrap the tape around the jar.

2. Find the line where the tape begins to wrap over itself.

3. Record the distance around the jar in centimeters.

Use a Metric Ruler

1. Place the ruler or the meterstick on the floor. Line up the end of the ruler with the heel of your shoe.

2. Notice where the other end of your shoe lines up with the ruler.

3. Look at the scale. Record the length of your shoe in centimeters and in millimeters.

Using a Thermometer

A thermometer is used to measure temperature. When the liquid in the tube of a thermometer gets warmer, it expands and moves farther up the tube. Different scales can be used to measure temperature, but scientists usually use the Celsius scale.

Measure the Temperature of a Cold Liquid

1. Take a chilled liquid out of the refrigerator. Half-fill a cup with the liquid.

2. Hold the thermometer so that the bulb is in the center of the liquid. Be sure that there are no bright lights or direct sunlight shining on the bulb.

3. Wait a couple of minutes until you see the liquid in the tube stop moving. Read the scale line that is closest to the top of the liquid in the tube. The thermometer shown reads 4°C (40°F).

Measuring
Volume

A graduated cylinder, a measuring cup, and a beaker are used to measure volume. Volume is the amount of space something takes up. Most of the containers that scientists use to measure volume have a scale marked in milliliters (mL).

Measure the Volume of Juice

1. Pour the juice into a measuring container.

2. Move your head so that your eyes are level with the top of the juice. Read the scale line that is closest to the surface of the juice. If the surface of the juice is curved up on the sides, look at the lowest point of the curve.

3. Read the measurement on the scale. You can estimate the value between two lines on the scale.

▲ The bottom of the curve is at 35 mL.

◀ This graduated cylinder has marks for every 5 mL.

This beaker has marks for each 25 mL. ▼

▼ **This measuring cup has marks for each 25 mL.**

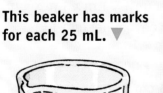

MEASUR

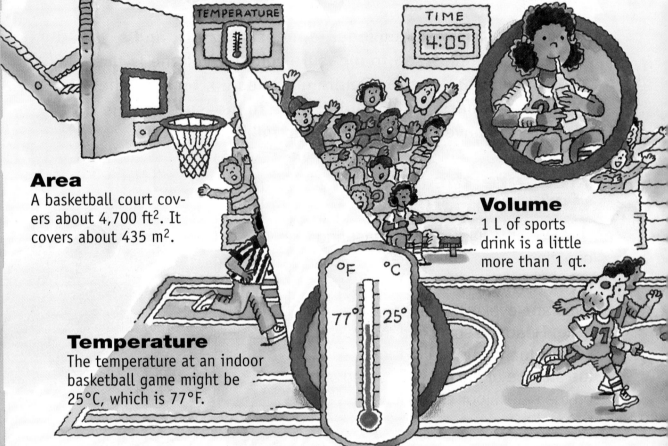

Area
A basketball court covers about 4,700 ft². It covers about 435 m².

Volume
1 L of sports drink is a little more than 1 qt.

Temperature
The temperature at an indoor basketball game might be 25°C, which is 77°F.

SI Measures

Temperature
Ice melts at 0 degrees Celsius (°C)

Water freezes at 0°C

Water boils at 100°C

Length and Distance
1,000 meters (m) = 1 kilometer (km)

100 centimeters (cm) = 1 m

10 millimeters (mm) = 1 cm

Force
1 newton (N) =
1 kilogram x meter/second/second
(kg x m/s²)

Volume
1 cubic meter (m³) = 1 m x 1 m x 1 m

1 cubic centimeter (cm³) =
1 cm x 1 cm x 1 cm

1 liter (L) = 1,000 milliliters (mL)

1 cm³ = 1 mL

Area
1 square kilometer (km²) = 1 km x 1 km

1 hectare = 10,000 m²

Mass
1,000 grams (g) = 1 kilogram (kg)

1,000 milligrams (mg) = 1 g

EMENTS

Mass and Weight
A basketball has a mass of about 650 g. It weighs about $1\frac{1}{2}$ lb.

Length/ Distance
A basketball rim is about 10 ft high, or a little more than 3 m from the floor.

Rates (SI and English)
km/h = kilometers per hour

m/s = meters per second

mph = miles per hour

English Measures

Volume of Fluids
8 fluid ounces (fl oz) = 1 cup (c)

2 c = 1 pint (pt)

2 pt = 1 quart (qt)

4 qt = 1 gallon (gal)

Temperature
Ice melts at 32 degrees Fahrenheit (°F)

Water freezes at 32°F

Water boils at 212°F

Length and Distance
12 inches (in.) = 1 foot (ft)

3 ft = 1 yard (yd)

5,280 ft = 1 mile (mi)

Weight
16 ounces (oz) = 1 pound (lb)   2,000 pounds = 1 ton (T)

GLOSSARY

Pronunciation Key

Symbol	Key Words	Symbol	Key Words
a	cat	g	get
ā	ape	h	help
ä	cot, car	j	jump
		k	kiss, call
e	ten, berry	l	leg
ē	me	m	meat
		n	nose
i	fit, here	p	put
ī	ice, fire	r	red
		s	see
ō	go	t	top
ô	fall, for	v	vat
oi	oil	w	wish
o͝o	look, pull	y	yard
o͞o	tool, rule	z	zebra
ou	out, crowd		
		ch	chin, arch
u	up	ŋ	ring, drink
ʉ	fur, shirt	sh	she, push
		th	thin, truth
ə	a in ago	*th*	then, father
	e in agent	zh	measure
	i in pencil		
	o in atom	
	u in circus	A heavy stress mark ′ is placed after a syllable that gets a heavy, or primary, stress, as in **picture** (pik′chər).
b	bed	
d	dog	
f	fall	

A

adaptation (ad əp tā′shən) A part or behavior that makes a living thing better able to survive in its environment. (C18) The polar bear's thick coat of fur is an *adaptation* that helps keep the animal warm in cold weather.

air (er) The invisible, odorless, and tasteless mixture of gases that surrounds Earth. (E10) *Air* consists mainly of the gases nitrogen and oxygen.

air mass (er mas) A large body of air that has about the same temperature, air pressure, and moisture throughout. (E64) When warm and cold *air masses* meet, the weather changes.

air pressure (er presh′ər) The push of the air in all directions against its surroundings. (E31) You can see the effect of *air pressure* when you blow up a balloon.

air sac (er sak) One of many tiny, thin-walled pockets in the lungs through which oxygen moves into the blood and carbon dioxide is removed. (F16) Each lung contains millions of *air sacs.*

amphibian (am-fib′ē ən) A vertebrate that usually lives in water in the early part of its life; it breathes with gills and then later develops lungs. (C49) Frogs, toads, and salamanders are *amphibians.*

anemometer (an ə mäm′ət ər) A device used to measure the speed of the wind. (E39) The *anemometer* showed that the wind was blowing at 33 km/h.

antibody (an′ti bäd ē) A substance, produced in the blood, that destroys or weakens germs, helping the body fight diseases. (F56) *Antibodies* attach to germs that invade the body, killing them.

artery (ärt′ər ē) A thick-walled blood vessel that carries blood away from the heart. (F26) The heart pumps blood to the *arteries.*

atmosphere (at′məs fir) The blanket of air that surrounds Earth, reaching to about 700 km above the surface. (E12) Earth's *atmosphere* makes it possible for life to exist on the planet.

atom (at′əm) The smallest part of an element that still has the properties of that element. (B30) Water forms when *atoms* of the elements hydrogen and oxygen combine in a certain way.

atrium (ā′trē əm) Either of the two upper chambers of the heart. (F27) Blood vessels lead to each *atrium*.

axis (ak′sis) An imaginary straight line from the North Pole, through Earth's center, to the South Pole. (E80) Earth makes one complete turn on its *axis* in about 24 hours.

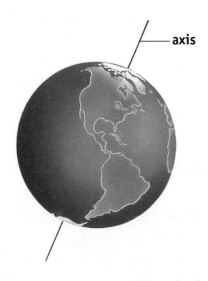

axis

bacteria (bak tir′ē ə) Certain one-celled organisms that can be seen only with a microscope. (F50) Some *bacteria* are useful, but others cause diseases, such as pneumonia and tuberculosis.

barometer (bə räm′ət ər) A device used to measure air pressure. (E32) Scientists use a *barometer* to gather information about the weather.

bay (bā) Part of a sea or lake extending into the land. (A14) The ship sailed through the *bay* into the Atlantic Ocean.

behavior (bē hāv′yər) The way in which a living thing acts or responds to its environment. (C28) Purring and washing themselves are two common *behaviors* of cats.

bird (burd) A vertebrate that has wings, is covered with feathers, and hatches from a hard-shelled egg. (C51) A *bird* is the only animal that has feathers covering its body.

blood (blud) A tissue made up of a liquid, called plasma, and several types of cells. (F29) *Blood* carries oxygen and nutrients to body cells.

boiling (boil'iŋ) The rapid change of state from a liquid to a gas. (B40) When water is *boiling*, bubbles of water vapor form.

breathing (brē*th*'iŋ) The process in which the body takes in fresh air, containing oxygen, and forces out used air, containing carbon dioxide. (F9) *Breathing* involves taking fresh air into the lungs.

breathing rate (brē*th*'iŋ rāt) The number of times a person inhales in one minute. (F10) Your *breathing rate* decreases when you fall asleep.

bronchial tube (bräŋ'kē əl to͞ob) One of the two tubes into which the windpipe branches; one tube goes to each lung. (F16) Air flows to and from the lungs through the *bronchial tubes*.

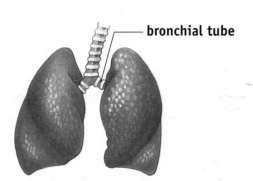

— bronchial tube

capillary (kap'ə ler ē) A tiny, thin-walled blood vessel that connects an artery and a vein. (F26) Nutrients pass through the walls of the *capillaries* into the cells.

carbon dioxide (kär'bən dī-äks'īd) A colorless, odorless gas. (E11) Plants use *carbon dioxide* to make food.

cartilage (kärt''l ij) A tough, flexible body material. (F10) The tip of your nose is made of *cartilage*.

cell (sel) The basic unit that makes up all living things. (F17) Every animal and plant is composed of *cells*.

chemical change (kem'i kəl chānj) A change in matter that results in one or more different kinds of matter forming. (B58) A *chemical change* occurs when paper burns and forms gases and ash.

chemical formula (kem'i kəl fôr'myo͞o lə) A group of symbols that shows the kind and number of each element in a single unit of a compound. (B35) The *chemical formula* for carbon dioxide is CO_2.

chemical property (kem'i kəl präp'ər tē) A characteristic of a substance that can only be seen when the substance changes and a new substance is formed. (B13, B58) A *chemical property* of iron is that iron can combine with oxygen to form rust.

chemical reaction (kem'i kəl rē ak'shən) The process in which one or more substances are changed into one or more different substances. (B59) A *chemical reaction* takes place when burning wood changes to ash.

chemical symbol (kem'i kəl sim'bəl) One or two letters that stand for the name of an element. (B30) The *chemical symbol* for gold is *Au*.

circuit breaker (sʉr'kit brāk'ər) A switch that opens or closes a circuit by turning off or on. (D52) When a circuit overheats, the *circuit breaker* switches off and the lights go out.

circulation (sʉr kyo͞o lā'shən) The movement of blood to the heart, through the network of blood vessels throughout the body, and back to the heart. (F26) Exercise causes *circulation* to speed up.

circulatory system (sʉr'kyo͞o lə-tôr ē sis'təm) The heart and the network of blood vessels, which work together to carry blood throughout the body. (F26) The *circulatory system* brings food and oxygen to the cells.

cirrus cloud (sir'əs kloud) A thin, feathery cloud made up of ice crystals high in the sky. (E57) *Cirrus clouds* often look like wisps of hair.

climate (klī'mət) The average weather conditions of an area over a long period of time. (E86) Some regions have a hot, rainy *climate*.

cloud (kloud) A mass of tiny droplets of water that condensed from the air. (E47) A dark *cloud* blocked the sunlight.

cold front (kōld frunt) The leading edge of a cold air mass that forms as the cold air mass moves into a warm air mass. (E64) Thunderstorms often occur along a *cold front.*

compass (kum′pəs) A device containing a magnetized needle that moves freely and is used to show direction. (D23) The north pole of the needle in a *compass* points toward Earth's magnetic north pole.

compound (käm′ pound) Matter made up of two or more elements chemically combined. (B33) Salt is a *compound* made up of sodium and chlorine.

condense (kən dens′) To change from a gas to a liquid. (E47) Water vapor from the air *condenses* on a cold window.

condensation (kän dən sā′shən) The change of state from a gas to a liquid. (B42) Drops of water form on the outside of a very cold glass because of the *condensation* of water vapor in the air.

conductor (kən duk′tər) A material through which electricity moves easily. (D42) Copper wire is a good *conductor* of electricity.

conservation (kän sər vā′shən) The preserving and wise use of natural resources. (A31) The *conservation* of forests is important to both humans and wildlife.

cumulus cloud (kyo͞o′myo͞o ləs kloud) A large, puffy cloud. (E55) White *cumulus clouds* can often be seen in an otherwise clear summer sky.

— D —

delta (del′tə) A flat, usually triangular plain formed by deposits of sediment where a river empties into the ocean. (A12) The largest *delta* in the United States is at the mouth of the Mississippi River.

diaphragm (dī′ə fram) A large dome-shaped muscle separating the chest from the stomach area. (F9) When you inhale, your *diaphragm* moves down, leaving a larger space inside your chest.

disease (di zēz′) A change or condition in the body, having a particular cause and signs, that keeps the body from working normally. (F50) Chickenpox is one of many *diseases* that cause a rash.

drug (drug) A chemical that affects or changes the way the body or mind works. (F61) Some *drugs* are useful medicines, while others are harmful, habit-forming substances.

electric cell (ē lek'trik sel) A device that changes chemical energy to electrical energy. (D62) A battery in a flashlight consists of one or more *electric cells*.

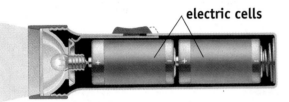

electric cells

electric charge (ē lek'trik chärj) The electrical property of particles of matter; an electric charge can be positive or negative. (D30) Rubbing a balloon with a wool cloth causes negative *electric charges* to move from the wool to the balloon.

electric circuit (ē lek'trik sʉr'kit) A path along which an electric current can move. (D41) We made an *electric circuit*, using a battery, wires, and a light bulb.

electric current (ē lek'trik kʉr'ənt) A continuous flow of electric charges. (D41) *Electric current* in wires allows you to run electric appliances, such as a refrigerator, in your home.

electric discharge (ē lek'trik dis'chärj) The loss or release of electric charge. (D33) A bolt of lightning is an *electric discharge*.

electromagnet (ē lek'trō mag-nit) A magnet made when an electric current passes through a wire coiled around an iron core. (D72) A large *electromagnet* can be strong enough to lift heavy metal objects.

element (el'ə mənt) Matter made up of only one kind of atom. (B30) Iron and oxygen are *elements*.

energy (en'ər jē) The ability to cause change. (B39) The bus uses *energy* from gasoline to move.

environment (en vī'rən mənt) Everything that surrounds and affects a living thing. (C9) Desert animals and forest animals live in very different *environments*.

equator (ē kwā'tər) An imaginary line circling the middle of Earth, halfway between the North Pole and the South Pole. (E80) The *equator* divides Earth into the Northern Hemisphere and the Southern Hemisphere.

erosion (ē rō′zhən) The gradual wearing away and removing of rock material by forces such as moving water, wind, and moving ice. (A10) Ocean waves cause *erosion* of the shore.

evaporate (ē vap′ə rāt) To change from a liquid to a gas. (E46) Some of the water boiling in the pot *evaporated*.

evaporation (ē vap ə rā′ shən) The change of state from a liquid to a gas. (B40) Under the hot sun, water in a puddle changes to water vapor through the process of *evaporation*.

excretory system (eks′krə tôr ē sis′təm) The body system that gets rid of harmful wastes produced by the cells. (F38) The kidneys, lungs, and skin are parts of the *excretory system*.

exhale (eks hāl′) To breathe out. (F10) When you *exhale*, air is forced out of your lungs.

exoskeleton (eks ō skel′ə tən) A hard outer structure, such as a shell, that protects or supports an animal's body. (C43) A lobster has a thick *exoskeleton*.

filament (fil′ə mənt) A long, thin coil of wire that glows when electricity passes through it. (D48) The *filament* in an incandescent light bulb gives off light.

filament

fish (fish) A vertebrate that lives in water and has gills for breathing and fins for swimming. (C48) Sharks and tuna are kinds of *fish*.

flash flood (flash flud) A sudden, violent flood. (E69) Heavy rains caused *flash floods* as the stream overflowed.

fossil fuel (fäs′əl fyōō′əl) A fuel formed from the remains of once-living things and that is nonrenewable. (A47) Oil is a *fossil fuel*.

freezing (frēz′iŋ) The change of state from a liquid to a solid. (B42) Water turns to ice by *freezing*.

front (frunt) The place where two air masses meet. (E64) Forecasters watch the movement of *fronts* to help predict the weather.

fuse (fyo͞oz) A device in a circuit that contains a metal strip, which melts and breaks when the circuit is overheated. (D52) The *fuse* blew because too many appliances were connected to the same circuit.

———— **G** ————

gas (gas) The state of matter that has no definite shape or volume. (B29) Helium is a very light *gas* that is used to fill some balloons.

generator (jen'ər ā tər) A device that changes energy of motion into electrical energy. (D60) The huge *generator* uses water power to produce electricity.

germ (jʉrm) A tiny organism that causes disease and can be seen only with a microscope. (F50) Some diseases are spread when one person passes on *germs* to another person.

gill (gil) A feathery structure on each side of a fish's head that lets the fish breathe underwater. (C48) A fish takes in oxygen through the thin walls of its *gills*.

glacier (glā'shər) A huge mass of slow-moving ice that forms over land; glaciers form in areas where the amount of snow that falls is more than the amount of snow that melts. (A22) As it moves, a *glacier* changes the surface beneath it.

greenhouse effect (grēn'hous e fekt') The process by which heat from the Sun builds up near Earth's surface and is trapped by the atmosphere. (E15) Some scientists fear that air pollution may increase the *greenhouse effect* and raise temperatures on Earth.

———— **H** ————

hazardous waste (haz'ər dəs wāst) A waste material that dirties the environment and that can kill living things or cause disease. (A65) Some chemicals used to kill insects become *hazardous wastes*.

headland (hed'land) A piece of land that extends out into the water and usually slows down the flow of water that passes it. (A14) The lighthouse stood on a *headland* overlooking the bay.

heart (härt) The muscular organ that pumps blood through the blood vessels of the body. (F26) The human *heart* normally beats about 70 to 80 times per minute.

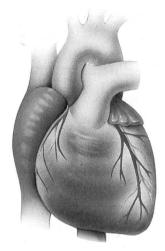

high-pressure area (hī′presh′ər er′ē ə) An area of higher air pressure than that of the surrounding air. (E33) Winds move from *high-pressure areas* to low-pressure areas.

humidity (hyo͞o mid′ə tē) The amount of water vapor in the air. (E46) Tropical climates have warm temperatures and high *humidity*.

hurricane (hur′i kān) A large, violent storm accompanied by strong winds and, usually, heavy rain. (E72) The *hurricane* winds blew at over 125 km/h.

ice age (īs āj) A period of time when glaciers covered much of Earth's land. (E91) During the last *ice age,* glaciers covered parts of North America.

illegal drug (i lē′gəl drug) A dangerous drug that is unlawful for people to have or to use. (F61) Marijuana is an *illegal drug.*

immune system (im myo͞on′ sis′təm) A body system that defends against germs by attacking and destroying germs as they enter the body. (F56) Antibodies are part of the *immune system.*

incineration (in sin ər ā′shən) Burning to ashes. (A61) You can get rid of trash by *incineration.*

inhale (in hāl′) To breathe in. (F10) When you *inhale,* your lungs expand and fill with air.

instinctive behavior (in-stiŋk′tiv bē hāv′yər) A behavior that a living thing does naturally without having to learn it. (C28) For a mother bird, feeding her young is an *instinctive behavior.*

insulator (in′sə lāt ər) A material through which electricity does not move easily. (D42) Rubber can prevent an electric shock because rubber is a good *insulator*.

invertebrate (in vʉr′tə brit) An animal that does not have a backbone. (C43) Jellyfish, sponges, insects, and worms are *invertebrates*.

kidney (kid′nē) One of a pair of organs that clean and filter the blood. (F39) As blood passes through the *kidneys*, waste materials are removed.

landfill (land′fil) An area where trash is buried and covered over with dirt. (A59) In some places towns build parks on the sites of old *landfills*.

learned behavior (lʉrnd bē-hāv′yər) A behavior that an organism is taught or learns from experience. (C28) Sitting on command is a *learned behavior* for a dog.

lines of force (līnz uv fôrs) The lines that form a pattern showing the size and shape of a magnetic force field. (D19) Iron filings sprinkled over a magnet form *lines of force* that show the strength and direction of the magnet's force.

liquid (lik′wid) The state of matter that has a definite volume but no definite shape. (B29) A *liquid*, such as water or milk, takes the shape of its container.

litter (lit′ər) The trash that is discarded on the ground or in water rather than being disposed of properly. (A66) The children cleaned up the park by removing all the *litter*.

lodestone (lōd′stōn) A naturally magnetic mineral found at or near Earth's surface. (D22) A piece of *lodestone* will attract iron.

low-pressure area (lō′presh′ər er′ē ə) An area of lower air pressure than that of the surrounding air. (E33) Storms are more likely to occur in *low-pressure areas*.

lung (luŋ) One of a pair of spongy, baglike organs of the body that expand when filled with air. (F9) The *lungs* give off oxygen to the blood and rid the body of carbon dioxide.

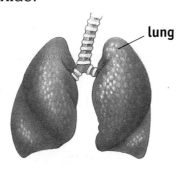

lung

magnet (mag'nit) An object that has the property of attracting certain materials, mainly iron and steel. (D11) The girl used a horseshoe *magnet* to pick up paper clips.

magnetic field (mag net'ik fēld) The space around a magnet within which the force of the magnet can act. (D20) The magnet attracted all the pins within its *magnetic field*.

magnetism (mag'nə tiz əm) A magnet's property of attracting certain materials, mainly iron and steel. (D11) *Magnetism* keeps kitchen magnets attached to a refrigerator door.

mammal (mam'əl) A vertebrate, such as a cat, that has hair or fur and that feeds its young with milk. (C52) Dogs, cats, rabbits, deer, bats, horses, mice, elephants, whales, and humans are all *mammals*.

mass (mas) The amount of matter that something contains. (B10) A large rock has more *mass* than a small rock that is made of the same material.

matter (mat'ər) Anything that has mass and takes up space. (B10) Rocks and water are two kinds of *matter*.

melting (melt'iŋ) The change of state from a solid to a liquid. (B40) As the temperature rises, snow and ice change to liquid water by *melting*.

metric system (me'trik sis'təm) A system of measurement in which the number of smaller parts in each unit is based on the number 10 and multiples of 10. (B20) In the *metric system*, length is measured in meters.

mineral (min'ər əl) A solid, found in nature, that has a definite chemical makeup. (A41) Salt, coal, diamond, and gold are *minerals*.

mixture (miks′chər) Matter that is made up of two or more substances that can be separated by physical means. (B52) This salad contains a *mixture* of lettuce and tomatoes.

molt (mōlt) To shed an outer covering such as hair, outer skin, horns, or feathers, at certain times. (C59) Snakes and insects *molt*.

natural resource (nach′ər əl rē′sôrs) Any useful material from Earth, such as water, oil, and minerals. (A31) One reason that trees are an important *natural resource* is because their wood is used to build houses and to make paper.

nitrogen (nī′trə jən) A colorless, odorless, tasteless gas that makes up about four fifths of the air. (E11) *Nitrogen* is used by plants for growth.

nonrenewable resource (nän-ri nōō′ə bəl rē′sôrs) A natural resource that can't be replaced once it's removed. (A43) Minerals are classified as a *nonrenewable resource* because there's a limited amount of them.

Northern Hemisphere (nôr′thərn hem′i sfir) The half of Earth north of the equator. (E81) Canada is in the *Northern Hemisphere*.

north pole (nôrth pōl) One of the ends of a magnet where the magnetic force is strongest; it points to the north when the magnet moves freely. (D13) The *north poles* of two magnets repel each other.

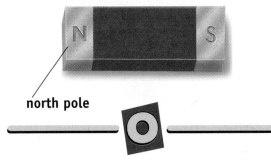

north pole

ore (ôr) A mineral or rock that contains enough of a metal to make mining that metal profitable. (A42) Gold, aluminum, and tin come from *ores*.

organism (ôr′gə niz əm) A living thing that can be classified as belonging to one of five kingdoms. (C36) Animals and plants are *organisms*.

oxygen (äks′i jən) A colorless, odorless, tasteless gas that makes up about one fifth of the air. (E11) *Oxygen* is essential to life.

packaging (pak'ij iŋ) The wrapping and containers in which items are transported or offered for sale. (A77) *Packaging* protects products from damage but adds to their cost.

parallel circuit (par'ə lel sʉr'kit) An electric circuit having more than one path along which electric current can travel. (D51) Because circuits in a home are *parallel circuits*, you can switch off one light and others will stay on.

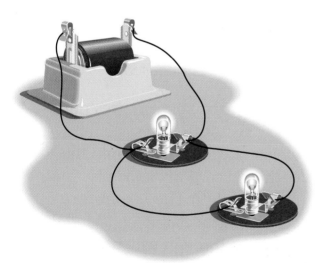

physical change (fiz'i kəl chānj) A change in size, shape, or state of matter in which no new matter is formed. (B50) Cutting an apple in half and freezing water into ice cubes are *physical changes*.

physical property (fiz'i kəl präp'ər tē) A characteristic of a material or object that can be seen or measured without changing the material into a new substance. (B12) One *physical property* of a ball is its round shape.

polar climate (pō'lər klī'mət) A very cold climate that does not receive much energy from the Sun. (E88) The Arctic has a *polar climate*.

pollutant (pə loot''nt) A substance that causes pollution. (A65) Exhaust gases from cars add *pollutants* to the air.

pollution (pə loo'shən) The dirtying of the environment with waste materials or other unwanted substances. (A65) Water *pollution* can result in death and disease in living things.

precipitation (prē sip ə tā'shən) Any form of water that falls from clouds to Earth's surface. (E47) Rain, snow, and hail are forms of *precipitation*.

property (präp'ər tē) A characteristic that describes matter. (B12) Hardness is a *property* of steel.

pulse (puls) The number of times that a heart beats in one minute; it is felt as a throbbing caused by blood rushing into the arteries each time the ventricles contract. (F28) The doctor took the patient's *pulse* by feeling the artery in the wrist.

R

rain gauge (rān gāj) A device for measuring precipitation. (E47) The *rain gauge* showed that 2 cm of rain had fallen in 24 hours.

recycle (rē sī′kəl) To process and reuse materials. (A74) Newspapers are *recycled* to make new paper.

relative humidity (rel′ə tiv hyo͞o mid′ə tē) The amount of water vapor present in the air at a given temperature compared to the maximum amount that the air could hold at that temperature. (E46) A *relative humidity* of 95 percent on a warm day can make you feel sticky and uncomfortable.

renewable resource (ri no͞o′ə-bəl rē′sôrs) A resource that can be replaced. (A42) Water is a *renewable resource* because rain increases the supply of water.

reptile (rep′təl) A vertebrate, such as a lizard, that has dry scaly skin and lays eggs that have a leathery shell. (C50) *Reptiles* can be found in both deserts and rain forests.

respiration (res pə rā′shən) The process in which cells use oxygen to release energy and give off carbon dioxide. (F17) During *respiration*, food is broken down and carbon dioxide is released.

respiratory system (res′pər ə-tôr ē sis′təm) The system by which oxygen is taken into the body and carbon dioxide is removed. (F9) The *respiratory system* includes the lungs and the passages through which air is brought to them.

river system (riv′ər sis′təm) A river and all the waterways, such as brooks, streams, and rivers, that drain into it. (A11) The Mississippi River and the many waterways feeding into it make up the largest *river system* in the country.

rock (räk) A solid material that is made up of one or more minerals and that may be used for its properties. (A41) Granite is a hard *rock* used in construction.

sand dune (sand do͞on) A mound, hill, or ridge of sand formed by the wind. (A21) *Sand dunes* are common in the desert.

sand dune

savanna (sə van′ə) A broad, grassy plain that has few or no trees. (C12) Nearly half of Africa is covered by *savannas*.

secondhand smoke (sek′ənd-hand smōk) The smoke given off by another person's burning tobacco. (F60) Breathing *secondhand smoke* from other people's cigarettes can make you sick.

sediment (sed′ə mənt) Sand, soil, and rock carried by water, wind, or ice. (A12) The rushing water deposited *sediment* along the riverbanks.

series circuit (sir′ēz sur′kit) An electric circuit in which the parts are connected in a single path. (D50) Electric current can follow only one path in a *series circuit*.

social animal (sō′shəl an′i məl) An animal that lives as part of an organized group or community. (C26) Ants and honeybees are *social animals*.

soil (soil) The loose material that covers much of Earth's land surface and is made up of three layers—topsoil, subsoil, and partly weathered rock. (A30) Plants, insects, and worms live in *soil*.

solar cell (sō′lər sel) A device that changes sunlight into electrical energy. (D66) *Solar cells* used in power plants can produce electricity without polluting the air.

solar energy (sō′lər en′ər jē) The clean and relatively low-cost energy from the Sun. (A50, D66) *Solar energy* is used to heat water in some homes.

solid (säl′id) Matter that has a definite volume and a definite shape. (B29) A *solid*, such as a rock or an ice cube, has a definite volume and shape.

solution (sə lo͞o′shən) A mixture in which the particles of different substances are mixed evenly. (B53) Stirring sugar into water makes a *solution*.

Southern Hemisphere (su*th*′ərn hem′i sfir) The half of Earth south of the equator. (E81) Australia is in the *Southern Hemisphere*.

south pole (south pōl) One of the ends of a magnet where the magnetic force is strongest; it points to the south when the magnet moves freely. (D13) The *south pole* of one magnet attracts the north pole of another magnet.

standard unit (stan′dərd yo͞on′it) A unit of measure that everyone agrees to use. (B19) Scientists use the gram as the *standard unit* of mass.

state of matter (stāt uv mat′ər) Any of the three forms that matter may ordinarily take: solid, liquid, and gas. (B29) When ice melts, it changes to a liquid *state of matter.*

static electricity (stat′ik ē lek-tris′i tē)) Electric charges that have built up on the surface of an object. (D31) Walking across a carpet on a cold, dry day can produce *static electricity.*

stratus cloud (strat′əs kloud) A low, flat cloud that often brings drizzle. (E57) Large sheets of dark *stratus clouds* covered the sky on the rainy morning.

substance (sub′stəns) A class of matter made up of elements and compounds. (B34) Salt and sugar are *substances.*

switch (swich) A device that completes or breaks the path a current can follow in an electric circuit. (D41) In order to turn on the light you must press the *switch* to complete the circuit.

temperate climate (tem′pər it klī′mət) A climate that generally has warm, dry summers and cold, wet winters. (E88) Most regions of the United States have a *temperate climate.*

thunderstorm (thun′dər stôrm) A storm that produces lightning and thunder and often heavy rain and strong winds. (E68) *Thunderstorms* often occur when the weather is hot and humid.

tornado (tôr nā′dō) A violent, funnel-shaped storm of spinning wind. (E74) The wind speed at the center of a *tornado* can be twice that of hurricane winds.

tropical climate (träp′i kəl klī′mət) A hot, rainy climate. (E88) Areas near the equator have a *tropical climate* because they receive the greatest amount of energy from the Sun.

troposphere (trō′pō sfir) The layer of the atmosphere closest to the surface of the Earth. (E12) The *troposphere* reaches about 11 km above the surface and is the layer of the atmosphere in which weather occurs.

vaccination (vak sə nā′shən) Shot given to provide immunity from a certain disease. (F57) *Vaccination* has stopped the spread of the disease of smallpox.

vein (vān) A blood vessel that carries blood to the heart. (F26) Blood flows from small *veins* into larger ones.

ventricle (ven′tri kəl) Either of the two lower chambers of the heart. (F27) The *ventricles* pump blood into the arteries.

vertebra (vʉr′tə brə) One of the bones that together make up the backbone. (C42) Each knob in your backbone is a *vertebra*.

vertebrate (vʉr′tə brit) An animal that has a backbone. (C42) Seals, snakes, and fish are all *vertebrates*.

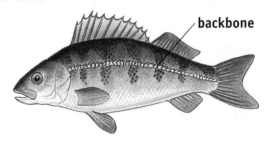

backbone

virus (vī′rəs) The smallest germ, about 100 times smaller than most bacteria. (F51) *Viruses* cause many diseases, including measles, AIDS, and rabies.

voltage (vōl′tij) The force of an electric current, measured in volts. (D65) Currents of high *voltage* travel through long-distance power lines.

volume (väl yo͞om) The amount of space that matter takes up. (B11) A baseball has a greater *volume* than a golf ball does.

warm front (wôrm frunt) The leading edge of a warm air mass that forms as the warm air mass moves forward into a cold air mass. (E65) Light rain often falls along a *warm front.*

water vapor (wôt'ər vā'pər) Water that is in the form of a gas. (E11) *Water vapor* from the air forms drops on cold glass.

weather (we*th*'ər) The condition of the atmosphere at a certain place and time. (E13) The *weather* today in Chicago is snowy.

weathering (we*th*'ər iŋ) The physical and chemical processes by which rock is broken down into smaller pieces. (A10) Cracks in rock produced by freezing rain-water are examples of *weathering.*

weather forecaster (we*th*'ər fôr'kast ər) A person who makes weather predictions or reports weather conditions. (E63) The *weather forecaster* predicted rain.

weather satellite (we*th*'ər sat''l īt) A human-made device in space that takes pictures of Earth and collects information about the weather. (E54) The *weather satellite* sent back pictures of clouds to weather stations in different locations on the ground.

wind (wind) The movement of air over Earth's surface. (E21) A strong *wind* lifted the kite high above the houses.

windpipe (wind'pīp) The air passage that connects the throat to the lungs. (F9) The *windpipe* is a tube through which air flows when you breathe.

windsock (wind'säk) A device used to show wind direction, consisting of a cloth bag that is open at both ends and hung on a pole. (E38) The *windsock* at the airport showed that the wind was blowing from the north.

wind vane (wind vān) A device, often shaped like an arrow, used to show the direction of the wind. (E38) The *wind vane* on the roof of the weather station showed that the wind was blowing from the southwest.

INDEX

air sacs, F17
bronchial tubes, F16
in circulatory system, F26
in excretory system, F38

M

Macaws, C32–C33
Maglev train, D14–D15
Magnetic force, D16–D17*,
  D18*, D19–D21
  force fields (lines of force),
  D19–D21, D23
  magnetic field, D18*,
  D19–D21, D23–D24
Magnetism, D10*, D11, D23,
  D68–D69*, D72
Magnets, D6–D7*, D8–D9*,
  D10*, D11–D12,
  D16–D17*, D18*,
  D19–D21, D22–D24,
  D25, D57*, D60, D72.
  See also Earth.
  attracting, D8–D9*, D13,
  D20
  bar magnets, D8–D9*,
  D10*, D16–D17*, D19
  electromagnet, D68–D69*,
  D72–D74, D79
  Magnetic Resonance
  Imaging (MRI), D4
  magnetic source, D57*
  poles of (north/south),
  D8–9*, D13
  permanent magnets, D12
  repelling, D8–D9*, D13,
  D20
  temporary magnets, D12
Mammals, C51–C53
Margulis, Lynn, C41
Mass, B10, B48*
Matter, B4, B6–B7*,
  B10–B11, B26–B27*,
  B28*, B29–B31,
  B40–B41, B58–B60
  air as matter, E10
  amount (mass), B8*, B10,
  B48*

building blocks of, B33
changes in states of, B36*,
  B37*, B40–B42,
  B46–B47*, B50–B51,
  B58–B59
invisible, B28*
particles of, B30–B31,
  B40–B42, D24,
  E31–E32
shape of, B26–B27*, B48*
space taken up by (volume),
  B9*, B11, B17*, B48*
states of, B26–B27*, B29,
  B36
Measurement, B14–B15*,
  B16*, B17*, B18–B22
  systems of, B19–B22
Measuring devices, B18,
  B20–B21
  balances, B20
  calendars, B18
  clocks, B18
  graduated cylinders, B21
  sundials, B18
  thermometers, B21
Medicines, F56–F57,
  F58–F59*, F61–F62
Melting, B36*, B40
Mercury, E30, E32
Metric system, B19–B22
  prefixes of terms, B22
Milk, C52
Minerals, A34–A35*,
  A38–A39, A41–A42
Mixture, B49*, B52–B53
Molecule, B35
Mollusks, C59
Molting, C59
Monerans, C37, C39
Moon, E4, E11, E15
Moraines, A23, A25. See
  also Glaciers.
Mountains, A24
Movement of animals, C37,
  C54–C55*, C56
Muscles, F27

N

Natural gas, A48–A49
Natural resources, A31,
  A36–A37*, A65
  nonrenewable, A43, A46
  renewable, A42
  U.S. Department of Natural
  Resources, C7
Nitrogen, E11
North/south poles
  of Earth, D22, D23–D24
  of magnets, D8–D9*, D13
Nycander, Eduardo,
  C32–C33

O

Ocean, A6–A7*, A13–A15
Odor, B28*
Oil. See Petroleum.
Oil spill, A63*
Ore, A42–A43
Organisms, C36, C42–C43,
  C63
Oxygen, E11, F9, F11,
  F14–F15*, F17–F18,
  F26, F27

P

Packaging, A77–A78
Paramecium, C39
Petroleum, A48–A49, A66,
  B54–B55
Pharmacist, B44
Photography, B61–B62
Physical change, B46–B47*,
  B48*, B49*, B50–B51,
  B52–B53, B54–B55
Physicist, B24
Plants, A20, A29*, A32,
  C37, C38
Plastic, A74–A75
Pollution, A63*, A65, D15
Power plant, D15, D61,
  D64, D66
Precipitation, E47
Prey, C19
Properties, B6–B7*,

* **Activity**

CREDITS

Cover: *Design, Art Direction, and Production:* Design Five, NYC. *Photography:* Jade Albert; *Photography Production:* Picture It Corporation; *Illustration:* Susan Swan. **TOC:** Mark Bender, Doreen Gay-Kassel, Nina Laden, Tom Lochray, Briar Lee Mitchell, Michael Sloan, Jackie Urbanovic.

ILLUSTRATORS
UNIT 4A Chapter A1: Skip Baker: 23; Susan Johnston Carlson: 10, 11, 12, 13; Jim Turgeon: 22, 23, 24; Jackie Urbanovic: 13, 15. **Chapter A2:** Terry Boles: 44; Brad Gaber: 30, 31, 40; Dave Joly: 38, 39; Debra Page-Trim: 46, 47; Rodica Prato: 46; Terry Ravenelli: 43; Jim Salvati: 32, 33. **Chapter A3:** Ken Bowser: 77; Randy Chewning: 79; Eldon Doty: 73; Greg Harris: 64, 71; Michael Ingle: 63; Scott MacNeil: 74, 75, 76; Bob Ostrom: 70, 72, 73; Robert Roper: 58, 59, 65; Jim Trusilo: 56; Ray Vella: 61.

UNIT 4B Chapter B1: Mark Bender: 19, 20, 21, 22; Terry Boles: 19; Nina Laden: 12, 13; Susan Simon: 4, 5; Dave Winter: 18. **Chapter B2:** Tom Buches: 33; Ron Fleming: 38, 40, 41; J.A.K. Graphics: 29, 30, 31, 34, 35, 43; Susan Johnston Carlson: 32; Nina Laden: 41. **Chapter B3:** Dartmouth Publishing: 62; Bob Doucet: 61; Patrick Gnan: 55; Andrew Shiff: 51.

UNIT 4C Chapter C1: Mark Bender: 26, 27; Richard Cowdrey: 18, 19, 20, 21, 22, 23, 29; Linda Howard: 12, 13; Julie Tsuchya: 8, 9, 10, 11; Jackie Urbanovic: 8; Phil Wilson: 4, 5. **Chapter C2:** David Barber: 42, 43; Jim Deal: 48, 50; Barbara Hoopes Ambler: 59; Susan Johnston Carlson: 46, 47; Susan Melrath: 40, 41; Lee Steadman: 36, 37.

UNIT 4D Chapter D1: Brad Gaber: 22; Patrick Gnan: 13; Dan McGowan: 15. **Chapter D2:** Jim Effier: 35; Patrick Gnan: 48; Dale Gustafson: 42, 43; Hans & Cassady Inc.: 41, 50, 51, 53; Robert Roper: 30, 31, 52; Andrew Shiff: 35; David Winter: 40. **Chapter D3:** Geoffrey McCormick: 64, 65; Robert Roper: 62, 63, 72, 74; Michael Sloan: 76, 77; Vincent Wayne: 70; Josie Yee: 66.

UNIT 4E Chapter E1: Randy Hamblin: 11, 13; Flora Jew: 22; Andy Lendway: 20; Robert Roper: 14, 15, 23. **Chapter E2:** Pamela Becker: 38, 39; Rob Burger: 31, 33, 49; Art Kretzschmar: 46, 47; Susan Melrath: 30; Tom Pansini: 32. **Chapter E3:** Patrick Gnan: 56; Susan Johnston Carlson: 62; Tom Lochray: 68, 70, 71, 72, 74; Robert Roper: 64; Nancy Tobin: 63, 64, 65; Gary Torrisi: 55, 73. **Chapter E4:** Susan Johnston Carlson: 86, 87; Uldis Klavins: 88, 89; Mark It For Design: 79; Julie Peterson: 92, 93, 94; Mike Quon: 80, 81; Josie Yee: 79, 81; John Youssi: 82, 83, 95.

UNIT 4F Chapter F1: Anne Greene: 13, 21; Jackie Heda: 9, 10, 11, 19; Kate Sweeney: 16, 17. **Chapter F2:** Art & Science Inc.: 38, 39, 40, 41, 45; Alex Bloch: 34, 35; Briar Lee Mitchell: 26, 27, 29, 42, 44; Leonid Mysakov: 30, 31. **Chapter F3:** Bob Brugger: 60; Doreen Gay-Kassel: 50, 51, 52, 53.

Glossary: David Barber, Dale Gustafson, Hans & Cassady Inc., Daniel McGowan, A.J. Miller.

Handbook: Terry Boles, Laurie Hamilton, Catherine Leary, Marjorie Muns

PHOTOGRAPHS
All photographs by Silver Burdett Ginn (SBG) unless otherwise noted.

Unit A Opener 2: Breck P. Kent. **Chapter 1** 4–5: *bkgd.* George Archibald/International Crane Foundation. *b.* Peter Weimann/Animals Animals. 10: *t.* E. R. Degginger/Color-Pic, Inc.; *b.* C. C. Lockwood/DRK Photo. 11: Cameron Davidson/Comstock. 12: *l.* TSA/Tom Stack & Associates; *r.* Manfred Gottschalk/Tom Stack & Associates. 13: Scott Blackman/Tom Stack & Associates. 14: *l.* Comstock; *r.* Breck P. Kent. 15: Bob Daemmrich. 20–21: Larry Ulrich/DRK Photo. 21: Breck P. Kent. 22: *l.* E. R. Degginger/Color-Pic, Inc.; *r.* © Porterfield/Chickering/Photo Researchers, Inc. 23: © Porterfield/Chickering/Photo Researchers, Inc. 24: Spencer Swanger/Tom Stack & Associates. 25: C. C. Lockwood/Bruce Coleman. **Chapter 2** 26–27: *bkgd.* Larry Ulrich/Tony Stone Images. 27: Harry Giglio. 28–29: Grant Huntington for SBG. 32: *t.* Harald Sund/The Image Bank; *b.* J. C. Carton/Bruce Coleman. 33: *t.* Kevin Schafer/Tom Stack & Associates; *b.* John Callahan/Tony Stone Images. 34–41: Grant Huntington for SBG. 43: *t.l.* Edward Bower/The Image Bank; *t.r.,* Lester Lefkowitz/Tony Stone Images. 44–45: Grant Huntington for SBG. 48: © Ludek Pesek/Photo Researchers, Inc. 49: *t.l.* J. Barry O'Rourke/The Image Bank; *t.r.* J. Barry O'Rourke/The Stock Market; *b.* Mike Abrahams/Tony Stone Images. 50: Chromo Sohm/Sohm/The Stock Market. 51: Larry Lefever/Grant Heilman Photography. **Chapter 3** 52–53: *bkgd.* Paul Conklin/Photo Edit. 53: Robert Holmgren. 62: © Andy Levin/Photo Researchers, Inc. 64: Frans Lanting/Minden Pictures. 66: *b.* Grant Heilman Photography. 67: *t.* Larry Lefever/Grant Heilman Photography; *b.* Runk/Schoenberger/Grant Heilman Photography. 76: *l.* © Donald S. Heintzelman/Photo Researchers, Inc.; *r.* © Will McIntyre/Photo Researchers, Inc.

Lee Rue III/National Audubon Society/Photo Researchers, Inc. 66–67: Richard Hutchings for SBG. 68: William Wantland/Tom Stack & Associates. 70–71: David Dennis/Tom Stack & Associates. 71: T. A. Wiewandt/DRK Photo. 72: NOAA/NESDIS/NCDC/SDSD. 74: Merilee Thomas/Tom Stack & Associates. **Chapter 4** 76–77: *inset* Richard Mahoney. 80: *l.* Terry Wild; *r.* Richard Hutchings for SBG. 84–85: Richard Hutchings for SBG. 90: North Museum, Franklin & Marshall/Runk/Schoenberger/Grant Heilman Photography. 91: *t.* © James L. Amos/Photo Researchers, Inc.; *b.* © J. G. Paren/Science Photo Library/Photo Researchers, Inc. 92: *l.* William Johnson/Johnson's Photography. 93: *t.* Anna E. Zuckerman/Tom Stack & Associates. *b.* © George Ranalli/Photo Researchers, Inc. 94: *t.* Rob Crandall/Stock Boston; *b.* Cary Wolinsky/Stock Boston.

Unit F Opener 1–3: *border* Robert Becker, Ph.D./Custom Medical Stock. 2: Merritt Vincent/PhotoEdit. **Chapter 1** 4–5: *bkgd.* Marine Safety Division/City of Huntington Beach, California. 6–20: Richard Hutchings for SBG. **Chapter 2** 22–23: Matt Meadows for SBG. 24–25: Richard Hutchings for SBG. 29: © Ken Edward/Science Source/Photo Researchers, Inc. 32: *inset* NASA. 32–33: *bkgd.* © NASA/Mark Marten/Photo Researchers, Inc. 33: *inset* George Hall/Check Six. 34: Inga/Tom Stack & Associates. 35: Rhoda Sidney/PhotoEdit. 36–37: Richard Hutchings for SBG. 43: M. Bridwell/PhotoEdit. **Chapter 3** 47–48: *bkgd.* E. R. Degginger/Color-Pic, Inc.; *inset* New England Medical Center. 48: Ken Lax for SBG. 50: *l.* © Dr. Tony Brain/Photo Researchers, Inc.; *r.* Phototake. 51: *t.* © CNRI/Photo Researchers, Inc.; *b.* Phototake. 53: *t.* E. R. Degginger/Color-Pic, Inc. 54: Tony Freeman/PhotoEdit. 54–55: *t.* Dan DeWilde for SBG; *b.* Merritt Vincent/PhotoEdit. 55: *t.* Richard Hutchings for SBG; *b.* Dan DeWilde for SBG. 57: Tony Freeman/PhotoEdit. 61–62: Ken Lax for SBG.